SOMETHING'S GOT TO GIVE

Something's Got to Give

Balancing Work, Childcare, and Eldercare

LINDA DUXBURY AND
CHRISTOPHER HIGGINS

UNIVERSITY OF TORONTO PRESS
Toronto Buffalo London

Rotman-UTP Publishing
University of Toronto Press
Toronto Buffalo London
www.utppublishing.com
Printed in Canada

ISBN 978-1-4426-4973-6

∞ Printed on acid-free, 100% post-consumer recycled paper with vegetable-based inks.

Library and Archives Canada Cataloguing in Publication

Duxbury, Linda, 1962–, author
Something's got to give : balancing work, childcare, and eldercare/
Linda Duxbury and Christopher Higgins.

Includes bibliographical references and index.
ISBN 978-1-4426-4973-6 (cloth)

1. Work and family – Canada.   2. Caregivers – Canada.   3. Work-life balance – Canada.   I. Higgins, Christopher Alan, 1949–, author   II. Title.

HD4904.25.D89 2017   306.3'6   C2016-908081-1

University of Toronto Press acknowledges the financial assistance to its publishing program of the Canada Council for the Arts and the Ontario Arts Council, an agency of the Government of Ontario.

Canada Council **Conseil des Arts**
for the Arts **du Canada**

ONTARIO ARTS COUNCIL
CONSEIL DES ARTS DE L'ONTARIO
an Ontario government agency
un organisme du gouvernement de l'Ontario

Funded by the   Financé par le
Government   gouvernement
of Canada   du Canada

Canada

Collectively we have many people to thank for their support. From peers, friends, family members, and study participants there have been many who have supported us throughout the years and championed our research. We thank you.

We dedicate this book to our parents who raised us and believed in us.

For you,
Roy and Alma Duxbury
Mary and Bill Higgins

We also dedicate this book to our families, who have been with us through thick and thin and have encouraged us to be the best people we can be. We could not have done this without you.

John Chinneck, Anne Duxbury Chinneck, Cheryl Duxbury, and Randy Moore
Barb Higgins, Shawn Higgins, Drew Higgins, Laura Higgins

CONTENTS

PREFACE

I go to an old-folks' home at suppertime four to five times a week to feed an invalid mother as well as working part time and taking care of a home, a husband, and a son who still lives at home. My own time is very limited. My health and my marriage are both suffering – but what can I do?

Just when you reach equilibrium, something new comes along. As the sole daughter of a progressively demented mother – her husband is dead – I have no one to share the responsibility with, and there is no structure to support my need to support her. This is the number-one source of my stress. Stressful things at work are easier to deal with – they are frustrating, but they don't hurt. Dealing with eldercare is much more personal – it hurts the heart!

These quotations, which were provided by respondents to the 2012 National Work, Life and Caregiving Study (Duxbury and Higgins, 2013a, 2013b, and 2013d), speak directly to the issues experienced by employees who are dealing with the demands and challenges associated with paid employment, care of at least one elderly dependent, and perhaps (for those in the "sandwich" generation) childcare as well. They describe the authors' lives (we both have elderly parents and children) and the lives of many employees in Canada today. They also describe the issue to be explored in this book: balancing work and caregiving.

Why Caregiving? Why Now?

In the new millennium, dependent care is not just a question of care for children. Demographic, social, economic, and policy changes have made family care of older relatives an issue of extreme importance to policy makers, families, researchers, and employers (Sims-Gould and Martin-Matthews 2007; Fast and Keating 2000). The increased interest in eldercare as a "work and family" issue can largely be attributed to its position at the nexus of a number of important socio-demographic trends that have increased the number of elderly dependents requiring care but decreased the number of potential caregivers. Taken in tandem these socio-demographic changes are increasing the probability that Canadians will simultaneously and/or sequentially be involved in combining paid employment with providing care and support to an ailing spouse/ partner, parent, in-law, or other older relative.

"Eldercare Is the New Childcare"

Faced with an influx of female employees in the 1970s and 1980s, many employers responded by implementing "family friendly" policies and practices to help women balance work outside the home with the demands associated with being a "mother." Academics responded by undertaking various studies to explore the impacts of this demographic shift on employers and employees alike. This interest has resulted in a vast academic literature dealing with the issues associated with balancing work and childcare. Unfortunately, an extensive review of the existing work-life literature revealed that researchers have not yet shifted their focus to include issues faced by employees who are caring for an elderly dependent. This is unfortunate, as Calvano (2013, 205) points out that, "Even though eldercare is likely to surpass childcare as a more pressing concern for organizations and their employees, management scholars have not embraced the topic." These gaps in our understanding of the issues associated with balancing work and caregiving informed the development of our research program on employed caregivers and motivated the writing of this definitive book on the topic of employed caregivers.

While caregiving is not an entirely new phenomenon (the term has been in use for several decades), at this point in time we have an incomplete understanding of how many employees are currently within this group. There does, however, appear to be a consensus within the literature that society has yet to feel the full effects of the challenges of providing care to seniors while also holding down a job. Demographic projections suggest that the number of people with such responsibilities will increase dramatically over the next several decades, while the number of people able to provide such care is likely to shrink as a confluence of factors pushes many developed countries in this direction. The trends contributing to this increase include increased life expectancy, aging baby boomers, delayed marriage and parenthood, decreased fertility rates, and changes in health-care policies and practices that have shifted responsibility for care from formal to informal caregivers (Duxbury and Dole 2014). These trends provide further evidence of the need for a book on employed caregivers.

About This Book

A myriad of diverse domains and disciplines have undertaken research on caregiving, including sociology, economics, psychology, social work, family studies, health studies, and gerontology, and at this time there is a very large academic literature on caregiving. The number of studies that focus on employed caregivers is, however, much smaller than the number on caregiving in general. The number of studies published in the management literature on employed caregivers, especially those in the "sandwich" generation, is smaller still (Calvano 2013). This book seeks to address this gap in our understanding by using both quantitative and qualitative data from the 2012 National Study on Work, Life and Caregiving (referred to throughout the book as "the 2012 Study") to articulate (and where possible quantify) how caregiving impacts employees, the organizations that employ them, the families that support them, and the society that they are a part of. This data set affords the most current and comprehensive examination of this topic at this time.

The goal in this book is not to provide a comprehensive review of the academic literature on caregiving (although we do use selected studies to provide context for our discussions). Nor do we seek to look at caregiving through a "gendered" lens. Rather, this book uses the rich data coming from the 2012 Study to compare the caregiving experiences of Canadian men and women in two family types: those seeking to balance work and eldercare (i.e., eldercare only) and those seeking to balance work, childcare, and eldercare (i.e., sandwich). Any discussion of the impact of gender on the issues being deliberated in the book has been integrated into the material being examined to reflect the fact that in today's society both men and women are experiencing challenges with respect to balancing work and caregiving.

The 2012 National Study on Work, Life and Caregiving

This book uses both quantitative and qualitative data from the 2012 National Study on Work, Life and Caregiving to explore issues associated with balancing work, childcare, and eldercare. The 2012 Study involved the collection of survey data from 25,000 Canadian employees, 8,000 of whom provided detailed information on their caregiving situation. We then did 111 in-depth follow-up interviews with both male and female employees who cared for one or more elderly dependents in order to gain a better understanding of the complexities inherent in the role of employed caregiver. Half of the people we interviewed also had children at home.

The use of data from the 2012 Study to explore issues associated with caregiving facilitates our ability to undertake an in-depth study of this complex issue. The 2012 Study represents one of the most comprehensive investigations to date of the challenges faced by employees as they seek to balance the demands of work with complex and ever-changing responsibilities at home (childcare and/or eldercare). Key strengths of the study are its use of psychometrically sound measures from the academic literature to quantify our respondents' situation at work and at home and the explanatory power provided by our in-depth discussions with 111 caregivers in a myriad of caregiving situations.

Who Should Read This Book?

The intended audience for this book is quite large and includes business and government policy makers; senior undergraduates/graduate students of gerontology, health studies, family studies, psychology, and business; as well as the caregiving public. Policy makers who are tasked with developing "family friendly" policies and practices to help employed caregivers cope with the demands on their time and energies imposed by the various roles in which they participate will find the focus on the costs of caregiving invaluable when making the business case for change in this area. They should also find the data and discussion of how employees cope with the challenges inherent in the caregiving role useful from a policy development perspective. Students in a variety of disciplines, particularly more senior students taking courses with a research focus, should find the multidisciplinary and multi-method approach used in this book helpful in developing their own research and practice in this area. Canadian employees who are caregivers themselves (or likely to be in the near future) and/or who manage employees who are engaged in the caregiving role should gain a deeper appreciation of the challenges associated with the role of employed caregiver as well as possible strategies that they can use to cope with (or help their subordinates cope with) the stresses associated with this role. Employees could also use the information in this book to make the case for changes within their organization to assist caregivers who are experiencing high levels of work-caregiving conflict. Canadians could also use the information in this book to lobby for political changes in this area.

Finally, it should be noted that, although the book focuses specifically on caregiving in Canada, the academic literature referred to is more global in nature, and the findings from this study can be generalized to other Western economies.

The Layout of the Book

The book consists of eight chapters, each of which shares a similar structure (i.e., the issue to be discussed; answers from academia; answers from the 2012 Study survey; answers from the interview study; conclusions, implications, and recommendations). Chapter 1 sets the stage for the rest of the book. At the end of this chapter the reader should: (1) be aware of how caregiving is defined, (2) have a greater appreciation of the number of employed caregivers in Canada at this time, (3) understand why a study of employed caregivers is particularly relevant just now, and (4) appreciate the impact caregiving has on key stakeholders, including caregivers themselves, their employers, and society in general. Information on the 2012 Study of relevance to this book is also provided in this chapter.

The second chapter in the book has two main objectives: (1) to help the reader appreciate the complexities inherent in the caregiving role, and (2) to enable the reader to better understand the stresses and frustrations experienced by caregivers as they undertake this role. To realize this goal we use information from a myriad of sources. We begin the chapter by using data from the interview component of the 2012 Study to paint a picture for the reader of the challenges facing employed caregivers in Canada in the new millennium and to familiarize the reader with the types of caregivers whose stories form the basis of this book. We then use data from a variety of sources (Statistics Canada's 2012 GSS; quantitative and qualitative data from the 2012 Study) to begin the process of profiling employed caregivers in Canada. The chapter presents data that address the following questions: "Who provides caregiving?" "Whom do they provide care for?" "What kinds of care do they offer?" "Why do employed Canadians take on the role of caregiver?" Such information is of critical importance to those who are tasked with developing policies and programs to support employed caregivers in the various activities they undertake in their role as caregiver. The chapter ends with a summary of key findings and a set of recommendations for employers and policy makers. At the end of chapter 2 the reader has a good understanding of the types of employees who provide care, whom they care for, why they have taken on the role, and what caregiving activities they perform as part of their role.

Chapter 3 builds on this information by (1) examining how much time employees spend in the various caregiving activities enumerated in chapter 2 and (2) exploring how employed caregivers balance the time commitments of the caregiver role with the other demands on their time. Three indicators of demands are presented and discussed in this chapter: (1) objective demands (e.g., the amount of time employed knowledge workers in Canada spend each week in childcare, caregiving, paid employment, and in their total role set), (2) subjective demands (role overload), and (3) work-life conflict. This focus on time, demands, and balance should give the reader insights into why, when asked to identify their biggest concern in their life, working parents and caregivers typically respond "time." The fourth and final section of chapter 3 provides a summary of key findings along with recommendations for policy makers tasked with helping employed Canadians balance work with the role of caregiver.

In chapter 3 we used compelling data from the 2012 Study to make the case that at this point in time many employed caregivers in Canada are overloaded and overwhelmed by the dual demands of work and family and report being time crunched by all they have to do. As Turcotte (2013, 5) notes, "Having too many tasks and responsibilities when caring for a family member or friend can be a major source of stress, especially when caregivers feel they lack the resources to meet the needs of their care receiver." Chapter 4 uses quantitative and qualitative data from the 2012 Study to explore the consequences of this "time famine" on the large majority of employed caregivers who are starved for time. Two questions are addressed: "What makes caregiving stressful?", and "What is the relationship between caregiving and employee well-being?" The answers to these two questions should help employers and policy makers identify policies and practices that can be put in place to reduce the challenges faced by employed caregivers in Canada at this time and in the future.

Chapter 4 is divided into seven sections. Section one is a brief review of the academic literature that links caregiving and employee well-being. Study data collected to help us better understand the various factors that make caregiving stressful are presented and discussed in section two (subjective caregiver burden, objective caregiver burden, and caregiver strain). In sections three and four we use qualitative data from the interviews to advance our understanding of the types of caregiver strain experienced by Canadian employees as well as our appreciation of the factors that make caregiving challenging and stressful. Sections five and six present data that further our understanding of the relationship between caregiving and employee well-being. The following indicators of employee well-being are presented in section five: perceived stress, depressed mood, and perceived health. This is followed, in section six, by a presentation of data from the interviews that looks more closely at why caregiving impacts employee well-being. Quotations from the interviews are used, as appropriate, to illustrate the realities behind the statistics presented in sections two and five. The chapter ends, in section seven, with a summary of key findings and recommendations that are supported by these data.

While most researchers agree that caregiving has the *potential* to interfere with employment, they disagree on the nature and extent of the disruption. While the uncertainty in the academic literature with respect to the relationship between eldercare and work is not surprising, given the many methodological issues plaguing research in this area (Calvano 2013), it makes it challenging for employees and policy makers alike to make a defendable case for change. This is unfortunate given the demographic data showing that the number of employees who provide care to elderly family members is likely to increase dramatically over the next several decades. Chapter 5 presents data from the 2012 Study on the relationship between caregiving and the organization's bottom line. Such information should help both employers and government policy makers understand how caregiving "threatens caregivers' employment and economic security and escalates employers' costs related to absenteeism and reduced productivity" (Fast et al. 2014, 1) and can result in lost tax revenues.

Chapter 5 is divided into four main sections. Section one provides a short summary of what the academic literature has to say about the impact caregiving has on an organization's bottom line. The impact of life-cycle stage on two key indicators of organizational performance – absenteeism and Statistics Canada's Employment Changes Index – are presented and discussed in section two of this chapter. The third section of chapter 5 features key findings on this issue from the interviews we conducted with employed caregivers. Key findings are summarized and implications for employers and policy makers outlined in the final section of the chapter.

While caregiving can be a rewarding and positive experience, the data presented in chapters 3, 4, and 5 establish, beyond a shadow of a doubt, that the role of caregiver can also be extremely demanding, stressful, physically taxing, and anxiety producing. A book that looks at the challenges employees face in balancing work and caregiving would be incomplete, therefore, if it did not also talk about how employees can cope with such stresses. Chapters 6 and 7 use insights gained through analysis of 2012 Study data to offer concrete suggestions on what can be done to reduce the adverse consequences of caregiving for Canadian employees.

"Coping" refers to strategies that people use, either alone or in conjunction with others, in order to avoid being harmed by stressors (Pearlin and Schooler 1978). Being able to deal with the inevitable stresses and strains of caregiving is part and parcel of being a truly effective caregiver, as people who do not care for themselves will be less able to care for someone else. Chapter 6 summarizes key findings from the "coping" section of the interview phase of the 2012 Study, which asked caregivers to reflect on their own caregiving experiences and identify how their *own* behaviour impacted their ability to cope effectively with their caregiving situation.

While caregivers can and do use a number of strategies to cope with the demands this role places on their time and the emotional strain that seems to be integral to caregiving, it is also important to recognize that caregivers are embedded within a number of social networks (e.g., family, work, community, Canadian society). Stakeholders from these various networks can (and often do) take actions that can either facilitate or make it more challenging for caregivers to execute their various roles:

caregiver, parent, employee, partner/spouse. Chapter 7 expands our examination of how employees cope with the demands and strains inherent in the employed caregiver role by including an analysis of how the actions of other stakeholders in this relationship may exacerbate or alleviate caregiver strain. The information presented in chapters 6 and 7 should facilitate the identification of strategies, programs, and policies to help caregivers cope more effectively with the various demands placed on their time and energy.

The book ends in chapter 8 with a call to action. The strong links between caregiving and employee well-being, the organizational bottom line, and government expenditures on health care identified in this book indicate that the current system is unsustainable over time and provide a wake-up call for change. It is hoped that governments and employers will heed this call sooner rather than later.

ACKNOWLEDGMENTS

We would like to acknowledge the thousands of people who patiently filled out a survey or sat through an interview as we bombarded them with questions about their lives. You are anonymous to the readers of this book, but many will relate to what you have said and take comfort from your advice and insights.

SOMETHING'S GOT TO GIVE

Chapter One

The Perfect Storm: Caregiving in Canada and Other Western Economies

I look after two elderly parents who live next door to me – 75 and 80 – as well as two children, 10 and 13. Efforts to get home care failed after my mom's surgery. I have hired individuals to help care for them who either quit or had to be fired. So I basically run two homes (yard work, shovelling, do my parents' laundry). I work a full time twelve-and-a-half-hour shift both days and nights. Time for myself is limited. Days off are usually doing errands, medical appointments for my parents, helping children with school, and household chores.[1]

In the new millennium, dependent care is not just a question of care for children. Demographic, social, economic, and policy changes have made family care of older relatives an issue of extreme importance to policy makers, families, researchers, and employers (Sims-Gould and Martin-Matthews 2007; Fast and Keating 2000). The increased interest in eldercare as a "work and family" issue can largely be attributed to its position at the nexus of several important socio-demographic trends that have increased the number of elderly dependents requiring care but decreased the number of potential caregivers. Taken in tandem, these socio-demographic changes are increasing the probability that Canadians will simultaneously and/or sequentially be involved in

---

1 Note: Unless otherwise mentioned, all the quotations provided in this chapter were given by caregivers who participated in the 2012 National Study on Work, Life and Caregiving (the 2012 Study) (Duxbury and Higgins, 2013a, 2013b, and 2013d).

combining paid employment with providing care and support to an ailing spouse/partner, parent, in-law, or other older relative.

This book focuses on employed caregivers – individuals who provide care to one or more elderly family members but also engage in paid employment. More specifically, this book examines the circumstances of two types of employed caregivers: (1) employees with responsibilities for the care of an adult dependent (i.e., employees who provide eldercare), and (2) employees in the sandwich group: "individuals who, by dint of circumstances, find themselves in the position of being caregivers for their young children and/or adult children as well as one or both of aging parents" (Chisholm 1999, 187).

This introductory chapter sets the stage for the rest of the book. At the end of this chapter the reader should: (1) be aware of how caregiving is defined; (2) have a greater appreciation of the number of employed caregivers in Canada; (3) understand why a book on employed caregivers is particularly relevant at this time; (4) appreciate the impact caregiving has on key stakeholders such as caregivers themselves, their employers, and society in general; and (5) understand how data from the 2012 National Study on Work, Life and Caregiving were collected and how they will be used in this book.

This introductory chapter is divided into four main sections: Answers from Academia; Answers from the 2012 Study; Answers from the Interview Study; and Conclusions, Recommendations, and Implications. The "Answers from Academia" section is divided into four subsections, each of which provides the reader with the necessary information to contextualize the material in this book. We begin the chapter by introducing the concept of caregiving. This is followed, in subsection two, with a discussion of how many employees find themselves balancing work and caregiving. The third subsection presents data related to the following two concerns: Why this issue? and Why now? In subsection four, data related to the impact of caregiving on key stakeholders (i.e., caregivers, their employers, and society in general) are presented and discussed. The goal of the second main section of this chapter is to familiarize the reader with the research initiative that provided much of the data used in this book: the 2012 National Study on Work, Life and

Caregiving (the 2012 Study). Section three of this chapter has three main objectives: (1) to familiarize the reader with the caregivers whose stories and data form the basis of this book, (2) to help the reader appreciate the complexities inherent in the caregiving role, and (3) to enable the reader to better understand the stresses and frustrations experienced by caregivers as they undertake this role. We accomplish this goal by using information from the interview component of the 2012 Study to paint a picture for the reader of the challenges facing employed caregivers in Canada in the new millennium. We close this chapter by providing the reader with a set of conclusions and recommendations arising from our review of the literature and our examination of the interview data.

Answers from Academia

What is caregiving?

In this book we use the term "caregivers" to refer to individuals who provide ongoing care and assistance, without pay, to family members and friends in need of support because of problems (physical, cognitive, or mental) related to aging. Included in our definition of caregivers are individuals who are primary caregivers and/or secondary caregivers who either live with or live separately from the senior receiving care (Duxbury, Higgins, and Schroder 2009). This definition of caregivers, is similar to that put forward by the Caregiver Coalition (Lum 2011, 1) and Statistics Canada (Sinah 2013, 4) but differs in that it excludes those individuals caring for non-seniors with limiting conditions (e.g., a disabled spouse or child).

In this book we do not include childcare within the "caregiving" umbrella. Caregiving (i.e., eldercare), is a complex phenomenon that relates to the special needs and requirements that are unique to senior citizens. Eldercare is different from childcare in that it tends to increase in amount and intensity over the course of caregiving (Morris 2001) and often entails meeting physical and psychological needs simultaneously (Calvano 2013). The timing of care is also different. Caring for children spans many years and has a fairly predictable pattern in that change typically occurs slowly over time as children become less dependent on their parents. Caregiving, on the other hand, is less predictable and varies widely in duration (Pavalko and Gong 2005). As Calvano (2013, 205) notes, "the need for eldercare usually occurs unexpectedly, increases over time, and entails the role reversal of children caring for their parents." Similarly, one of the respondents to our study noted the following differences between the two roles:

> *Every new thing your child does is growth. With my mother it is loss; her personality is dissolving before my eyes.*

The challenges of studying caregiving

Before beginning the research project described in this book we undertook an extensive review of the caregiving and work-life literatures (Duxbury and Dole 2014). This review revealed that current research in this area suffers from a number of critical deficiencies, including wide variation in how the caregiving construct is defined and operationalized. Issues with respect to measurement can be attributed partly to the fact that research on caregiving appears to have "fallen between the gaps" in terms of research agendas (Calvano 2013). Most research on caregiving has been confined to the gerontology and family studies literatures and has focused on caregiver burden and caregiver strain (Sims-Gould and Martin-Matthews 2007). While some management and employee well-being researchers have studied the balance between work and caregiving, most of the research in these disciplines has focused on the balance between employment and caring for younger children (Pavalko and Gong 2005). Research on the experiences of those combining the competing needs of paid work, childcare, and eldercare is, however, rare (Pyper 2006; Calvano 2013; Duxbury and Dole 2014).

Our review (Duxbury and Dole 2014) determined that the first (and perhaps greatest) problem facing researchers looking at issues associated with caregiving is the lack of a single, agreed-on measure of the caregiving construct. The lack of consistency and clarity in definitions of caregiving and the lack of agreement on what constitutes "caregiving" introduce wide variation into who is included in eldercare and sand-wich generation samples (Calvano 2013) and limits comparability and generalizability within the field (Pavalko and Gong 2005).

A number of researchers identify the definitional issue as challeng-ing. Rubin and White-Means (2009), for example, note that many of the most highly cited papers on the subject of the sandwich generation use different definitions for the term. In a similar vein, Keene and Prokos (2007) speak to the challenges associated with defining membership within the sandwich group. They note that there are degrees of being "sandwiched" that current measures of the construct do not capture. Keene and Prokos (2007) also note that samples (and hence results) vary depending on whether or not the researcher is considering poten-tial versus actual caregiving behaviours and argue that just because an individual has dependent children as well as parents of a certain age does not imply that the individual is an active caregiver. The measure-ment issue is worsened by the lack of a clear theoretical framework to guide research (Pavalko and Gong 2005) and difficulties with interpret-ing the concept of "family" in "family caregiving" that can be attribut-ed to societal shifts with respect to how families are identified and defined (Duxbury and Dole 2014).

Challenges are exacerbated by the fact that the terminology used in the academic literature to denote the activities undertaken by caregivers is quite variable. To better capture the meaning of the term, Fast and Keating (2000) categorized caregiving activities into four groups: person-al, physical, organizational, and emotional. Other terms commonly used to describe caregiving activities include "basic care," "personal care," "activities of daily living" or ADLs (e.g., dressing, feeding, and bathing), and "instrumental activities of daily living" or IADLs (e.g., grocery shop-ping, transportation, handling finances) (Mature Market Institute 2011). Furthermore, the terms "informal" or "unpaid" care are also used in the literature to emphasize that the caregiving is undertaken on a volunteer basis by family members, friends, and neighbours (Lum 2011). From the caregivers' perspective, however, much of this debate over terms is ir-relevant because they often cannot tell at which point the assistance they provide to the elderly turns them into a "caregiver" (Chappell 2011).

The Prevalence of Employed Caregiving

How many employees engage in caregiving? How many employees can be considered part of the sandwich generation? These important questions remain largely unresolved at this time because of inconsistencies in how researchers and governments treat the following basic parameters when making decisions as to whom they could identify as caregivers: the age of the caregiver, the type of care provided, the age of children in the home, and employment status. Our review of the literature and government records indicates that at this point in time we do not know the precise number of individuals who are involved in caregiving, let alone the number of employees who are involved in this role. Moreover, existing estimates vary widely.

Age of Caregiver: When preparing their estimates of the number of employed caregivers, most researchers assume that parents of individuals younger than 45 years of age will likely not need assistance with their daily activities. Based on this assumption they focus on samples of employees aged 45 and older (Turcotte 2013). This decision, however, is likely to result in an underestimate of the number of employees in the eldercare and sandwich generation groups, as recent evidence shows that adults under the age of 45 may also assume some of the caregiving responsibilities for grandparents and other elderly relatives (Albert and Schulz 2010; Turcotte 2013).

Type of Care Provided: Estimates also very depending on how researchers define "type of care." Our review of the literature identified three common ways to define "type of care" (Duxbury and Dole 2014): anyone who cares for an elderly dependent (including a spouse's parents, a family friend, a neighbour), anyone who is caring for their own parents, and anyone who is caring for a disabled child or adult. Lack of agreement on how to define "type of care" makes it difficult to give an accurate estimate of the prevalence of informal caregivers in the Canadian population, let alone the prevalence of employees in the eldercare and sandwich generation groups.

Age of Children at Home: Estimates of the number of people in the sandwich generation also vary depending on how researchers operationalize childcare. Some sources include those households where children are 18 and younger (e.g., Rajnovich, Keefe, and Fast 2005; Spillman and Pezzin 2000), while other sources include young adults up to age 25 who still live with their parents (e.g., Cranswick 2002; Hicks, Rowe, and Gribble 2007).

Employment Status: The above concerns make it difficult to come to any kind of consensus with respect to the number of caregivers in Canada at this time. These problems are compounded in any study of employed caregivers by the fact that many researchers do not provide data on either employment status or hours in paid employment per week for the populations being studied in their reports or articles.

Despite these challenges several estimates of the number of people in the eldercare and sandwich groups are provided below. These data serve both to illustrate the wide degree of variability in the existing estimates and to point out the significant number of citizens in this group.

At least one in four Canadians are caregivers

In Canada, the most recent data on family caregivers are found in Statistics Canada's 2012 General Social Survey (GSS) on Caregiving and Care Receiving (Sinah 2013; Turcotte 2013). These estimates suggest that the prevalence of employed caregivers in Canada is substantial. Consider the following data taken from the 2012 GSS:

- In 2012, about 8.1 million individuals, or 28 per cent of Canadians aged 15 years and older, provided care to a family member or friend with a long-term health condition, disability, or aging needs (Sinah 2013).
- The majority (6.1 million individuals or 60 per cent of the total caregiver population) of these caregivers were also juggling the demands of caregiving with paid work (Sinah 2013).

Data from the United States paint a very similar picture

Two large recent studies done in the United States, one by PEW Social Research and the other by the Families and Work Institute (the U.S. National Study of Employees), suggest that the prevalence of caregivers in the U.S. population is very similar to that observed in Canada. For example:

- The 2005 U.S. National Study of Employees notes that "29 percent (of employers) provide employees with information about elder care services" (Bond et al. 2005, 17).
- The 2008 National Study of the Changing Workforce (NSCW), a nationally representative study of the U.S. workforce, determined that 42 per cent of employed Americans (nearly 54.6 million employees) have provided eldercare in the past five years (Autman et al. 2010).
- The 2013 PEW study reports that "Four in ten adults in the U.S. are caring for an adult or child with significant health issues, up from 30% in 2010. Caring for a loved one is an activity that cuts across most demographic groups, but is especially prevalent among adults ages 30 to 64, a group traditionally still in the workforce" (PEW 2013, 2).

Estimates suggest that more than 2 million Canadian employees are "sandwiched"

As noted earlier, the "sandwich generation" is a subset of caregivers who still have children in their home but are also taking care of their aging parents. Relatively little is known about this cohort of caregivers, including their prevalence. The most current estimates in Canada are reported by Sinah (2013), who used Canada's 2012 GSS to estimate the number of Canadians in the sandwich group. She notes that over one-quarter (28 per cent) of caregivers, or 2.2 million individuals, could be considered "sandwiched" between caregiving (they provided assistance to parents or parents-in-law) and raising children (they had at least one child under 18 at home). Sinah (2013) also reports that the majority (81 per cent) of these individuals were also juggling the demands of paid work.

How has the number of people with caregiving responsibilities changed over time?

Unfortunately, it is difficult to tell how the number of caregivers has changed, as Statistics Canada have changed their sampling criteria over time – from individuals who were 45 to 65 years of age to all Canadians 15 years of age or older. That being said, the available data suggest that the number of Canadians engaged in caregiving has increased over time.

The 2002 GSS (Cycle 16), for example, reported that in 2002 more than 1.7 million Canadian adults aged 45 to 64 (or 16 per cent of this age group) were caregivers to almost 2.3 million seniors suffering from long-term disabilities (Cranswick 2002). A substantial number of these caregivers were employed (77 per cent of men and 63 per cent of women), most of them full time (Cranswick 2002).

Unfortunately, the 2002 GSS does not differentiate between employed caregivers who also have children at home (i.e., the sandwich group) and those who do not (the eldercare group). Using approximations from Canada's 2002 GSS, Williams (2004) estimated that there were 712,000 Canadians between the ages of 45 and 64 (25 per cent of the labour force) who would be considered "sandwiched." Using the same data set, Cranswick and Dosman (2008) also noted that almost 43 per cent of caregivers to the elderly were between 45 and 54 years old and very likely to have children living with them.

Estimates of the number of employees in the sandwich generation in the United States also vary widely depending on the source of the data. Spillman and Pezzin (2000), for example, reported that in the United States in 1994 there were almost 3.5 million people in the sandwich generation (1.8 million men and 1.7 million women). This group represented approximately 24 per cent of all potential caregivers in the United States. Rubin and White-Means (2009) cite a 2001 survey from the American Association of Retired People (AARP) suggesting that 40 per cent of people in the United States between the ages of 45 and 55 could be considered sandwiched. Hammer and Neal (2008) estimated that between 9 per cent and 13 per cent of U.S. households are made up of dual-earner, sandwiched-generation couples. The authors characterized the sandwich group as being a sizable minority of the U.S. workforce but not the norm. Finally, the recent PEW (2013, 1) study reported that "nearly half (47%) of adults in their 40s and 50s have a parent age 65 or older and are either raising a young child or financially supporting a grown child (age 18 or older)." Unfortunately, PEW does not report the employment status of the individuals in this group.

Lastly, it is interesting to note that both Williams (2004) and Sinah (2013) reported that a higher percentage of "sandwiched" Canadians were employed than of those who cared only for an elderly individual. Both authors attributed this difference to the fact that those in the sandwich group are younger than other caregivers. Sinah notes that in 2012 the median age of an individual in the sandwich group was 41 years of age versus a mean age of 52 years for someone in the eldercare group.

The Perfect Storm: Why Focus on Employed Caregiving? Why Now?

It is not a matter of "if you become a caregiver," but when.
                                    Canadian Caregiver Coalition (2001)

As noted above, there is significant variance in our estimates of how many employees are currently caregivers. There is, however, a high degree of consensus within the literature that society has yet to feel the full effects of the challenges of providing caregiving. Demographic projections suggest that in many developed countries the number of caregivers will increase dramatically over the next several decades, while the number of people able to provide such care is likely to shrink. The trends contributing to this increase include increased life expectancy, aging baby boomers, delayed marriage and parenthood, decreased fertility rates, and changes in health-care policies and practices that have shifted responsibility for care from formal to informal caregivers (Duxbury and Dole 2014). In the section below, Canada is used as an exemplar in our discussion of the factors likely to contribute to significant growth in the number of employees with responsibilities for caregiving. Most of these same trends can, however, be observed in most Western economies. Given the inexorable nature of many of these trends, it is hoped that the material in the sections below can be used by interested employers and policy makers to build a "burning platform" for change with respect to how employed caregivers are supported within the workplace.

Canada's population is aging

The global population is becoming increasingly older (World Bank 2012) and "ageing is one of the most challenging megatrends of the 21st century." In fact, preparing for an aging society is now a critical part of policy agendas throughout the world. Consider the following data. In Canada, from 1950 to 2010, the proportion of the population aged 65 and older grew from 8 per cent to 14 per cent. Recent census data (Statistics Canada 2014) determined that on 1 July 2013, the Canadian population included approximately 5.4 million people aged 65 and over (15.3 per cent of the total population). In 2036, it is estimated that this age bracket will represent 23 per cent to 25 per cent of the population. In fact, according to the medium-growth scenario of the most recent population projections put forward by Statistics Canada (2014), in 2017 the proportion of seniors in Canada's population could start to exceed the proportion of children, with a subsequent widening of the gap over time. The sheer number of people living longer will mean that in the not-too-distant future many employed Canadians will need to provide some form of assistance to at least one elderly relative.

The aging phenomenon observed in many countries, including Canada, is attributed to something that is referred to as the "rectangularization" or "compression" of mortality. This phenomenon occurs when there is an increase in the proportion of persons surviving to an advanced age (Statistics Canada 2014). Three factors are contributing to this rectangularization in Canada: increased life expectancy, reduced fertility, and the size of Canada's baby boom cohort.

Population aging is partially due to an increase in life expectancy

The Canadian trends with respect to an increase in longevity over time are quite clear. Life expectancy at birth in Canada for the 2009–2011 period was 79.1 years for males and 83.4 years for females (Statistics Canada 2014), a substantial increase over the 71.1 years of life reported for the total population in 1960 (World Bank 2012). According to the median mortality assumption in the most recent Canadian population projections, the life expectancy at birth of males and females will reach 84.0 years and 87.3 years, respectively, in 2036 (Statistics Canada 2014).

Also noteworthy is the projected increase over time in the number of Canadians 80 years of age and older (the "fragile elderly"). In 2001, there were 430,000 people aged 85 or older in Canada, double the number of people in this population group observed in 1981 and a twenty-fold increase since 1921 (Krett 2008). This trend has continued, and at this point in time the number of individuals 80 years of age and older has become a sizeable portion of the Canadian population. In 2010, out of 4.8 million seniors there were 1.3 million individuals aged 80 or older and 6,500 individuals aged 100 years or older. Recent projections (Statistics Canada 2014) show that this trend will continue unabated over time with the chances of a newborn in Canada in 2014 reaching 90 years of age being estimated at 21.7 per cent for males and 35.7 per cent for females. This is significantly higher than the chances of reaching 90 reported in 1931 (3.6 per cent for males and 4.7 per cent for females).

Declining fertility rates in the developed world have also contributed to population aging

On average, Canadian couples are no longer having enough children to replace themselves. In fact, the total fertility rate in Canada has been below the replacement level (which is currently 2.1 children per woman) for more than forty years. This low-fertility era follows the postwar baby-boom period (1946 to 1965), when the total fertility rate was much higher, reaching 3.94 children per woman in 1959 (Statistics Canada 2014). Many reasons are given for this decline in fertility, including a sudden increase in the amount of higher education pursued by both sexes and the increased number of women in the labour force (Lesthaeghe 2010). Cravey and Mitra (2011) report that, post-1970, as women became more educated and engaged in the labour market, they also postponed childbirth so that over time the highest rate of childbirth was observed in women between the ages of 30 and 34 while the second highest rate was detected in women between the ages of 35 and 39.

The most recent Canadian census provides current data on Canadian fertility rates. According to Statistics Canada (2014), the total fertility rate in Canada increased slightly from 1.51 children per woman in 2002 to 1.68 in 2008, before falling to its present value of 1.61 children per woman in 2011. Declining fertility rates mean that Canadian families are smaller today than they were thirty years ago, which means that, within the next few decades, children may be required to provide support for a larger number of elderly family members.

Population aging trends are likely to be intensified by the baby boom

The proportion of the Canadian population 65 years of age and older (i.e., seniors) has been steadily increasing in Canada over the past fifty years as a result of below-replacement fertility and the lengthening of life expectancy. Of note are projections showing that the proportion of the population in this group will increase dramatically in the coming years as more baby boomers reach 65 years of age (Statistics Canada 2014). The baby boom was a noticeable temporary increase in the birth rate that occurred in western and northern Europe as well as Canada, the United States, New Zealand, and Australia between 1946 and 1964 (Lesthaeghe 2010). The first baby boomer turned 65 in 2011. Increased longevity in this significant population cohort is likely to lead to a significant increase in the next several decades in the number of frail or dependent seniors in our population who will potentially require care from their family. Moreover, the fact that Canada has a larger number of baby boomers than most other countries means that we will see more pronounced changes in age demographics compared to other nations over time (Conner 2000; Statistics Canada 2011a, 2011b). What kind of numbers are we talking about here? According to Statistics Canada,[2] "the demands and expectations for care will continue to grow with the number of Canadians over 65 expected to double by 2026." This implies that as the baby-boom generation moves towards middle age, and their parents towards old age, a higher proportion of workers will simultaneously and/

---

2 Statistics Canada, The Daily: http://www.statcan.gc.ca/daily-quotidien/120529/dq120529a-eng.htm.

or sequentially be involved in combining paid employment with providing care and support to an ailing spouse or partner, parent, in-law, or other older relative (Lero and Lewis 2008, 391).

Similar trends can be observed in the United States

Similar trends can be observed in the United States. In 2012, 13 per cent of the U.S. population was aged 65 and older. While an individual born in 1900 had an average life expectancy of 49.2 years, by 2001 life expectancy had increased to 76.9 years, an increase of 27.7 years in longevity over time (Rice and Fineman 2004). According to the U.S. Census Bureau, by 2030 there will be approximately 60 million Americans between the ages of 66 and 84 (Cravey and Mitra 2011). Other estimates put the number of U.S. baby boomers expected to be living in 2030 at 70 million, or one in five of the U.S. population (Rice and Fineman 2004). Perhaps more significantly, by 2030 there may be as many as 8.9 million people aged 85 and over (Rice and Fineman 2004).

The demand for caregiving is projected to increase over time

The above trends (longer life expectancy, decreases in fertility) make it likely that the proportion of the Canadian population who require assistance from others will continue to grow over time (Cranswick 2002; Johnson and Lo Sasso 2000). While the oldest cohort of the Canadian baby boom generation has just achieved the traditional retirement age of 65 (in 2011), it is projected that in the years ahead the number of individuals in this retirement age bracket will show noticeable growth as more and more baby boomers make this transition. By 2036, the number of "seniors" (Canadians 65 years of age or older) will more than double, while the number of individuals aged 80 and over will increase by 2.6 times. One out of every three seniors will be 80 or older in 2036 (Statistics Canada 2010).

Poor health often accompanies aging, especially in the 80 and older age group. Improvements in medical science and assistive technology that enable people with disabilities and health problems to live longer and new patterns of chronic illness and disability suggest that we will likely see a greater number of people living longer with chronic ailments than in the past (Albert and Schulz 2010). Consider the following. Statistics Canada (2011a) reported that in 2009, 25 per cent of Canadian seniors suffered from more than one chronic condition. Neufeld and Harrison (2000) report that dementia is also on the rise, with estimates from the 1990s suggesting that approximately 8 per cent of all senior Canadians suffered from some form of dementia. Statistics Canada (Greenburg and Decady 2014) also noted that while Canadians are living longer, for many the ability to perform key health functions declines as they age. After age 65, this decline in functional health tends to accelerate, with more severe disability/activity limitations occurring, on average, around age 77. These trends will likely contribute to an increased need for employees to take on the role of caregiver (Statistics Canada 2011a; Fast and Keating 2000) and will have serious implications with respect to the requirement for continuous care (Chappell 2011).

The burden of caregiving is shifting from formal to informal caregivers

The above data indicate that over the next several decades Canada will need to devote more resources to eldercare. Unfortunately, the restructuring of the Canadian health-care system has reduced the ability of public health services to respond to this increase in demand. The lengths of stay in hospital are shorter, wait times are longer, and costs for nursing homes and other professional services are higher (Johnson and Lo Sasso 2000; Neufeld and Harrison 2000). While the data show that patients are being transitioned back into the community from hospitals at an expedited rate, they also show that: (1) the provision within the community of social service resources and supports for these patients has not kept pace with the discharge rate, (2) the need for informal caregiver support increases concomitant with early discharge of the elderly from hospitals into the community, and (3) an increasing number of elderly individuals who need help with activities of daily living are living in the community (Johnson and Schaner 2005).

It would appear that health-care reforms that emphasize early discharge and community-based care have shifted responsibility for care from formal to informal caregivers. They have also redistributed a considerable amount of eldercare to the community and to informal caregivers who now need to provide higher levels of care for frail, ill, and disabled people at home (Fast and Keating 2000). Although living in the community is considered a physically and psychologically healthier option than being institutionalized, it can be expected that the demands for care will increase the anxiety, stress, and burnout levels of informal caregivers (Frederick and Fast 1999).

Also relevant to this discussion are data showing that improvements in medical science and assistive technology have enabled people to coexist with debilitating illnesses and disabilities for a longer time than in the past (Albert and Schulz 2010). These trends also place more of a burden on family caregivers, as these elderly will not only need assistance with their daily activities but will also require types of medical care or therapy that untrained informal helpers might not be comfortable with providing (Armstrong and Kitts 2004).

A review by Guberman (1999) concluded that family and friends provide 75 to 90 per cent of total care to their loved ones. There is no reason to suspect that this level of support will decline in coming years. Rather, it is anticipated that unpaid care by family and friends will continue to be a substantial part of eldercare in the future (Chappell 2011). It also implies that a higher proportion of our workforce will take on this burden.

As greater numbers of elderly are residing in the community, there is a strong tendency towards a shared responsibility of care from informal sources such as family, friends, and neighbours, with limited support from formal sources. Informal sources of care are predominantly close family members, most of whom are women. It is anticipated that unpaid care by family and friends will continue to be a substantial part of eldercare in the future (Chappell 2011). Unfortunately, the data show that the rise in the need for informal caregiving is occurring concomitant with a decline in the supply of this important resource. Smaller family sizes, later marriages, remarriages, higher divorce rates, an increase in the proportion of elderly within the family unit, a decline in free time, and an increase in the number of women pursuing career ambitions rather than having children have contributed to this shift (Grunfeld et al. 1997; Lesthaeghe 2010). More importantly, the available data suggest we can expect these trends to hold steady into the future.

Recent work by Statistics Canada (2014) provides further support for the idea that in the very near future this higher demand for caregiving will fall on a smaller number of employed children. From the 1950s to the early 1970s, there were approximately eight working-age persons (aged 15 to 64) for each person aged 65 and over. This ratio has since declined over time to its current level of 4.5 working-age persons for each person aged 65 and over (Statistics Canada 2014). Furthermore, population projections suggest that this ratio could decline by about half in the next fifty years such that by the late 2050s, there could be only two working-age persons for each person aged 65 and over (Statistics Canada 2014).

Other demographic changes may also increase the number of "sandwiched" Canadians

Originally, people used the term "sandwich generation" to refer to people who supported children under the age of 18 while also providing care to one or more seniors. Recent data indicate, however, that the "sandwiched" may remain sandwiched even after their children reach 18 years of age, as today parents' progeny take a more prolonged path to mature adulthood and do not "leave the nest" until they are older. In practical terms, many adult children of the sandwiched group continue to live at home and rely on financial support from their parents, who are increasingly weighed down by their own filial responsibilities to their aging parents (Igarashi et al. 2013).

Why should we care about caregivers?

Why should Canadians care that the number of employed caregivers in Canada is both substantial and likely to increase over time? In the section below we make the "case for caring" by outlining what is currently known about the consequences of caregiving for key stakeholders in the caregiving relationship. We used Harlton, Keating, and Fast's (1998, 281) list of key stakeholders (i.e., "older adults themselves, their family members, friends and neighbors, those who provide services to older adults and those who develop policies for seniors' benefits and services") as the starting point for our discussion. To this list we add employers (many caregivers are employed) and society in general, which is impacted through public policy and the allocation of resources.

The body of literature on this topic is large, and a complete review is beyond the scope of this book. We elected, therefore, to present only a few key findings on the consequences of caregiving that are representative of the literature as a whole. Interested readers who want more details on the material summarized in the section below, as well as a list of relevant references in each of the areas discussed, are directed to the following three articles, which served as the source of much of the data presented in this section:

- the review of Canadian research on the causes, consequences, and moderators of caregiver strain among employed caregivers undertaken by Duxbury and Higgins (2013b)
- the comprehensive review by Calvano (2013) of the research on the relationship between eldercare and employment published in peer reviewed academic journals since 1995
- the systematic review by Duxbury and Dole (2014) of peer reviewed academic articles on the sandwich generation published after Stoller's highly cited 1983 article on parental caregiving

The Impact of Caregiving on Caregivers

Family caregiving is a resource-intensive responsibility, as caregivers' time, energy, and financial resources are diverted from their normal activities to caring for their loved one. Evidence indicates that caregiving is especially taxing for caregivers who are also engaged in paid employment, as such individuals need to balance multiple roles and responsibilities – a balancing act that may result in higher levels of physical, mental, emotional, and economic strain (Duxbury and Dole 2014).

Individuals can be affected by their caregiving responsibilities in a variety of ways. Cranswick (2002) contends that caregiving can contribute to physical and mental health problems for caregivers, negatively impact caregivers' work situations as well as their economic well-being, influence caregivers' social consequences, and effect their living arrangements. In the section below we provide evidence that caregiving impacts outcomes in each of these given areas. We then provide a brief discussion of positive outcomes that have been found to be associated with the caregiver role.

*Caregiving is associated with a variety of physical
and mental health problems*

There is ample evidence in the literature linking caregiving to a variety of health problems for the caregiver. First, providing personal care to severely disabled elderly person (e.g., bedridden or in a wheelchair) typically involves lifting and turning and may cause muscle strain and back problems. Second, sleep deprivation or disrupted sleep patterns can also occur, leading to various physical and mental health problems, including fatigue, headaches, ulcer, inability to concentrate, and hypertension. Third, the health of caregivers can be further affected by the behaviours they engage in to cope with caregiver strain such as smoking and alcohol use. Finally, employed caregivers tend to ignore preventive health check-ups and, in general, neglect caring for their own health. From the limited literature that is available, it appears that multigenerational caregivers are experiencing the same physical consequences from caregiving as those individuals in the eldercare-only group.

The research findings linking caregiving and caregiver mental health are somewhat mixed. While a number of studies report that caregivers claim that providing care to an elderly dependent is stressful, other studies show that such stress does not necessarily always lead to adverse mental health outcomes. This discrepancy has been attributed to two ideas: that caregiving also has a number of positive outcomes that can outweigh the challenge, and that caregivers are able to adapt to their situation over time.

A number of studies support a link between caregiving and poor mental health. In cases where mental health is affected, caregivers have consistently reported higher rates of depression than non-caregivers, as well as increased levels of anxiety, fatigue, anger, resentment, hostility, and eating problems. The literature identifies a number of reasons why caregiving may negatively impact mental health, including the following:

- Caregivers often feel trapped and helpless.
- Caregiving tends to be unpredictable, and caregivers experience a loss of control over their lives (e.g., are forced to reduce time spent in social activities and hobbies, to change travel and holiday plans, and/or to shift or reduce their work hours, resulting in lost income).
- Caregivers tend to worry about their own finances as well as the financial security and physical and mental health of those they care for.
- Caregivers often feel guilty about not being able to devote sufficient attention to the care recipient, other family members, work, and themselves.
- Caregivers often feel pressed for time and find it difficult to balance work and family demands.

Double the demands does not necessarily lead to double the stress

Do middle-aged employees providing care to both seniors and children at the same time experience higher levels of strain than their counterparts who only have to care for a child or an elderly dependent? The evidence with respect to this issue is not clear-cut. One set of studies supports the view that excess load results in negative consequences for the caregivers in the sandwich group. A second set of studies endorses the idea that the burden of multiple caregiving roles is offset by the positive aspects of caregiving, which lessen the negative impacts of either role. Having reviewed the findings of a series of studies on this topic, Chumbler, Pienta, and Dwyer (2004) concluded that both perspectives are supported in the literature and that there are "just too many factors at play" for the relationship between multigenerational caregiving and employee mental health to be simple and straightforward.

Studies reporting that employees in the sandwich group are at higher risk of experiencing depression, stress, and mental strain than their counterparts in other family situations (e.g., childcare only, eldercare only) dominate in the research literature. While initially it was felt that these negative outcomes stemmed from the higher time demands faced by those in this group, the research in the area now suggests that it is not the work per se that increases depression and stress but rather the number and range of seniors that caregivers have to look after. More specifically, the skills needed to care for seniors are often quite different from those needed to care for children, and it may be that it is easier for an individual to care for more than one senior or more than one child than for a mixture of the two.

There is also a smaller body of research that supports the idea that the burden of multiple caregiving roles is offset by the positive aspects of caregiving. Such research notes that, when physical care demands are high, children have also been found to help with lifting and other caregiving chores. They also help look after each other. Mothers in the sandwich group who reported that their children helped out and supported their efforts to care for the elderly family member reported an improvement in their psychological well-being.

Caregiving can affect the caregiver's social and family life

Caregiving also has the potential to affect the caregiver's social and family life. Several studies report that caregivers find it more difficult to balance their work and personal demands than those without such duties. Caregivers often make up the time that they need to take off during the work day to deal with caregiving emergencies by taking work home to complete in the evenings and on weekends. Care duties have also been found to interfere with caregivers' ability to spend time in leisure and social activities, or on hobbies, visits with friends, and vacations. Finally, research has also established a link between caregiving and an increased incidence of family conflict. More specifically, time in caregiving may damage relationships within the family, as time alone with one's spouse becomes limited and family vacation times are restricted.

The economic consequences of caregiving for the caregiver

Other research supports the idea that the caregiving role may have a negative impact on the caregiver's financial situation. Missed days of work, unpaid leaves, transitioning to part-time work, or quitting a job may result in lost income and hurt the long-term economic well-being of caregivers. The 2002 General Social Survey noted that 11 per cent of women and 9 per cent of men aged 45 to 54 lost income as a result of their care duties. The opportunity costs of these reductions in employment are considerable and include diminished chances of future employment, reductions in savings and investments, reduced contributions to pension funds, smaller pension benefits, and lower standards of living during retirement. Mature Market Institute (2011) calculated that over an American's lifetime, all of the income losses due to caregiving add up to U.S. $283,716 for men and $324,044 for women. Any economic recession puts caregivers at an even greater financial risk, as they have to maintain their own financial stability while using up their savings or incurring additional debt to cover caregiving expenses (Evercare Survey 2009).

Other research shows that the costs of caregiving often come out of the caregiver's pocket. Caregivers may, for example, incur extra expenses because they need to purchase adaptive equipment, medication, special diets, care services, home modifications, and grocery delivery and pay for travel and phone bills for the person(s) they are caring for. Decima Research estimated that caregivers spent more than $100 per month on caregiving, amounting to $80 million per year for all Canadians

(Lum 2011). According to a more liberal estimate by Evercare (Evercare Survey 2009), caregiving to the elderly costs more than 10 per cent of a caregiver's annual income, and at least half of all caregivers experience difficulty paying for their own necessities as a result of these extra expenses. According to Mature Market Institute (2011), annual out-of-pocket expenses for caregiving may reach U.S. $5,531 per caregiver. Despite the rising costs associated with caregiving, 65 per cent of Evercare Survey (2009) respondents said that financial burden had not decreased the quality of care they provided to their family members.

Caregiving responsibilities may also hurt employees' career advancement and promotional opportunities. Research in the area has found that employed caregivers are more likely than their counterparts without such responsibilities to have declined training, challenging new assignments, and job transfers that involve relocation. These decisions severely hinder career advancement (and earning potential), as they limit an employee's ability to acquire new skills. Men appear to be somewhat more vulnerable to this risk than women.

Finally, it should be noted that no information could be found regarding the financial costs or lost income associated with caregiving for those in the "sandwich generation." This makes it impossible to compare their economic burden to those in the eldercare-only group.

The positive side of caregiving

Despite all of the burdens that caregivers face, the extant research in the area suggests that there are also beneficial outcomes associated with caregiving, especially when the care recipient is a parent. A number of studies have reported, for example, that caregivers describe a number of positive feelings associated with caregiving, including a closer relationship with the care receiver, the ability to show their love and gratitude to their relative, the ability to display competence to their parent, the ability to make a difference and to fulfil their sense of duty. Caregivers also felt thankful that their relative had lived to an old age and obtained satisfaction from seeing their elderly dependent happy, in feeling that their elderly family member appreciated them, and in seeing their condition improve. Others reported feeling fulfilled that they had helped their elderly family member preserve their dignity and self-esteem by keeping them at home longer.

Impact on Employers

In the 1990s, very few employers paid attention to the issues faced by employees who had to provide care for elderly dependents. Those employers who did consider the issue as potentially important took the view that caregiving would have essentially the same impact on work-life conflict as childcare. A decade later, while caregiving has become a growing reality for many workplaces, research in the area suggests that eldercare carries a certain stigma and is not acknowledged and supported by employers to the same extent as childcare. In the section below, we review research showing how caregiving may impact a number of key work outcomes, including intent to turnover, absenteeism, and succession planning, all of which are linked to the organization's bottom line.

Caregiving may negatively impact an organization's bottom line

From the employer's perspective the fact that employees with eldercare responsibilities miss work more often than their colleagues without such duties is well documented. The data also show a strong link between absence due to ill health and taking on the roles of caregiver and employee at the same time, suggesting that an inability to balance these two roles negatively affects caregivers' health. While the data indicate that younger employees find it particularly difficult to combine all of life's demands with eldercare, there is very little information in the literature about why this might be the case. Such information is necessary given the fact that the number of younger caregivers is expected to rise in the future (i.e., delaying parenting until one is older means that 25-year-olds can have older parents).

In the MetLife (2003) study, taking time off, coming in late, and leaving early were common practices in the workplace for those with caregiving responsibilities. This trend appears to be on the rise. Mathew

Greenwald and Associates (2009), for example, stated that in 2009, 65 per cent of employed caregivers engaged in these types of behaviours – a significant increase from the 57 per cent who reported these forms of work interruption in 2007.

Geographic proximity between caregivers and care recipients also plays a role in workplace dynamics. About 40 per cent of caregivers who lived more than half a day away from their parents were found to miss full days of work, while only 28 per cent of caregivers who lived in the same neighbourhood as their parents did so (Statistics Canada 2011a). Little attention has been given to the effects of multigenerational caregiving on workplace behaviours, and it is unclear if caregivers in the "sandwich generation" are more likely to be absent from work than employees who have only childcare or eldercare responsibilities.

Research in the area also supports the idea that work performance is compromised when employees have significant caregiving demands. This reduction in work performance is often attributed to the idea that caregivers are more likely to encounter distractions at work (e.g., phone calls to coordinate care) and/or to experience a lack of energy and focus that is associated with their role as a caregiver. Other research reports that employed caregivers find it difficult to accept promotions, attend meetings outside regular working hours, take on extra work, and work longer hours. Employed caregivers have also been found to be more likely to refuse overtime, forgo work-related travel, consider a job change, or consider quitting work altogether. Work disruptions are especially common when the caregiver is looking after someone with some form of dementia or mental health problems. Also important are data showing that employees of all ranks and job types experience a significant reduction in workplace productivity due to eldercare responsibilities

Several attempts have been made to assign a monetary value to the costs that employers experience as a consequence of having employees with eldercare responsibilities. Direct costs from absenteeism and an employee's utilization of health benefits (e.g., from hospital admissions for stress-related illnesses) are more explicit and therefore easier to measure. The health problems most frequently reported by those with caregiving responsibilities include depression, diabetes, hypertension, and heart disease. Metlife Institute in the United States included absenteeism, partial absenteeism, workday interruptions, crisis in care, supervision (covering for absent employees), replacements, unpaid leave, and reducing hours from full-time to part-time in their calculation of costs attributable to caregiving. The total estimated cost to employers for all full-time caregivers in this study was $33.6 billion annually or an average annual cost of $2,110 per employed caregiver (Wagner, Lottes, and Neal 2006). Indirect costs, such as lost productivity, are much harder to estimate but are also incurred by employers as a result of an employee's eldercare responsibilities (Albert and Schulz 2010). Further costs may be incurred by employers if co-workers become involved as an informal source of support for their caregiving colleagues.

Finally, the research suggests that women approach responsibilities around caregiving very differently from men, and that this could account for gender differences in how caregiving impacts the organizational bottom line. More specifically, when an elderly family member, especially a parent, is in need of assistance, women are more likely than men to make the provision of such assistance (even helping with the more intensive activities of daily living) a priority, regardless of their employment status. As a consequence, female employees with caregiving responsibilities are more likely than their male counterparts to report that their work demands conflict with their caregiving responsibilities and to cope with such conflict by (1) reducing the amount of time they spend in paid employment, (2) quitting their jobs, (3) letting their caregiving duties interrupt their work, and (4) missing work altogether (i.e., increased absenteeism). Male caregivers, on the other hand, are less involved in intensive caregiving and are less likely to give up their jobs to provide care.

Other studies paint a more positive picture as they suggest that paid employment may provide a respite from caregiving activities for women. For example, a number of case studies have reported that most women who quit their jobs to provide care were regretful because they missed the social interactions with co-workers and their sense of achievement from the job and felt badly about forgoing personal development. Other studies show that employment also allowed female caregivers to spend money on formal sources of care instead of providing all of the intensive care themselves. Finally, the fact that female caregivers who are not employed often report poorer mental health outcomes than their female counterparts who are employed provides further support for the idea that paid work may help females cope with the demands of the caregiver role.

Social consequences

The care provided by informal caregivers is one of the significant "hidden costs" associated with the public health-care system. If not for family caregivers, society would be responsible for providing these services. The economic value provided by family caregivers is enormous. Over a decade ago it was estimated that informal help and care for seniors saved the public system over $5.3 billion per year, which was deemed to be equivalent to the work of 276,500 full-time employees (Fast and Keating 2000). More recently, Hollander and colleagues (2009, 48) concluded that "a reasonably conservative estimate of the imputed economic contribution of unpaid caregivers for Canada, for 2009, would be $25–$26 billion."

Despite the significant cost savings associated with informal caregiving, there are also expenditures. In the paragraphs below we provide a short summary of the costs of caregiving to the caregiver and society. It should be noted, however, that a lot has been written on this topic in the past several years, and a complete review of this topic is beyond the purview of this book. The interested reader is therefore referred to the following two excellent articles on this topic that describe the various costs in detail: Fast (2015) and Keating and colleagues (2014).

The societal costs of caregiving are most apparent when caregivers who cannot balance caregiving and work responsibilities end up leaving their jobs. This is especially apparent for women, who constitute the majority of caregivers. Forgone employment income results in decreased tax revenue and in turn imposes limits on public spending. Jacobs and colleagues (2013) calculated the annual costs of informal caregiving for Canadians aged 45 and older. They found that the costs to the government of having employees engaged in informal caregiving increased concomitant with the amount of time per week the individual spent in caregiving and noted that, at higher levels of caregiving intensity (more than five hours per week), there was a net cost to the government of $641 million per year. They attributed these costs to decreased tax revenues and an increased use of social assistance for caregivers who had left the labour market because of their caregiving demands. Keating and colleagues (2014) identified the following costs to caregivers of the provision of such care: reduced or forgone income, lost employment benefits, reduced pension benefits, reduced savings and investments, and reduced overall financial security. Other research shows that caregivers' health is often adversely affected because they are subject to multiple strains and tend to neglect their own health. Ultimately, they end up seeking health services themselves and placing an additional burden on the health-care system.

Answers from the 2012 National Study on Work, Life and Caregiving

In this book, we use quantitative (i.e., survey) and qualitative (i.e., interview) data from the 2012 National Study on Work, Life and Caregiving (referred to throughout the book as "the 2012 Study") to inform our discussion of the challenges faced by Canadian employees who are also engaged in caregiving. The 2012 Study is one of the most comprehensive investigations done to date on the challenges faced by Canadian employees seeking to balance the demands they face at work with the complex and ever-changing conditions they face at home (childcare and/or eldercare). The ability to use both quantitative and qualitative data from this study to broadly explore the topic of employed caregiving is one of the strengths of this book. Complete details on the methodology used to collect and analyse the data from "the 2012 Study" can be found in Duxbury and Higgins (2013a, b, and d). For ease of reference, key details of relevance to this book are summarized below.

Quantitative data: The Total Sample

A questionnaire (the 2012 National Work, Life and Caregiving Survey; hereafter, "the 2012 Survey") was used to collect the quantitative data presented in this book. The survey instrument was divided into seven sections: your job and your organization; your manager; work-life balance; management of work and family demands; caregiving; physical and mental health; and "information about you." All of the scales used in the questionnaire are psychometrically sound research instruments that have been well validated in other studies. A complete summary of all the measures included in the survey, including the working definition of each of the variables, the source of the measure, and its interpretation, are included in Duxbury and Higgins (2013a). The measures used to quantify the constructs of relevance to this book are listed, along with their source(s), in the appendix.

The use of a survey to collect quantitative data on issues associated with caregiving offers a number of advantages from a research perspective. First, it allows us to collect information from a large number of individuals, thus enhancing the generalizability of the results. Second, the use of reliable and valid measures and well-established statistical procedures allows us to objectively test numerous hypotheses pertaining to caregiving.

Just over 25,000 Canadian employees who worked full-time for a sample of larger (100-plus employees) public (federal, provincial, and municipal governments), private, and not-for-profit organizations responded to this questionnaire. We use the term "the Total Sample" throughout the book to refer to this sample of 25,000 employees. A majority of these respondents are highly educated managers and professionals (i.e., knowledge workers) who work for larger firms and for whom money and job security are less likely to be issues. As such, the findings from this study represent a best-case scenario of the work-caregiving relationship.

Quantitative data: The Caregiver Sample

The 2012 National Work, Life and Caregiving Survey included an optional section entitled "Caregiving." This section of the survey was designed to give us a greater understanding of how combining the roles of employee and caregiver impacts work-life conflict and the organizational bottom line. Rather than predefine who should and should not be in the caregiving group, we allowed respondents to self-define as to whether or not they considered themselves to be caregivers. This self-definition process involved the following two steps. First, we put the following prompt into the survey:

As our population ages many Canadian employees find themselves providing some kind of care, be it financial, help with chores or concrete caregiving activities, for their elderly parents or in-laws. The following questions deal with the challenges of providing such care. If you do not have any caregiving responsibilities, please skip to ...

Respondents had to click a radio button acknowledging that they engaged in caregiving before they were allowed to see the questions in the Caregiving section. Second, to confirm that these individuals had selected appropriately we included the following question at the beginning of the Caregiving section:

If you are providing care for an elderly family member (i.e., you provide emotional care and/or concrete caregiving activities) please answer the following questions. If you are not, please skip to ...

As a final check we asked respondents to *"think of a specific individual for whom you provide care when answering the questions in this section"* and to *"Please confirm that you provide care to an elderly family member: (a) yes, (b) no."* Only then were the respondents asked to fill out the questions included in the Caregiving section of the survey. This last step also enabled us to include several open-ended questions in the survey to collect information on the care recipient as well as to give the respondent a reference point to think of when responding to the questions. Just under 8,000 (n = 7,966) of the 25,000 respondents also completed the optional Caregiver section of the survey. We use the term "the Caregiver Sample" throughout the book to refer to this sample of 7,966 employees.

Qualitative data: The Interview Sample

Survey data have a number of limitations when it comes to examining an emotion-laden, highly complex topic like caregiving, and often do not adequately answer the question of why people responded to the survey the way they did. These issues are more adequately addressed in interviews, where the researcher is able to explore people's attitudes, feelings, and behaviours in greater depth.

To give us a better understanding of the role of employed caregiver (i.e., what employed caregivers do, why they do it, and the joys and pressures that come along with assuming the role of employed caregiver), we undertook a follow-up interview study of a select group of caregivers who responded to our survey. The qualitative data complement the quantitative data in that they helps us better understand why some employees find caregiving to be burdensome and stressful, while others find joy in the role (Montgomery, Gonyea, and Hooyman 1985). Such information (i.e., what contributes to these variations in experiences) should help policy makers and employers to design effective intervention strategies.

The interview sample was obtained as follows. At the end of the survey we asked respondents to give us their names if they were willing to participate in follow-up interviews on their caregiving experiences. Fifteen per cent (n = 1,175) of the 7,966 employees who completed the Caregiver section of the survey indicated that they would be willing to participate in our interview study. To minimize the impact of uncontrolled confounds on the relationships under study we selected from this initial set of volunteers men and women who (1) were married/living with a partner, (2) worked full time (i.e., 35 or more hours per week), and (3) spent at least an hour a week in caregiving. We did this so that we could consider the impact of three key possible caregiving differentiators on the outcomes being studied: the intensity of caregiving duties (operationalized using our measure of subjective caregiver burden), life-cycle stage (sandwich, eldercare), and gender. Respondents in the sandwich group were required to spend at least an hour per week in childcare in addition to the one hour per week spent in eldercare. We use the term "the Interview Sample" throughout the book to refer to the 111 employed caregivers who participated in the interview phase of the study.

As shown in table 1.1, the interview sample is balanced with respect to gender (48 per cent men, 52 per cent women), caregiving intensity

Table 1.1 Interview Sample Distribution

	Sandwich		Eldercare		Total
	Men	Women	Men	Women	
High Intensity	12 (11%)	15 (14%)	9 (8%)	17 (15%)	53 (48%)
Low Intensity	17 (15%)	13 (12%)	15 (14%)	13 (12%)	58 (52%)
Gender	29	28	24	30	
Total		57 (51%)		54 (49%)	

(48 per cent high intensity, 52 per cent low intensity), and life-cycle stage (51 per cent sandwich generation, 49 per cent eldercare). In fact, with one exception (males, high intensity, eldercare), the interview cell sizes were all approximately equal. The fact that males in the high-intensity eldercare group were also under-represented in the survey sample of caregivers suggests that fewer employed men find themselves in this situation.

We used a semi-structured interview format to collect our qualitative data. The complete interview script can be found in Duxbury and Higgins (2013d). We referred to the cognitive process of stress appraisal (Lazarus and Folkman 1984) when designing our interview script. According to this model, distress does not necessarily result from a potentially stressful episode (e.g., caring for an elderly dependent). High stress results when something (i.e., a stressor) is appraised by an individual as threatening or harmful in some way, resulting in negative emotions. On the other hand, when individuals appraise a situation as "challenging" or "beneficial" and report positive emotions, they will not experience higher levels of stress. This is consistent with the fact that some employees experience high levels of stress when performing the caregiver role while others, in very similar situations, do not. The cognitive model of stress thus provides a theoretical basis for understanding negative, positive, and mixed reactions to the role of employed caregiver (Gilboa et al. 2008).

Using this model of stress as a framework for the design of the interview offers a number of benefits. First, we can examine in more detail the process by which caregiving is appraised as stressful and, in particular, how the context in which the caregiving experience unfolds determines the level of stress experienced. Second, this approach will help to identify coping strategies and forms of support that result in positive appraisals. Such information will be useful to both employers and policy makers who seek to reduce stress within the workforce.

All interviews were done by telephone and recorded. The interview took people approximately forty-five to ninety minutes to complete. Most respondents noted that they found the experience to be "cathartic" and useful and thanked us for doing the study. After all the interviews were conducted, we transcribed the information on the tapes into Word documents. Content analysis (Charmaz 2014) was used to analyse the data. Throughout this book, we italicize direct quotations from the interviews and also use italic type for the content categories.

Orienting Framework: Life-Cycle Stage

Given the sheer amount of data collected in this study, we needed to draw up a number of protocols governing how the data are presented and discussed in this book. We elected to use the concept of life-cycle (or life-course) stage as an orienting framework. Life-cycle stage is an analytic concept commonly used in sociology to study changes over time in patterns of individual (life stage) and family (family cycle) development. Underlying the life-cycle concept is the recognition that (1) an individual's social roles (such as work or having a child) define the human life cycle, (2) role occupancy (i.e., spouse, parent, grandparent) tends to be age related, and (3) people tend to transition from one life-cycle stage to the next (i.e., move from one set of social roles to another) as they age. We examine the impact of the following life-cycle stages in various parts this book:

- *No dependent care:* This group is made up of employees who work full time but spend no time in any form of dependent care. Employees in this group are considered as a control group in this analysis.
- *Childcare:* Childcare consists of the supervision and nurturing of a child, including casual and informal services provided by a parent.

In this study, employees are considered to be in this life-cycle stage if they spend one or more hours per day in childcare/activities with their children but no time in eldercare activities.

- *Eldercare:* Eldercare is a form of caregiving that relates to the special needs and requirements unique to seniors (i.e., caregiving). Employees who supply eldercare typically provide a broad range of financially uncompensated ongoing care and assistance (either by necessity or choice) directly to family members who are in need due to physical, cognitive, or mental health conditions. In this study employees are considered to be in this life-cycle stage if they spend one or more hours per week providing care to an elderly dependent but no time per week in childcare.
- *Sandwich generation:* Individuals who are dealing with their own dependent children while also tending to the needs of aging parents are referred to as belonging to the "sandwich" generation. Such employees have "multigenerational" caring responsibilities. In this study, employees are considered to be in this life-cycle stage if they spend one or more hours per day in childcare activities with their children and one or more hours per week in eldercare.

The use of a life-cycle stage framework in this book supports the reporting of findings and comparisons that are particularly relevant for policy makers and employers, as it facilitates the development of solutions that are specific to the various groups in their workforce. The breakdown of the 2012 Study Total Sample with respect to gender and life-cycle stage is as shown in figure 1.1. The large number of employees in each of the groups of interest means that even relatively small differences between groups are statistically significant. As such we focus our discussion on findings that are also substantive in nature.

Generalizability of the findings

Data from the 2012 Study provide us with a unique opportunity to undertake an in-depth study of the issues faced by employed caregivers. The sample is geographically representative but skewed with respect to

Figure 1.1: Caregiving: Total Sample (n = 25,021) (percentages)

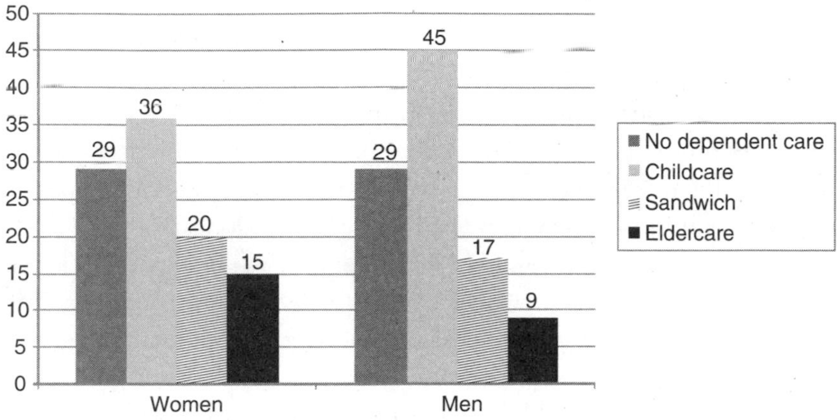

job type and socio-economic status. The fact that most of the employed caregivers in this sample were highly educated managers and professionals working for larger firms (firms with more than 500 employees) has two important implications with respect to the generalizability of the findings. First, the findings presented in this book are of relevance to organizations which are interested in recruiting, retaining, and engaging knowledge workers. Second, findings using data from the 2012 Study are likely to represent a "best case" scenario with respect to the relationship between employment and caregiving, as the employees in this sample can afford to purchase goods and services to help them manage their responsibilities outside of work. Respondents are also more likely to have access to flexible work arrangements, a fact that could also help them cope with the challenges they face with respect to balancing work and caregiving. Job security is also less likely to be an issue for the individuals in our sample. Our interview sample was selected to reduce the impact of uncontrolled confounds on our findings. While this strategy helps us understand the challenges faced by caregivers in dual-income families, it limits our ability to understand the experiences of employed caregivers who are not employed full time or who are in different family types.

Answers from the interview study

This section has no statistics or data. Instead we take a "storytelling" approach to give a voice to those who are currently providing care and provide the reader with a better appreciation of what is behind the numbers presented in the rest of the book. Such an approach also encourages the reader to empathize with those in the caregiving situation in a way that is unlikely when one relies on data alone.

The eight case studies profiled in this part of the book were selected from the 111 interviews we conducted with Canadian caregivers and illustrate "typical" challenges facing employees in the four main caregiving groups featured in this book: men and women in the sandwich group, and men and women in the eldercare group. The scenarios were selected because in many key ways they "typify" what we heard in the interviews.

In each of the case studies, we describe the caregivers (age, marital status, and number and age of their children) and the people they care for (who they are, their age, and where they live). Then, to help the reader understand the kinds of situations faced by employed caregivers in this country we provide a short synopsis of what they told us – why they provide care; how much time they spend in caregiving; how much time their partner spends in caregiving; the types of caregiving activities they perform; the extent to which they experience physical, financial, and emotional strain as a result of their caregiving activities; and what makes caregiving emotionally overwhelming.

In addition, we briefly summarize findings from the scenario analysis section of the interview (see Duxbury and Higgins 2013d), which asked people to describe a time when they were overwhelmed by their caregiving role. Examination of these scenarios gives the reader an appreciation of why caregiving can be extremely stressful for those engaged in such activities. Finally, it should be noted that when writing up this section we made every effort to protect the anonymity of the respondents.

Mary, sandwich generation

Mary is 43 years old. She is married and has two children of her own (15- and 16-year-old boys). In addition to her two children, a 16-year-old friend of her son's has also moved in with her recently: *"and I have a young lad that I'm actually taking care of. He's having some problems at home, so he moved in with us in May. So right now I've got three children."* Even though her boys are teenagers, she spends twenty hours a week in child-care – because *"the boys are in hockey ..."* Her husband spends about the same amount of time in childcare as she does and also acts as chauffeur to the boys.

She is also currently looking after three elderly dependents: *"My mother, and my aunt, and my mother-in-law."* Her mother, who is 85, re-quires the most care, and Mary has been caring for her *"intensely"* for the past two years (spending between ten and twenty hours a week in care) because she is an only child and she feels it is her duty to look af-ter her mother: *"She's my mom and there is basically nobody else to do it."*

Over the last six years she has also been providing care for her moth-er-in-law (her husband is the primary caregiver and she *"helps out"*) and her aunt (*"they did not have children and her husband has died"*). Both of these women are in their late eighties.

For Mary, caregiving involves a myriad of different activities. She talks to her mother on the phone every day – *"I'd say half an hour on the telephone each day – she doesn't talk much, except asking the same question over and over... "* – and generally does whatever else is required: *"So, groceries; bath; socialization; cleaning the house. I bring her laundry home to do. I try and make sure that bills are getting paid. I go to the bank for her when she needs it – just stuff like that. It's all so mundane that I'm not even sure anymore."*

Her husband spends an additional two hours a week on care of Mary's mother doing the things that she cannot get around to doing that week: *"Basically, the same stuff that I do with the exception, obviously, of bathing."*

While financial caregiver strain does not appear to be problem for Mary or her family, Mary reports that caregiving is a real physical strain on her – which she attributes to the fact that she is waiting for back sur-gery for an injury that has been exacerbated by caring for her mother.

Mary reports that she is overwhelmed by her caregiving situation on a daily basis because *"it's work, home, dinner, Mom, home, hockey or some extra-curricular activities for the boys ..."* Mary's caregiving scenario describes a number of factors that are common sources of stress within our sample of caregivers: her mother's physical health has deteriorated over time; she cannot get appropriate care for her mother within the community and is constantly worried that her mother is not safe living in her home; her mother's mental health is worsening; she cannot find a suitable facility to care for her mother; she continually experiences anxiety that she attributes to her caregiving situation.

Approximately half of the caregivers in our sample discussed issues associated with dementia when relating their eldercare scenario. Mary describes it as follows: *"I was still worrying about that because, when there wasn't anybody there ... I can't be on the phone with her every waking hour of the day to make sure that she's not fallen down, or whatever, so not knowing what or where or how she's doing is very stressful. With her level of dementia now, she can't remember numbers, so she's forgotten how to use the phone and how to call the house. It really was up to me to make that phone call every night when I got home, and say, how was your day, and what did you do, have you eaten, have you taken your medication? You've got to make sure you use your walker because you cannot be walking around without your walker anymore. It was everything that you had to remember to do, and say it over and over and over."*

She became overwhelmed when her mother fell: *"The last month left me feeling very overwhelmed because she fell about six weeks ago and ended up back in the hospital. The Ontario government has mandated that doctors cannot make the choice anymore for seniors to not go home. That's been taken out of their hands. CCAC's mandate is home first – so she had to go home. I said, 'The care that you're going to give her is not enough care.' Two weeks later, she fell again and was on the floor for hours. So now she's back in the hospital, and she will not be going home."*

When her mother fell a second time it was on a weekend when she had gone out. She phoned her mother when she got back but got no answer, so she went to her mother's house: *"and that's when we found her on the floor. I had to call 911 and so on ... and I came back from the hospital to call her care providers to say, what was she like at noon? Was she walking fine? Only to find out that morning and afternoon care had not been able to get in and nobody phoned me ... so she had been on the floor, probably, for about eight hours, if not longer. Again, it's the emotions. It's the guilt and everything that goes along with not being there."*

When we did the interview, Mary had yet to find a place for her mother: *"I've been out three times this week looking at potential places. I had a rather bad experience, and perhaps it was just because I was emotionally tired. One of the homes was just overwhelming for me."* She attributes the emotional strain she is under to the following: *"I think too much. Coulda, shoulda, woulda. Had I only been stronger at this point; had I only said this; had I only made her do this; had I only done this."* This is a response we heard from many caregivers.

Fiona, sandwich generation

Fiona is 40 years old. She is married with one child, a 6-year-old son. She spends approximately twenty to thirty hours a week caring for him. Her husband does some childcare (*"a couple of hours here and there"*), but the main responsibility for his care falls on Fiona.

She cares for her mother, who is 60 years old and has just had a stroke. Her mother originally lived in a different city, but there was no one to look after her so she moved in with her daughter. Fiona spends fifteen to twenty hours a week caring for her mother, in addition to caring for her son and working full time. She does her mother's shopping, makes sure she does her exercises, takes her for walks, talks to her, makes her meals, and keeps her room clean.

In her caregiving scenario Fiona describes the months after her mother's stroke when her mother lived in a different city but needed care: *"It was overwhelming because I had to shuffle between the two cities, so on the weekends, after work, I then had to go and take care of her, when she was living in XXX. So that was hard, because I had to go pretty much every weekend."* Again, this scenario is one that can be considered typical for the caregivers we talked to – and one that virtually everyone who lived through it (i.e., health problem with a parent in a different city) found to be overwhelming and stressful.

What exacerbated the situation for Fiona was the fact that her son also became ill and required hospitalization at the same time as her mother but in a different city. This situation made Fiona feel very anxious, *"because I thought that I couldn't deal with all the different things in my life at the same time – my child, my mom, my work … one at a time, maybe, but not everything together … I was very tired and as well, I wasn't in control because everything was falling apart and I was very concerned about my mom and my son."*

Ultimately the situation was resolved successfully. Her son recovered, and her mother survived and moved in with Fiona on what was supposed to be a temporary basis. She is currently trying to place her mother in a facility near her home but, like Mary, is finding this task very challenging because of difficulties in finding information on what kinds of government supports and benefits her mother is entitled to. She is frustrated by the time it is taking to get answers to "very basic" questions and the amount of contradictory information she is receiving.

Fiona talked in her interview about feeling incredibly tired, anxious, and helpless because of her current situation. When asked what it was about the caregiving situation that made her feel this way, Fiona stated: *"Well, time management and things like the emotional investment too. Because you have to stay really positive for long periods of time, even when you're not feeling positive, that's hard sometimes."* Again, our analysis of the interview data reveals that lack of time and difficulties in remaining positive in the face of an unpredictable situation over which one has little control exemplify many caregiving situations and contribute to higher levels of stress and anxiety for the employee providing the care.

Robert, sandwich generation

Robert, 52, is a married father of two children (one son, one daughter) who are both in university. He has been looking after his 84-year-old mother since his father passed away six years ago. His mother currently lives twenty-five kilometres away from Robert. Robert's brother lives closer to their mother than Robert but is unwilling to provide care as *"they just do not get on at all."*

While his children require little actual care, they are a source of stress. As Robert notes: *"[Y]ou'd think when the kids go to university they'd be less work for you, but you would be wrong … now we have with car-pooling and everything that goes along with it … more vehicles at home now and I'm more of a fleet manager than anything else … six vehicles at home right now. Yes, so in addition to the eldercare, other things are contributing to make my life less enjoyable at this phase than it would be normally."*

Robert spends about fifteen hours a week in caregiving activities – five of these hours on the phone: *"Between two and five hours each week talking to her on the phone, that's just emotional support on the phone. When I'm there, in person, I take her grocery shopping and I take her to lunch; I go through her apartment to look at what needs to be done. Everything from watering plants to cleaning out her fridge to, maybe, starting a meal for her … I do all her finances, pay her bills, and make appointments for doctors and whatnot. I don't have to help her dress herself or bathe her, or those types of personal care issues."*

His partner does not help with the care of his mother, as they also do not get on with each other. According to Robert, this is a source of stress within their family: *"Because my wife does not get along with my mother, it causes additional strain and stress on me."* It is worth noting that a substantial number of the men in our interview sample talked about the fact that their wife did not get on with their mother – a stereotype that seems to be borne out by fact. None of the women in the interview sample, however, mentioned that their husbands did not get on with their in-laws.

While caregiving is not a source of physical or financial strain for Robert, he reports feeling emotionally overwhelmed several times a week or more: *"her main issue is mental, or mental/emotional, you might lump those together. She'll call up many times a day to look for someone to talk to, emotional support because of her condition. I mean, she is partway to dementia … even before that, she didn't relate well to many other people … now she has very few friends or relatives that she can call and look to for support. She's constantly calling me with additional mini-crises, whether real or not …"*

Robert's caregiving scenario involved a situation where his mother's apartment *"managed to contract bedbugs,"* which required him to *"go through all her clothes and all her drawers … I threw out twenty garbage bags full of clothes stuff and processed twenty more through the dryer to try and kill the bugs."* While this may seem like an unusual scenario to feature in our discussion, it is representative of the fact that many caregivers we interviewed were coping – though barely – until something unpredictable and out of their control occurred to tip the scale into the "high stress zone" – the proverbial straw that broke the caregiver's back.

Finally, Robert mentioned that much of his frustration revolved around his mother's deteriorating mental capacity – a concern that was mentioned by many of the other caregivers we talked to. He noted that, *"I need to go through all my mum's papers, anything that comes in her door. While she is clearly suffering from dementia she hasn't been declared incompetent yet, so some of her mail still goes to her. And when she gets it out of the mailbox she'll squirrel it away in different places in her apartment. So, you have to go through different drawers and piles of papers and whatever, to, often, find what you're looking for. And let's just say it's frustrating ..."*

To summarize, it is the accumulation of a lot of stressors that is contributing to Robert's high levels of stress and caregiver strain. He describes it as follows: *"I think that I am just frustrated that more can't be done quicker or better. Frustrated and somewhat depressed, because I can't see a quick end to it and I know that many other things are also being neglected at the same time. I still haven't done my income taxes for last year ..."*

Josh, sandwich generation

Josh is a married father of three children aged 11, 13, and 15. He spends approximately ten to fifteen hours a week in childcare. Most of this time involves helping out with the competitive sports teams his children play on.

He spends significant time each week (approximately one to two hours per dependent) looking after four elderly dependents – his parents (they live an hour away from him, and no one else in his family lives in the same province) and his spouse's parents (they live in same city). Josh personifies what we refer to in this report as sequential caregiving, as he has been caring for one or more elderly dependents for just over ten years: *"at first there was just one, then two, now all of them to one degree or another."* His wife spends the same amount of time in providing care as he does. Activities undertaken by Josh and his wife include driving his parents/in-laws to medical appointments and keeping them company.

Josh notes that neither eldercare nor childcare separately would cause him a problem. Rather, he feels that it is trying to do a good job of all the different roles at the same time that makes things challenging: *"The problem is time. We have three kids and ourselves that are extremely active and take up way too much time ... there's far more stress right now with our kids than there is with the eldercare – but it is the combination, really."*

He noted during the interview that the challenges he has had to face with caregiving have waxed and waned over the past ten years: *"Things come and go ... right now we are in a period of lull before the storm. I've got three kids that play competitive sports, and right now I can mention, things have been pretty quiet. I mean ten years ago if you had called, my dad was in the middle of a heart attack, triple bypass, life was hell, kids were extremely young ..."*

The storm he anticipates was the one he talked about in his eldercare scenario and also involves dementia: *"[M]y wife's father has just been diagnosed with dementia ... and it's quickly progressing, so he's just been told he's losing his driving license and stuff and my mother-in-law doesn't drive and that's going to cause lots of challenges for us."*

This situation is causing conflict within the family, as neither of his in-laws wants anyone to know about the dementia, making it more challenging to access or provide care. Josh also admits to feeling worried and anxious about what the future will bring: *"I'd say it's a fear worry. I mean once my father-in-law passes on ... we don't know if my mother-in-law can afford to stay where she's living right now. So there's certainly that worry ..."*

Joyce, eldercare

Joyce is a 61-year-old married mother of three adult children and grandmother to three teenagers/young adults. Up until last month, when her father died, she was caring for her parents. Now she provides care to just her 87-year-old mother, who is *"quite frail"* and lives ten kilometres away. Joyce shares caregiving duties with her sister because *"I believe that's what families do."* Each of the sisters spends about twenty hours a week in caregiving – *"Phoning her, visiting her, taking her out for meals. We're really concerned about the eating right now because she's not eating well. Until last month when her husband died, we were taking her to the hospital or to the hospice every day, my sister or myself, to see her husband because she can't drive anymore."*

Joyce anticipates that the death of her father will mean that the amount of time that she and her sister spend caring for their mother is likely to increase significantly in the future: *"I think we're going to be spending a lot of time in the next little while just making sure that all of the bank accounts are consolidated and all of the tax things are done There's a lot of fiduciary things to do that she can't handle. So we'll be doing a lot of that. And then I think it's just going to be a fair bit of care after that, actual physical care, because she wants to stay on her own and we're really concerned about that."*

Joyce's husband is retired and also spends about five hours a week caring for her mother: *"He takes her out for breakfast, and he took her to get her toenails done last week."* Why toenails? Again, personal care tasks like cutting their own toenails can often become an issue for the elderly: *"she had a fall and was just lying there all night, and EMS came and they said her feet look like ... well, they didn't say, like hell, but that's what they were. They were terrible. So they suggested a place where she could go and have a pedicure and get her feet fixed up and stuff. So he does stuff like that."*

From her interview, it became apparent, that both Joyce and her sister are "serial caregivers." She talked about how, prior to her father's death from cancer and heart issues, she and her sister had taken on the burden of care for him – caregiving that was made more stressful by the fact that he was suffering from dementia that was aggravated by the drugs and the stress of the cancer treatments.

Joyce's caregiving scenario revolved around providing care for her father in the last several months of his life: *"For my father, it was just overwhelming ... It was even overwhelming when I took time off work to deal with it."* While the scenario given here is from Joyce's point of view, it echoes what we heard from many of our other interviewees, who also talked about the stresses associated with dealing with an end-of-life situation. Joyce noted that she was overwhelmed during this time period even though her own family was incredibly supportive: *"I also have my kids here and they try to do things; like my daughter took food over. So they help us too with them. And I noticed when my father was dying, my son, he said, 'Grandpa, I just want to let you know that we're going to look after Grandma for you.' Like I said, I just think that's what families do. But it is hard."*

What made it stressful for Joyce and her sister was her father's insistence on driving his car despite the fact that *"he wasn't supposed to drive his car because he had just had this stroke ... We started off reasoning, then yelling and screaming and fighting and having horrible conflicts. Then we stole his car. We hid the keys. He was so furious. We had to go through this big, long process to get his license taken away."*

According to Joyce the situation she and her sister face with her mother is different than the one she faced with her father. More specifically, with her father it was his dementia: *"At the end ... I knew that my dad wasn't really my dad anymore ... but then he was ... and then he wasn't. It was really, really sad."* With her mother, on the other hand, it is the mother's desire to live in her own home that contributes to the stress and worry of caregiving: *"You just feel so bad ... you're worried because it's not that safe and you know that there's going to be a time where it's going to be a real crisis. You just know it."*

Joyce went on to talk about the challenge of getting her older mother to consider moving to a retirement care facility – a dispute that was mentioned by more than half of the caregivers we talked to: *"with my mother what I feel is the main challenge is that as they get older they still want to be independent. And you want to give them what they want, but what you'd really like to do is to just put them in a place where other people will be looking after them all the time and they will be safe. Then all you have to do is go and visit them. So that would be really nice and that was how we were hoping it would be ... she would be in a hospice where she could be fairly independent. There are places like that, but for some reason they just get so they don't want to go."*

Joyce expressed the frustrations of her situation very eloquently: *"You become the parent when you really want to be the child, I guess. You want to have your parents say, yes, we can take care of ourselves, and we can and we're going to do this and we're going to do that. You'd really like that, but you see them getting forgetful and unable to... [I] would say the most stressful is just knowing where to go next ... We're the ones, the actual children of the elderly, that have to sometimes make some hard decisions, and it's horrible."*

Nathalie, eldercare

Nathalie is a married women in her late fifties who has been providing care for her mother *"of one sort or another"* for fifteen years. Her mother is 89 years old and now living in a nursing home twenty minutes from her house. Nathalie's children are older and have left home, so childcare is not an issue.

The challenge facing Nathalie (and many of the caregivers we talked to) relates to the fact that English is not her mother's first language, and her ability to communicate with others is very limited. This means that her daughter has to be constantly available to "translate." Even though her mother now lives in a home, Nathalie still spends about five hours a week in caregiving: *"Buying supplies; taking care of medical appointments – making appointments and taking her to the appointments; connecting with the nursing staff to make changes to medication; doing her banking."* Her mother's lack of English also means that Nathalie needs to be there for all medical appointments, medical assessments, and so on.

Natalie's husband helps her if he can with doctor visits, but it is hard for him to get time off work. He also helps by providing a lot of emotional support, but he cannot really help Nathalie with the care of her mother because he does not speak the only language that her mother speaks.

Nathalie experiences high levels of physical and emotional caregiver strain, which she describes as occurring when she has to take her mother out of the house for specialist appointments in the winter (something that she describes as happening quite regularly). Her mother's gait is unsteady, and Nathalie describes the process of getting her into and out of the car along with the walker as both a physically and an emotionally stressful exercise. She notes that the stress is associated with worries about the consequences of falling for her mother and for herself (broken bones, hospitalization). Nathalie attributes the back and hip problems she is currently experiencing to the physical stress of steadying her mother and helping her in and out of the car.

What makes caregiving stressful for Nathalie? *"It's the responsibility for caring, and being the only support for another human being. She treats me as the only person who can give her support – which is not true, there are a lot of people around her at the nursing home – but I am the go-to. To be the source of providing everything that a person thinks she needs, she wants, she dreams of – I'm it, because I'm an only child. I'm it. And it impacts my life. Recently I was offered a great new job, but it was in another province and I can't take it because I cannot move my mother."*

Her high-stress caregiving scenario involved one such visit to a specialist during an ice storm – a visit that if cancelled meant her mother would go back on the doctor's waiting list for an undetermined amount of time. This experience was so stressful Natalie vowed *"never again."*

For Natalie and many like her, caregiving is a high-demand, low-control situation: *"and I'm trying to avoid – unless there is an absolute emergency – to go out in winter. I try to avoid it, yes … but I cannot control the situation. I am trying to avoid, but you cannot avoid everything, so I don't have control. Even if my mother is sick, I don't have control. And that applies not only in this particular situation that you made me think of, but in every other situation where there is reason for apprehension and worry. It's because I cannot control it. My mother's health is not under my control. The weather is not under my control. And even her mood when I go there and she starts bitching at me and making me feel guilty, like I'm not a good daughter, and whatever, and that's also not under my control. My mother's mood, my mother's getting older and older, is not under my control."* Many of the caregiving scenarios described by the employees in our interview sample can be described as ones characterized by high demands and low control. There is a vast body of research (see for example, work done by Karasek 1979 and Karasek and Theorell 1990) linking such situations to very high levels of stress.

Doug, eldercare

Doug is a 61-year-old married man with three children aged 25, 30, and 32. At this point in time there are no grandchildren. Nor do Doug or his wife spend any time in childcare. Doug and his brother are currently co-caring for their 92-year-old father. They have been providing such care for just over ten years. He notes that his father has been losing first physical and then mental capacity over the years. According to Doug the situation has got so challenging that his father has been placed in a nursing home that is four kilometres from Doug's house. Doug spends approximately five hours a week in caregiving activities. Doug describes his caregiving activities as follows: *"basically visiting and social interaction and we also will go for a walk so there's a bit of physical activity as well, and a bit of supervision while feeding, while eating."* Doug says that his brother spends about the same amount of time in caregiving as he does, but his wife spends no time at all.

The caregiving scenario described by Doug involved his father's move from a retirement home to a nursing home – a stressful situation that many of our respondents experienced and talked about during the interviews. Doug describes the situation as follows: *"in the last three years he's had to go from a retirement home to a nursing home, and the reason is that he does need a high level of physical nursing care attention – bathing, dressing, toileting, to some extent feeding ... so they look after all of those needs."* The move increased the amount of time Doug and his brother had to spend in caregiving: *"So it meant I had to spend more time making sure he was eating the right food, making sure that they were looking after him the right way, that they weren't just sticking him in front of the TV and letting him sit there all day long. And it's almost a management kind of situation that, if you go there and do it yourself, then they'll back off, but if you don't go then nothing happens ... he's in a wheelchair most of the time – and you're sitting vertically in the wheelchair, you'll end up getting bed sores, and bed sores can be very serious at that age ... So, you need to go in at different times to make sure that they tilt the wheelchair back; that they keep him moving and so on a little bit, is important for his long-term well-being."*

Doug identified different factors that made things stressful as well as challenging. What made things stressful? *"I guess it was the potential for the nursing home not reacting and not doing anything. Or, having a difficult relationship with the nursing home, and other issues happening."* What makes the situation challenging? *"I guess the time involvement; it's only a few hours a week, but I'm working full time, and my wife's working full time. Even two/ three hours a week can be a fair chunk out of your free time, your hobby time."*

Doug says that in his case caregiving is emotionally stressful rather than a physical strain or a financial strain *("father is well off financially so that is not an issue").* He articulates the stress of caregiving as follows: *"Well, it's more of an emotional issue, it's just kind of a depressing feeling as you see his physical condition and mental condition deteriorating. You can appreciate at age 91/92, he doesn't have Alzheimer's but he's got various forms of dementia and physical problems, and it's just harder and harder to talk and interact."*

Many of the caregivers in our sample were highly paid professionals and could afford to purchase services to reduce the strains they were experiencing. In Doug's case, the family pays several thousands of dollars a month (in addition to the amount charged by the nursing home) to pay someone to help with the care of their father: *"we do have a personal care worker that we pay for or that my father pays for, and she comes in two to three hours probably five days or six days a week and spends time with him. You know you asked how much time I spend with my father; I probably would spend a lot more if we didn't have the personal care worker and the financial resources to pay for that personal care worker. Because, again, you've got to appreciate the situation at any nursing home ... they look after the basic physical medical issues, they don't really provide a lot of quality social time."*

And what if the next generation does not feel obligated to care for their parents? Doug ended his interview with us by musing on this very issue: *"Unfortunately, my two sons don't show a lot of interest in visiting him. And that's an interesting philosophical question, because I say to myself, well, if they don't care about my father who's 90 years old, are they going to care about my wife and me when we're 90 years old?"* The fact that the granddaughter *"does her bit"* suggests, however, that the gendered division of care may carry on to the next generation.

Serge, eldercare

Serge is a 45-year-old divorced male with four children aged 20, 22, 24, and 26. He provides care for his 94-year-old grandmother and has been doing so for the past four years. She lives in a retirement home ten kilometres away from him. Why does Serge care for his grandmother? *"Because ... my father was an only child, and I am an only child, and my father's deceased, and [her] husband passed away, and ... she had a sister who was looking after her, but her sister is obviously getting older, too, and she had some medical complications, so ... it fell on me."* Serge spends eight to ten hours a week in caregiving: *"Mostly conversation, sometimes doctors' appointments or meetings with other medical care or general care people. Business, financial stuff. Mainly family-related and just general company-keeping."*

Serge says that in his case caregiving is not a physical or financial stressor. It does, however, result in high levels of emotional stress several times a week or more. He attributed this stress to the following factors: *"Why? Because even though when I calculate the time, it sounds very small on a large scale, it happens that the time that I have to devote is time taken out of my own personal life outside of work ... time that I don't have to accomplish the things that I need to get done for myself or for other family members or whomever. That would be one source of my stress. Then it is the fact that it's seldom fun to be looking after somebody older, so it can be just a strain to go through some motions that can be not what you'd like to be doing."*

Serge's overwhelming caregiving scenario involved a time when his grandmother was ill and had to be hospitalized for a period: *"This meant that I had to spend a lot more time going to hospital and, of course, paying the costs associated with that. Plus I had the conflicting concerns about wanting the best care for my grandmother and wanting to be able to keep her company and keep her cheery through a difficult ordeal while she was in the hospital ... but at the same time, a hospital is an awful place to be, and when you're visiting somebody or looking after somebody who's in there, it can be a challenge to stay cheerful yourself. And you leave feeling exhausted and wishing to never go back."*

What caused him to feel overwhelmed? *"Guilt ... Because ... as I said before, you are dealing with conflicting emotions ... you want the best for the person you love and you care for ... but at the same time, you feel resentful that you have to devote so much time when it falls on you and there's no alternative. And so you feel sorry for yourself, but then the immediate reaction to that is to feel guilty for even considering the fact that you would rather be doing other things or not have to be bothered with it. So, despite the fact that there are four emotional components to caregiving* [he identified worry, fear, annoyance, guilt], *I think the one that leads to feeling overwhelmed the most – for me would be guilt."*

Conclusions, Implications, and Recommendations

A number of conclusions can be drawn from the information presented in this chapter. These conclusions, along with the implications they hold for policy makers and employers, are presented below.

The number of employed caregivers is substantial and likely to increase over time

According to the 2012 General Social Survey (Sinah 2013), in 2012 about 8.1 million individuals, or 28 per cent of Canadians aged 15 years and older, provided care to a family member or friend with a long-term health condition, disability, or needs related to aging. The majority (6.1 million) of these caregivers were also juggling the demands of caregiving with paid work, and 2.2 million were "sandwiched" between caregiving and raising children.

The data reviewed in this chapter also point to a significant growth in the number of employed caregivers in Canada in the very near future – particularly the number of employees in the sandwich group. The following data support this prediction. First, the growing number of aging baby boomers combined with decreased fertility rates and increased life expectancy are likely to result in an increase in the number of families with elderly dependents who need care (Hicks et al. 2007). Second, the sheer size of the baby boom teamed with advances in medical sciences mean that there will be more frail seniors suffering longer from chronic health conditions in our populations. This can be expected to increase both the number of years employees spend as caregivers and the increased complexity of that role (Chappell 2011). Third, declining fertility rates among the baby boom and Generation X cohorts mean that over the course of the next several decades there will be fewer and fewer children available to take care of their own aging parents (Cravey and Mitra 2011). Fourth, the tendency to postpone childbearing until after age 30 will lead to an increase in multigenerational families (Grundy and Henretta 2006) and thus an increase in the number of employees with children at home who also provide eldercare. These trends also have implications for those in the sandwich group. Not only will the need to provide care likely swell over time (more older people), but the burden of providing such care is also likely to increase as a smaller cohort of family caregivers will need to provide increasingly more complex types of care to seniors with chronic illness and dementia.

Consequences of caregiving – the good, the bad, and the ugly

Our review of the literature shows that the effects of caregiving are pervasive, potentially impacting those requiring care, their informal caregivers and other family members, friends, neighbours, service providers, policy makers, employers, and society. Caregiving can challenge the care provider (physically, mentally, economically, and socially) but may also be a rewarding experience. For employers, eldercare can impact the organization's bottom line costs both directly (through health benefits, absenteeism) and indirectly (through lost productivity). Research in the area has determined that women's work roles are more strongly affected by caregiving than those of their male colleagues. Societal impacts are also apparent. If it were not for family caregivers, the cost of eldercare would become a burden to the public health-care system.

Caregiving is complex and complicated

The stories presented in this chapter support a number of conclusions with respect to the challenges faced by employed caregivers in Canada. More specifically, they support the idea that the role of caregiver is complex and complicated.

But there are also commonalities with respect to the challenges these caregivers face

While our interviews showed that each caregiving situation was unique, it was also easy to identify a number of commonalities across the different caregiving situations we examined that help inform our understanding of the issues facing employed caregivers of both genders in Canada at this time. First, our data support the idea that the need to provide physical and emotional support to one or more family members who are experiencing problems looking after themselves because of age-related physical or mental health problems forms the foundation of the role of caregiver. Virtually everyone we talked to spoke about the amount of time and energy required to do a good job of caregiving – and all interviewees were focused on fulfilling the caregiver role to the best of their ability. Second, the interviews also helped us identify a number of factors that could exacerbate caregiver strain, including the following:

- family dynamics (lack of family support for the caregiver role, conflict with family members)
- a lack of support for the caregiver role (in the community, at work, at home)
- the need to combine childcare and eldercare (the roles are not the same, and time and energy given to one of the roles makes performance of the other role more difficult)
- caring for a family member with dementia and/or diminishing mental capacity (many caregivers struggled with the fact that the person they were caring for no longer recognized them and talked about how dementia had "stolen" their family member from them)
- the stresses associated with dealing with an end-of-life situation
- the challenges of getting older family members who want to live on their own to move out of their home into a retirement home or a care facility
- communication issues (the person needing care spoke neither of Canada's official languages, which severely limited the ability to communicate with others and increased the reliance on the caregiver)

These findings suggest that, to really understand caregiver strain, we need to better appreciate how the accumulation of various stressors contributes to the outcomes of interest.

*For many Canadians caregiving is overwhelming, stressful,
and triggers guilty feelings*

It is also interesting to note that virtually all of the employees we interviewed used the following terms to describe their caregiving situation:
"stressful," "depressing," "overwhelming," "frustrating," and "worrying." Many also talked about feeling guilty that they could not do more
for the person they were caring for and being fearful for the future.
These descriptors indicate that caregiving is a very emotional experience for many Canadians.

Caregiving can be sequential or concurrent

In speaking to caregivers it also became apparent that caregiving is a
role that can be performed sequentially (e.g., care for mother, then care
for father, then care for mother-in-law, and so on) or concurrently (e.g.,
care for mother and father-in-law at the same time). This diversity adds
to the complexity of the caregiver situation and may also impact the
amount of resources caregivers bring to the role as well as their ability
to cope with the demands of the role. In fact, the interview data support
the idea that the caregiving role comes with high demands and low
perceptions of control – a combination that has been shown to be associated with higher levels of stress (Karasek 1979).

Implications and recommendations

The trends identified in this chapter represent a "perfect storm" for employers seeking to recruit, retain, and promote employees now and in
the future and for governments and policy makers who have responsibility for designing and delivering affordable community and health-
care services to support Canadians with caregiving responsibilities.
The number of Canadians who are unable to balance the demands at
work with the demands of their caregiving role is substantial and likely
to increase in the near future.

The academic data reviewed in this chapter, which show very clearly the costs to all involved of taking on the role of caregiver, can be used by impacted stakeholders to make the business case for change. These data also reinforce the need for employers and government policy makers to pay greater attention to issues associated with caregiving when developing their strategic plans and setting resource priorities.

We would, therefore, recommend that both employers and governments at all levels concretely recognize caregiving as a legitimate business issue and undertake to develop and implement a set of policies designed to support caregivers' desire or need to care for family members and friends who are in the twilight of their lives. We would also recommend that employers, communities, and service providers undertake research to quantify the "hidden" costs of informal caregiving. The benefits of having family members provide care are obvious, while the costs are often hidden and delayed. Such data are, however, critical to policy makers' and employees' ability to make informed decisions on how best to move forward with respect to this issue. Such data are also essential if we wish to change the dialogue from "How much will it cost us to change how we deal with the issue of caregiving?" to "Can we afford not to take action with respect to this issue?"

A number of important implications and recommendations for Canadian employers and policy makers can also be drawn from the qualitative data reviewed in this chapter. First, the complexity of the caregiving situation indicates that there is no one-size-fits-all solution to this issue and supports the need for governments and employers to provide a wide variety of supports and to be flexible with respect to their application and use. Second, the fact that caregiving is a very emotional experience for many Canadian employees emphasizes the need for two types of support: concrete policies and programs to help employees with the tasks of caregiving, and counselling and community support groups to help employees deal with the emotional aspects of this role. Third, the fact that caregiving can be considered a high-demand, low-control job means that employers and policy makers who wish to reduce caregiver strain need to concentrate on strategies that either reduce the demands faced by employees in this group (e.g., increase the type and amount of caregiver support services in the community) and/or increase the amount of control they have over their situation (e.g., provide for flexible work arrangements and extended physician hours, and make information on what to do more easily available).

Chapter Two

Profiling Canadian Caregivers: Who Are They? What Do They Do? Why Do They Do It?

There are four types of people in this world:
Those who have been caregivers
Those who are currently caregivers
Those who will be caregivers
Those who will need caregivers

Rosalyn Carter

The demographic projections reviewed in chapter 1 showing that most Canadians will, at some point in their lives, have responsibility for the care of an elderly family member lend weight to Rosalyn Carter's predictions about caregiving. The caregivers' stories also presented in chapter 1 illustrate quite vividly the juggling acts typically performed by employed caregivers in this country. Taken together, these two sets of data reinforce the need for organizations, governments, and communities to address issues around caregiving, particularly when considered in light of the data presented in chapter 1 suggesting that the greatest proportion of this caregiving will likely occur in mid-life, a time when most employees are also juggling work and other family responsibilities (Pavalko and Gong 2005).

This chapter moves beyond the projections and stories and begins the process of profiling employed caregivers in Canada. Data from the 2012 National Study on Work, Life and Caregiving (the 2012 Study; see Duxbury and Higgins 2013a, 2013b, and 2013d), as well as findings from the academic literature in the area, are used to provide answers to the following questions: Who provides care? For whom? Why do they provide care? What do they do? The chapter is divided into five main sections. Sections one to four present data from the academic literature as well as quantitative and qualitative data from the 2012 Study that speak to each of the following four questions: "Who provides care? Whom do employed caregivers provide care for? Why do employed Canadians take on the role of caregiver? What kinds of care do Canadian employees provide?" The fifth and final section of this chapter summarizes what we know about employed caregivers in Canada at this time and provides recommendations for employers and policy makers based on these insights.

The 2012 Study provides us with a very rich and comprehensive set of quantitative and qualitative data on working caregivers in Canada. Our ability to draw on three quite different information sources to draw conclusions with respect to the important issues covered in this chapter is a key strength of this book. Sections one to four all have a similar structure. We begin each section by presenting a short summary of what the academic literature has to tell us about this particular topic (i.e., "Answers from academia"). This is followed by the presentation and analysis of survey data from the 2012 Study that speak to the question being posed (i.e., "Answers from the 2012 Survey"). The third part of sections one through four discusses data from the interview study that pertain to the subject being addressed (i.e., "Answers from the interview study").

Who Provides Care?

Who provides care? Answers from academia

The General Social Survey (GSS) is conducted by Statistics Canada with two objectives in mind: to gather data on social trends in order to monitor changes in the living conditions and well-being of Canadians over time; and to provide information on specific social policy issues of current or emerging interest (Statistics Canada 2012). The information from

the GSS is used by Canadian policy makers to develop policy and programs to support Canadians. The GSS was started in 1985 and targets
all non-institutionalized Canadians 15 years of age or older living in the
ten provinces of Canada. In the GSS, all respondents are contacted and
interviewed by telephone. The GSS repeats cycles by topic every five
years. The 2012 GSS Cycle 26 was undertaken to provide a snapshot of
the lives of caregivers and care receivers in today's Canada. Cycle 26 is
the fourth cycle of GSS that deals with this topic, the first three having
been conducted in 1996, 2002, and 2007 (Statistics Canada 2012).

Data from the GSS Cycle 26 (Sinah 2013) give us a better appreciation
of the demographic characteristics of caregivers in Canada in 2012.
Consider the following:

- Slightly more women than men were caregivers in 2012 (54%
  female).
- Although the median number of caregiving hours was similar
  between men and women (between three and four hours per week,
  respectively), women were more likely than their male counterparts
  to spend twenty or more hours per week on caregiving tasks
  (17% versus 11%).
- The plurality of caregivers was between the ages of 45 to 54 years
  (24%) and 55 to 64 years (20%) and provided care for their parents.
- Almost one in five (15%) young Canadians aged 15 to 24 years were
  caregivers. This group was most likely providing care to grandparents (48%) and parents (25%).
- Just over one in four (28%) caregivers were "sandwiched" between
  caregiving and childrearing, having at least one child under
  18 years living at home. In the majority of these cases (82%),
  caregivers were raising children under the age of 15. Thirty-one per
  cent had children aged 4 and under; 38 per cent had children aged
  5 to 9; and 42 per cent had children aged 10 to 14.
- Despite the dual role, caregivers with children reported similar
  hours of caregiving as those without children.
- Women were more likely than their male counterparts to engage in
  high-intensity caregiving activities. For instance, they were twice as

likely as their male counterparts to provide personal care to the primary care receiver, including bathing and dressing (29% versus 13%).

For further information, the reader is referred to two very recent Canadian publications on this topic that draw on the 2012 GSS: Sinah's (2013) *Portrait of Caregivers* and Turcotte's (2013) *Family Caregiving: What Are the Consequences?* It should be noted that both of these reports focus on all caregivers – not just employed caregivers.

Who provides care? Answers from the 2012 Survey

Just over 25,000 people responded to the 2012 National Work, Life and Caregiving Survey. Almost 8,000 employed Canadians (n = 7,966) filled in the "Caregiver" section of the 2012 Survey, and 111 of these caregivers then participated in follow-up interviews. As noted earlier, the sampling criteria used in the 2012 Study ensured that the employees who responded to the caregiving section of the survey were caregivers in the strictest sense of the word. In the following section we describe the three samples of employed caregivers featured in this book. These descriptions should help the reader to contextualize the material in the rest of the book.

The data discussed in this section of the chapter can be found in Duxbury and Higgins 2013a and the Desjardins Report (Duxbury and Higgins, 2013c).

Caregivers: The total sample

Just over 25,000 people responded to the 2012 Study. The sample is geographically diverse but, as noted in chapter 1, skewed by job type and socio-economic status. Respondents were very well-educated (22% with a college diploma, 38% with one university degree, 17% with at least one postgraduate degree) and socio-economically advantaged (two-thirds of the respondents had personal incomes of $60,000 or more per year). More than half of the respondents were "knowledge workers" with just over 60 per cent of the sample working in managerial and professional positions. While life-cycle stage is associated with age and dependent-care responsibilities, it is not associated with where the caregivers live (e.g., population of community, province) or their socio-economic status (education, job type, income).

Of note are the data showing that there has been somewhat of a shift within Canadian dual-income families with respect to which partner is considered to be the primary breadwinner, with just under half (45%) of our respondents saying breadwinner status is a shared responsibility within their family. Gender norms with respect to childcare, on the other hand, appear to be more firmly rooted, as only 20 per cent of our respondents indicated that responsibility for childcare is shared equally in their family.

Who is in the sandwich generation of employees?

Our research gives us a better understanding of the demographic characteristics of professional employees in the sandwich generation. The men and women in this group are fairly evenly split between the Generation X (30 to 45 years of age) and baby boomer (46-plus years of age) cohorts: 28 per cent are between 31 and 40 years of age; 34 per cent are between 41 and 50 years of age; and 26 per cent are over 50 years of age. One in ten are below 30 years of age. Most are married (88%) and live in dual-income families (i.e., both partners work full time outside the home). Although most respondents earn more than $60,000 per year (above the Canadian average) many (just over one in four) state that financial resources are tight in their family. In terms of dependent care, employees in the sandwich generation balance the demands of parenting pre-adolescent (aged 5 to 12) and teenage children with often onerous eldercare demands.

There are also a number of interesting gender differences in the data that are worth noting. First, the women in the sandwich generation were more likely than the men to have primary responsibility for childcare in their families and to say that their spouse was the primary breadwinner in the family. The men in the sandwich group, on the other hand, were more likely than their female counterparts to earn more than $80,000 per year, to say that they were the primary breadwinner in their family, and to live in a "traditional" male-breadwinner family.

Who is in the eldercare-only group of employees?

While the majority of employees in the eldercare group are married and live in dual-income families, one in three are single and have never married. While those in the eldercare group tend to be older (41% over 50 years of age), a substantial number are in their thirties and forties. The breadwinner role tends to be shared within these families, and just over half of the employees in the eldercare life-cycle stage say that money is not an issue in their families – a finding that is consistent with the fact that their incomes are relatively high and childcare expenses are virtually nil. In terms of dependent care, employees in the eldercare-only group either have no children (33%) or have children over the age of 18 who no longer live at home.

The men and women in the eldercare stage of the life cycle were very similar with respect to age, financial status, and their perceptions that breadwinner status was shared within their family. There was, however, one gender difference within the eldercare sample that is important to note: the women in this group were more likely than the men to be single. This finding might be due to the high number of years these women have spent in caregiving.

Money is more likely to be an issue in families
with multigenerational caregiving

Employees' assessment of their families' financial situation (money is tight/we live comfortably/money is not an issue) is strongly associated with their caregiving situation. More specifically, employees with multigenerational caregiving responsibilities were more likely than employees in the childcare and eldercare groups to say that money was tight in their family (just under one in three indicated that this was the case). Employees in the eldercare only group, on the other hand, were more likely to say that money was not an issue in their family (just over 40% gave this response). This finding is particularly interesting given the data showing that when gender is taken into account, employment income is not associated with caregiver group and supports the idea that taking on the role of eldercare is more likely to be a financial strain in families with children still living in the home.

Caregivers: The caregiver sample

As noted earlier, the sampling criteria used in the 2012 Study ensured that the 7,966 employees who responded to this section of the survey were caregivers in the strictest sense of the word. In the following section we describe the employed caregivers in the Caregiver Sample.

The Caregiver Sample was well distributed with respect to age, supporting the conclusion that employees of all ages (not just older employees) engage in caregiving activities. More specifically: 5 per cent of the respondents in the caregiver sample were under the age of 30; 35 per cent were between 30 and 45; 44 per cent were 46 to 55; and 17 per cent were 56 or older. The higher number of younger workers in the Caregiver Sample is likely reflective of our focus on Canadians who are still in the workforce. Employees in the eldercare group tended to be older than those in the sandwich group (see figure 2.1), a finding that is consistent with the fact that, by definition, those in the sandwich group still have children at home.

The majority (70%) of the employees in the Caregiver Sample were women. While the higher number of women in our sample may be partially due to the fact that women were more likely than men to respond to the 2012 Survey (58% of the Total Sample were female), it is also consistent with the GSS 2012 data, which also found that women are still more likely than men to provide caregiving. It may also reflect the fact that women were more likely than men to see themselves as caregivers and chose to answer this caregiver section of the survey.

Employed caregivers are a demographically diverse group

The employed caregivers who responded to our survey live in all provinces of Canada and work in a wide variety of jobs. Most have some form of postsecondary education and are financially secure (earn incomes of $60,000 per year or more). A majority of the employees in the

Figure 2.1: Age by Caregiver Group (Caregiver Sample, n = 7,966) (percentages)

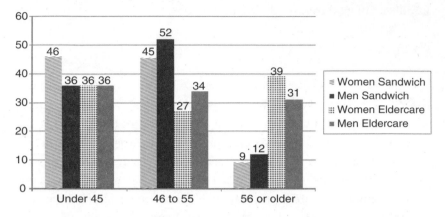

eldercare group have children who are over 18 years of age and no longer live at home. A plurality of the employees in the sandwich group are parents of teenagers (approximately 40%) and pre-adolescents (35%). One in five of the employees in the sandwich group are parents to children under the age of 5. Half of the men and women in the sandwich group are parenting two children.

A number of interesting conclusions on the family circumstances of employed caregivers in Canada (particularly of well-educated professionals who provide care) can be drawn by looking at the demographic data describing those in the Caregiver Sample. First, it is interesting to note that a substantial number of the employed caregivers (35% of women and 25% of men) in our sample are single. Second, employees in the sandwich group (35% of women and 25% of men) are more likely than their counterparts in the eldercare-only group to be in dual-career families. While these families are more likely to have the financial resources to help them cope with their caregiving demands, the respondents in this group are also more likely to have challenges with balancing the time demands of managing two careers with two sets of dependent-care needs. Third, one in three employees in the sandwich group live in a family where their partner is deemed to be the primary breadwinner (earns more income than they do), suggesting either that these individuals are taking on the eldercare role because their partner has a secure income and/or that these individuals have reduced their commitment to their career as a way to manage their dual set of family demands (i.e., childcare, eldercare). Finally, the data suggest that caregiving responsibilities may be contributing to a change in who does what within many Canadian families. This conclusion is supported by looking at how our caregivers evaluated how breadwinning and caregiving responsibilities were distributed within their families. One in three of the women in the sandwich group responded to this question by stating that within their family their partner had primary responsibility for childcare. This was double the percentage of women in the "childcare only" stage of the life cycle who gave this response. This finding suggests that eldercare may be shifting who does what at home in families with multigenerational caregiving responsibilities.

Who provides care? Answers from the interview study

In total, 111 people took part in the interview process. The sample was selected to ensure diversity with respect to age, gender, family type, and caregiving intensity and as such cannot be considered to be generalizable to all Canadian caregivers. Caregivers who participated in the interview process came from across Canada and lived in a wide variety of sizes of communities (approximately 25% in communities of 24,999 or less; approximately 34% in communities of 25,000 to 499,999; approximately 43% in communities of 500,000 plus). Virtually all of the employees in the sample were married or lived with a partner (90%) and were parents (86%), although most of those in the eldercare group indicated that their children no longer lived at home. Eight per cent of those in the eldercare group were grandparents and could also be considered to have multigenerational caregiving responsibilities (admittedly of a different sort from those experienced within sandwiched families). While the majority of respondents (58%) provided care for one dependent, a substantial number cared for two (28%) or three (14%) elderly dependents. A plurality of the sample (44%) were parents of two children.

The Care Recipient

Whom do employed Canadians care for? Answers from academia

Data from the 2012 GSS also give us information on the recipients of informal caregiving. According to Sinah (2013), almost half (48%) of the caregivers in their sample reported caring for their own parents or parents-in-law over the past year. Adult children were almost four times more likely to report caring for a parent than for a parent-in-law, and 2.5 times more likely to report caring for their own mother than father. Other recipients of care included friends or neighbours (16%), grand-parents (13%), siblings and extended family members (10%), spouses (8%), and sons or daughters (5%) (Sinah 2013).

Whom do employed Canadians care for?
Answers from the 2012 Survey

To help us understand more about employees' caregiving situations we included questions in both the 2012 Survey instrument (Caregiver Sample only) and the interview script on the dependent(s) the respondent was providing care for. In those cases where the respondent cared for multiple dependents, we asked them to think about the "dependent who occupies most of your time and energy" when responding to all questions (the pre-test indicated that the survey and the interview were much too long if we did not use this strategy). Key findings with respect to the care recipient are summarized in table 2.1 and discussed in the section below. It should be noted that the Interview Sample was selected from the Caregiver Sample and that findings with respect to who is being cared for are virtually identical between the two data sets. As such only one set of findings from the 2012 Study are presented in this section of the chapter.

Whom do Canadian employees care for? The data from the 2012 Study have one simple answer – their parents. The majority of the employees in our sample (75%) indicated that they were providing care for one of their parents (58% cared for their mother and 17% their father).

Table 2.1 Characteristics of the Care Recipient
Who Requires the Most Care (n = 7,966)

Relationship to Respondent	Total (%)
Mother	58
Father	17
Mother-in-law	12
Father-in-law	5
Other relative	5
Other	4
Gender of Dependent	
Male	25
Female	75
Age of Dependent	
65 and under	13
66 to 75	22
76 to 85	42
86 and over	23
Years Caring for Dependent	
Less than 2 years	18
2 to 5 years	46
6 to 10 years	22
More than 10 years	15
Distance to Dependent's House/Residence	
Less than 30 km	68
31 to 100 km	8
100 to 200 km	6
201 to 500 km	8
501 to 1000 km	6
1000+ km	3

Others cared for one of their in-laws (16%) or an extended family member (12% cared for an aunt, an uncle, or an older sibling). Less than 1 per cent of the respondents cared for someone who was not related to them. The fact that most (70%) employees in this sample care for their mother or mother-in-law is consistent with the fact that women in Canada have higher life expectancy than men. It also mirrors the findings from the 2012 GSS.

The survey data also show that the majority of the employees in our sample provided care for someone in their late seventies. The age of the care recipient is not surprising given the fact that just over 60 per cent of the employees in our sample were 45 years of age or older and were caring for their parents. While the mean age of the care recipient for the employees in our sample was 77.9 years of age, a substantial number of employees (13% of the sample) provided care for someone much younger (i.e., under the age of 65), and one in four cared for someone over 86 years of age (what is typically referred to in the literature as "the fragile elderly"). The employees in this latter group can be expected to experience more challenges balancing work and caregiving, given the research showing that caregiving intensity increases with the age of the care recipient.

Also noteworthy are the survey data showing that the employees in our sample have spent an average of 6.3 years in caregiving, a finding that supports the idea that caregiving is not a transitory, end-of-life phenomenon but rather an activity that can impose challenges for a substantial period of time. These data support the need for employers to address this issue, as the demands of caregiving have been found to increase in intensity over time as care recipients age and their health declines.

Issues related to work-life balance are likely to be more complex in families that need to balance employment with the care of multiple elderly dependents. While the majority of respondents (58%) provided care for one dependent, a substantial number provided care for two (28%) or three (14%) elderly dependents. Respondents in the sandwich group were more likely than those in the eldercare group to feel responsible for the well-being of three or more dependents. This difference is likely due to the fact that the respondents in the sandwich group are younger, which increases the chances that their parents and in-laws are still alive.

We also included questions in the 2012 Survey to help us understand where the recipient of care lived relative to the caregiver. The following data speak to this issue. The majority of employees (68%) care for someone who lives nearby (i.e., within 30 km of their house). Employees in the sandwich generation are slightly more likely to provide care for a parent and/or in-law who lives nearby. This finding might be attributed to the fact that either the respondent's parents and/or in-laws have moved to live in the same community as their children and/or the fact that the younger employees in this sample are more likely to live in the community where they grew up. It should also be noted that this is the most common "care arrangement" in this sample.

Half of the employees in the sample, on the other hand, indicated that they provide care to at least one dependent who lives far away from them (i.e., more than 1,000 km). Most of the employees who gave this response said that they had responsibility for one (20%) or two (16.3%) respondents who live elsewhere. One in ten stated that they felt responsible for three or more dependents who live at a distance.

Finally, data from the 2012 Survey reveal that very few employed caregivers in our sample provide care for someone who lives with them. That being said, it is worthwhile noting that a substantial number of employees (8%) care for one dependent and just under 3 per cent care for two family members who live in their home.

Why Provide Care?

There is no single answer to this question. People become caregivers for a combination of emotional, psychological, moral, and logistical reasons. Some take on the role joyfully, some feel pressured into providing care, while others have mixed feelings. This section is divided into three parts. Part one summarizes what the literature has to say about this issue. Part two uses data from the 2012 Survey (Caregiver Sample) to inform this issue. Finally, in part three we hear from caregivers themselves about their motivations to take on this role (Interview Sample).

Why provide care? Answers from academia

It is not well understood why employees decide to assume the demanding role of caregiver. When one considers the options available for caregiving (e.g., the public health-care system, community services, private agencies, caregiving networks) it might appear that they have made a free choice in assuming this role. Our review of the literature indicates that the situation is far more complex than this, and that in many cases people take on the role for a combination of the following reasons: their parents/in-laws are old and their health is deteriorating; formal sources of care are not available; formal sources of care are not affordable; no one else in the family is willing and/or able to take on the role; cultural expectations; emotional reasons; and societal expectations. Details on each are given below.

The most frequent condition that necessitates a senior's dependence on other people is a decline in physical or mental (typically some form of dementia) health (Cranswick and Dosman 2008; Cranswick and Thomas 2005; Johnson and Lo Sasso 2000; Mathew Greenwald and Associates 2009; Uhlenberg and Cheuk 2008). In most cases, these declines in health that resulted in the need for care were age-related. This is important, as these findings, when considered in light of the demographic data presented in chapter 1, support the idea that the aging of the Canadian population will result in a substantial increase in the need for caregiving in the next several decades.

The academic literature shows that the availability (or lack) of formal sources of care also has a bearing on the decision to take on the caregiving role and the amount of caregiving provided by family members. Formal sources of care are increasingly limited, as the number of beds in care institutions is insufficient to meet current demand and hospitals are under pressure to discharge patients as quickly as possible (Armstrong and Kitts 2004; Guberman 1999). Since the focus of Community Care Access Centres is on post-acute care, continuing care for elderly with chronic conditions is often placed in the hands of informal caregivers (Lum 2011). This situation appears to be particularly problematic in rural areas in Canada (Keefe 1997).

The literature also suggests that the availability (or lack) of affordable care is an equally important consideration for potential caregivers. The cost of nursing homes and paid home care is on the rise. It is consistently reported across studies that families with lower incomes cannot afford to purchase services for their frail kin and therefore rely on informal sources of care. The socio-economic status of informal caregivers is quite variable, but in many cases (e.g., poor women, rural residents, recent immigrants) the household incomes of caregivers are below the national average (Health Canada 2002). Limited financial resources reduce the options available for providing care and often mean that caregivers have to rely more heavily on their own efforts as they cannot afford to purchase expensive services (Conner 2000). While all Canadians would benefit from access to public-health-system resources, community support, and workplace policies aimed at eldercare providers, such initiatives would be especially helpful to those who live in families where money is an issue (Centers for Disease Control and Prevention 2008; Johnson and Schaner 2005; Keefe 1997; Mathew Greenwald and Associates 2009).

The relative affluence of the dependent also factors into the caregiving situation. According to the 2002 GSS, seniors with higher education and more financial resources from previous employment did not require as much informal care as those with lower education and less wealth. They were also more able to afford to purchase formal sources of care (Cranswick and Thomas 2005; Spillman and Pezzin 2000).

The need for individuals to assume the role of caregiver often depends on their position in the family and their gender. Many Canadians fall into the role of caregiver if no one else in the family is willing or able to assume the caregiver role. As noted earlier, most Canadians provide caregiving for a family member, which means that individuals who have no sibling(s) are more likely than those in larger families to have to take on the role of caregiver. Gender is also a critically important determinant of caregiving. Johnson and Lo Sasso (2000) demonstrated that having sisters reduced the likelihood that a woman would have to provide care for her parents, but having brothers did not. The likelihood that a man would be intensively involved in caregiving for his parents, on the other hand, decreased when he had female relatives or a wife to whom he could delegate the hands-on caregiving responsibilities (Montgomery, Borgatta, and Borgatta 2000).

Ethnicity may also be an important determinant of caregiving, although research evidence with respect to this issue is scanty. The research that is available does, however, suggest that some ethnic groups provide more caregiving to their kin than the national average (Uhlenberg and Cheuk 2008; Evercare Survey 2009). Lack of knowledge about available services and language barriers are additional difficulties faced by minority groups, especially if they are recent immigrants (Rajnovich, Keefe, and Fast 2005; Remennick 1999).

Personality characteristics have also been found to influence the caregiving decision, especially for women. Research has identified compassion, feeling a calling to care, a need to feel useful, and a need to help others as strong motivators to assuming a caregiving role (Briggs 1998; Guberman 1999).

For some, caregiving is a labour of love – for others, a duty they cannot shirk

A recent Health Canada (2002) study reported that the majority (60%) of caregivers in their sample said that they provided care to a family member because they chose to do so – because they loved and felt close to the care recipient. Interestingly enough, it would appear that even adult children who do not feel great affection towards their parents still want to provide care. Briggs (1998) notes the following factors as influencing the decision to care in such cases: a feeling that caregiving is a familial responsibility or a duty that children owe their parents and feelings of gratitude and reciprocity. In a similar vein, Abel (1991) notes that children either want to return the care they once received from their parents or want to provide the good care that they did not receive in their childhood. This motive might have roots in a person's value system, personal characteristics, or the need to confirm one's self-image.

Family members are also often dissatisfied with the services provided by public agencies or paid care (Briggs 1998) and believe that the home environment is the best place for their loved one, especially when they live close by (Briggs 1998; Keefe 2002; Rosenthal et al. 2004). They also want to accommodate their elderly parents/in-laws, who often prefer living in the community and receiving care from family members to relying on more formal care arrangements (Soldo and Freedman, 1994). Johnson and Lo Sasso (2000) found that all respondents who indicated that their parents needed assistance also provided it regardless of their family circumstances (e.g., young children, a frail spouse, and/or in-laws also required care). Children were, however, less likely to care for a parent if their other parent was alive and perceived to be capable of providing care (Cranswick and Dosman 2008).

For others, particularly women, socialization plays a major role in the decision

Since women are more likely than men to assume the role of caregiver, it is interesting to look more closely at the reasons that motivate them to assume this role. Although affection and personal characteristics are strong motivators, women are also more likely than men to feel pressured by societal expectations and upbringing to take on the role, even if they are employed (Rosenthal et al. 2004; Margolies 2004). It has been observed that even if there are several family members available, daughters will be the first to emerge as the primary caregiver, followed by other women, and then by men (Henderson 2002; Margolies 2004). While women often admit that responsibilities should be shared equally between working siblings and that it is better to pay for care rather than quit their jobs, in practice they often do not follow these beliefs (Brody 1990).

So what does research tell us about why Canadians engage in caregiving?

It is evident from the discussion above that motivation to provide care is based on multiple considerations rather than just pure choice. Motives might be emotional, psychological, or moral, or may depend on logistical considerations, income level, socio-economic dependence, or reasons entirely unknown to the caregiver. In any case, rarely is the caregiver role assumed purely by choice. Most often multiple motivators are involved.

It should also be noted that the extant research in the area has drawn a link between reasons for care and caregiver mental health outcomes. These studies report that people who feel that they have no choice in the caregiving decision (formal care not available or too expensive) were more likely to find the role exhausting, stressful, and depressing

(Health Canada 2002). Those who are employed are less subject to such pressures, but daughters who have left employment to take care of a parent may end up becoming caught in the former condition of providing care out of necessity (Guberman 1999).

Why provide care? Answers from the 2012 Survey

The above review of the literature indicates that we do not really understand why employees, predominantly women, decide to assume the demanding role of caregiving for their elderly parents/in-laws. To provide greater insight into this important issue we included a research instrument developed by Decima Research Inc. (2004) to examine "Choice to Care" in the caregiving section of the 2012 Survey. Respondents were given a list of six reasons why someone might care for an elderly dependent and asked to what extent they agreed that each of these reasons applied in their case: believe it is a family responsibility, it is a personal choice, there is no one else available, there is a lack of homecare services, there is a lack of health-care services, and no one else is willing. The responses given to this question by the almost 8,000 employees in the Caregiver Sample are discussed in the sections below.

Why do people take on the role of caregiver? The survey data indicate that most employees can identify a number of reasons for taking on the role. The two most common reasons by far, both mentioned by virtually all respondents in the sample, is the perception that caregiving is a family responsibility (90% agree), and one that they choose to take on (83% agree). That being said, a substantial portion of the sample said that they took on the caregiver role because no one else was either available (42% agree) and/or willing (35% agree) to take it on. Finally, 30 per cent of the sample indicated that they took on the role of caregiver because of a lack of homecare and appropriate health services. Also noteworthy is the fact that neither gender nor life-cycle stage had much of an impact on why the employees in this sample indicated that they took on the caregiving role.

Factor analysis of the above six items showed that there are essentially three main reasons why employees take on the caregiver role:

Figure 2.2: Reasons Employees Take on Caregiver Role (Caregiver Sample, n = 7,966) (percentages)

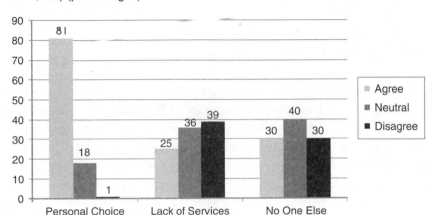

- *Lack of services:* A lack of homecare/health services.
- *There is no one else:* No one else is available/willing.
- *Personal choice:* Choose to provide the care/Believe it is a family responsibility.

Data showing how often the employees in the Caregiver Sample were motivated by each of these factors to assume the role of caregiver are shown in figure 2.2 and discussed below.

Why do Canadian employees take on the role of caregiver? They choose to because they see it as a family responsibility (81%); they do it because there is no one else available to take on the role (29%); and they do it because there is a lack of services to support the elderly within the community in which they live (25%). The employees in these last two groups may feel that they have been *pushed* into the caregiver role because of a lack of other alternatives. Given the strong link between choice to care and employee well-being, these findings imply that almost a third of the employed caregivers in this sample are at high risk with respect to stress and depression.

Interestingly enough, the data from this study do not identify any gender differences in the findings with respect to why employees choose to provide eldercare, which suggests that there has been an increase over time in the number of men who feel that caregiving is a family responsibility. This finding will be validated in chapter 3 when we look at the amount of time the men and women in our sample spend in caregiving.

Why provide care? Answers from the interview study

We asked the 111 employees who participated in the interview process, *"Why have you assumed the role of caregiver?"* The caregivers we spoke to identified ten reasons why they "chose to care." These reasons, along with quotations that exemplify the types of things we heard are given below in descending order with respect to the frequency they were mentioned.

One in four caregivers said they provided care because they were *the nearest, physically to the elderly dependent*. The importance of proximity as a reason for caring is clear from the following quotation:

> *Well, we're just here, right? We're the closest ones so when he had the stroke we were the ones that were here when the ambulance came.*

One in five caregivers linked their decision to assume the caregiver role to *their place in the family structure* (e.g., they were the only child, the eldest child, the only daughter). As one woman in our sample noted:

> *I think, of my siblings and myself, I'm the one that is closest to my parents, and because I'm the female out of two brothers I think that fell more to me.*

And, in a response that combines the first two reasons, one employee justified the choice to care as follows: *"I lived the closest, and I was the baby."*

One in five employed caregivers stated that they felt that they had *no choice but to provide care*. The following quotation illustrates how this could happen:

> He [respondent's uncle] *asked me to look after them because he couldn't look after his wife who had severe Alzheimer's and he was in poor health … it was a complex situation. I never thought that I would get into this type of thing, and it came as a total surprise. But I felt I had no choice.*

Just under one in five of the employees who were interviewed talked about how their *family member (typically their mother or their father) needed help* caring for their spouse. They noted that they had been motivated by this felt need to "step in" and assume the role of caregiver. The following quotations typify these types of situations:

To give my dad a break – he is finding it hard to care for Mom.

My dad had a massive stroke and he's in a long-term care facility … Mom suffers from anxiety and arthritis, and things like that. I have to be there for her so she can be there for him.

Just over one in ten of the interview respondents talked about how caregiving fell to them by default, as their *siblings/other family members could not or would not help out*. The following comment conveys the frustration of people in this situation:

You can check the absentee siblings box for sure … The other siblings ran away from the responsibility, so my wife and I were left with it.

Another one in ten of the employees we talked to stated that they provided care because the *person they looked after (again, typically a parent or in-law) was having health issues and could no longer look after themselves.* For example:

She had injuries. She had a fall and sustained injuries.

My mum is not very old, but she had a stroke last year, so I'm taking care of her.

One in ten caregivers felt an obligation to care for their parents because their parents had cared for them when they were young (e.g., "*I love them and it's my turn to look after them*"). People who gave this response used terms like "*payback*," "*what goes around comes around*," and "*it's my turn now*." They also talked about how much they loved their parents.

My mum was a single mum and she raised us … and I always said when she got older and stuff like that, I would be there for her … and I am.

One in ten caregivers noted that they did not provide care on their own. Instead they talked about how the family had made the decision to share responsibility for the care of their parents between siblings. This group of employees were motivated to provide care because they did *"not want to leave their siblings with all the responsibility."* Many who gave this response (both men and women) talked about how guilty they would feel if they did not do *"their share."* For example:

> *It's my own choice ... I'm fortunate that I have four other siblings who live a little bit closer to Mom and so they certainly do a lot more ... but I certainly try to take some of their burden as well, doing anything I can from a distance.*

Finally, a small number of the employees we talked to said that they took on the role *to support their partner* who had assumed the role of primary caregiver – either because they had no choice or because they wanted to. The following quotations illustrate the variety of circumstances impacting these employees:

> *No one else in the family wanted to take care of the uncle in question, and he* [my husband] *decided that he didn't want him to be placed in a home, or in a facility somewhere, so we decided to take care of him ... He cannot take care of a home, or pay bills or stuff like that – so he moved in with us.*

> *They were no longer capable of caring for themselves because, well, my father-in-law had bone cancer which ended up being terminal and my mother-in-law is a chronic alcoholic. She just couldn't keep her house. Her house was going to go into receivership, so she lost her house and moved in with us.*

Why do employees assume the caregiving role? When reading the quotations it becomes clear that often it is not just one factor that contributes to the employee's decision to provide care. Rather people take on the role for a myriad of reasons. For some the decision to care is quite personal. For others, circumstances drive them into a role that it is clear from their comments they had not anticipated assuming. In the section below we talk about what taking on the role of caregiver means in term of the activities undertaken by those in this role.

What Do Caregivers Do?

What do caregivers do? Caregiving can include a wide array of helping activities, which vary with respect to intensity as well as the physical and emotional demands they place on the caregiver (Duxbury, Higgins, and Schroder 2009; Calvano 2013). The following section addresses this very important question by reviewing three sets of data that speak to this issue: the academic literature in this area, quantitative data from the 2012 Survey (Caregiving Sample), and qualitative data from the 2012 Study (Interview Sample).

What do caregivers do? Answers from academia

"Caregiving" is a very general term pertaining to a variety of caring activities. To better capture the meaning of the term, a number of researchers have developed frameworks for categorizing informal caregiving tasks. They differ slightly in their level of detail but are generally quite similar. Most frameworks (Fast and Keating 2000; Henderson 2002; Wagner and Lottes 2006) include the following caregiving tasks:

- *Activities of daily living (ADL):* Includes support for day-to-day "personal care" activities such as bathing, dressing, feeding, toileting, and transferring from chair or bed.
- *Instrumental activities of daily living (IADL):* Includes activities such as housekeeping, meal preparation, home maintenance, banking, shopping, and transportation.
- *Nursing:* Includes activities such as help with medications and basic routine medical procedures.
- *Care management:* Includes activities such as identification of care providers and coordination of their activities.
- *Emotional care:* Includes things like emotional support and reassurance.
- *Psychological care:* Includes things like encouraging communication and involvement in activities.
- *Spiritual care:* Includes activities such as listening, talking about life, praying together, and going to church.

Fast and Keating (2000) categorized the above activities into four groups: personal, physical, organizational, and emotional. Rosenthal and Martin-Matthews (1999) grouped all caregivers into two groups based on the activities they performed: care providers (performing hands-on care tasks) or care managers (coordinating and managing services performed by others).

How often the caregiver engages in these various activities depends on the care recipient

Our review of the academic literature indicated that the frequency with which the caregiver engages in many of the above tasks depends on factors associated with the care recipient. Decima Research Inc. (2004), for example, noted that although a large majority of caregivers perform a wide range of tasks in looking after family members (the most common being providing medication, paying bills, driving them to destinations, and assisting with lifting and moving), fewer than half of all caregivers report that they engage in such tasks on a daily basis. Two key determinants of the frequency with which these different tasks are performed have been identified: the care recipient's age and the level of disability. At the stage when more help is needed with personal care, informal caregiving is often replaced with more formal or institutional care if financial resources are available (Uhlenberg and Cheuk 2008). Parents who are perceived as being more dependent receive more financial assistance (especially mothers) and more help with transportation, meal preparation, and personal hygiene (Nichols and Junk 1997).

With the oldest group of Canada's population growing in size, an increasing number of individuals will gradually lose their ability to perform the activities of daily living without help, and more seniors will require basic care. The Longitudinal Health and Retirement Study of caregivers aged 55 and older found that in 1994, 3 per cent of male caregivers and 9 per cent of female caregivers provided help with basic care. In 2008, these numbers had increased to 17 per cent and 28 per cent, respectively (Mature Market Institute 2011). Interestingly, caregivers continue to help with personal care even when the care recipient moves into a long-term care facility. Two factors motivate them to provide such care: a desire to improve the quality of care and/or a desire to reduce the cost of "assisted living" (Cranswick and Dosman 2008).

Caregiving activities: Key findings from the 2012 GSS

Sinah (2013) uses the 2012 GSS data to sketch out the various activities performed by Canadian caregivers. Unfortunately, she makes no distinctions related to whether or not these caregivers are employed and how employment status impacts what caregivers do. According to Sinah, caregivers performed a range of tasks in caring for their family member or friend, with providing transportation (73%) being the most commonly reported. Transportation involved conveying ill or disabled care recipients to run errands, shop, attend medical appointments, or participate in social events. Other tasks commonly undertaken by caregivers included housework (51%), house maintenance and outdoor work (45%), scheduling and coordinating appointments (31%), managing finances (27%), helping with medical treatments (23%), and providing personal care (22%).

Importantly, the GSS data show that caregiving is generally not limited to one specific task or activity. More than six in ten (63%) caregivers helped their family or friends on a regular basis, and most who did so helped with a variety of tasks. More specifically, 71 per cent of caregivers providing regular assistance helped with two or more tasks. Emotional support often accompanied other help to the care receiver. Nearly nine in ten caregivers (88%) reported spending time with the person, talking with and listening to them, cheering them up, or providing some other form of emotional support. Virtually all caregivers (96%) ensured that the ill or disabled family member or friend was okay either by visiting or calling.

Intensity of caregiving and caregiver mental health

Research suggests that the challenges faced by employed caregivers largely depend on the intensity of the caregiving experience. There has been considerable debate in the academic literature as to how intensity should be measured. In chapter 3 we present data that speak to one of the common indicators of intensity of caregiving: the number of hours spent on caregiving. In the section below we take a different approach and review literature linking what caregivers do (and how long they do it for) to the intensity of the caregiver role.

With respect to the types of tasks involved, a significant positive relationship has been found between providing intensive basic care (what we referred to earlier as ADL or acts of daily living) and caregiver strain. Intensive basic care requires the frequent presence of the caregiver and a lack of personal boundaries between the caregiver and the care recipient (Cranswick 2002; Evercare Survey 2009; Frederick and Fast 1999). Caregivers who have provided assistance for many years also feel more strained and often replace their informal caregiving with formal care services (Johnson and Lo Sasso 2000).

The severity of the care receiver's condition has also been found to affect caregiver outcomes. Different health conditions pose different demands on caregivers. The strain is much higher when dementia is involved, as compared to providing care for someone who is recovering from a hip fracture, for example. It is also emotionally more difficult to watch the deterioration of a closely related person, especially a spouse or a parent, than of a more distant relative (Amirkhanyan and Wolf 2006; Kramer and Kipnis 1995; Vitaliano, Young, and Russo 1991).

What do caregivers do? Answers from the 2012 Survey

Caregiving intensity was measured in this study by asking employees who had indicated that they were caregivers (i.e., respondents in the Caregiver Sample) to consider a list of seven caregiving activities and indicate, for each of these roles, the level of demands (i.e., time, energy) that the role placed on them in a typical month. The respondent was given the following choices in terms of response: do not spend time/energy in the role, spend almost no time/energy, spend a little time/energy, spend a moderate amount of time/energy, and spend a lot of time/energy. When analysing this measure we first looked at the percentage of

Table 2.2 What Do Caregivers Do? Per Cent Performing the Following Caregiving Tasks (n = 7,966)

	Men		Women		Total
	Sandwich	Eldercare	Sandwich	Eldercare	
Moral/emotional support	96.3	95.0	97.5	96.0	96.6
General care (transportation, running errands)	85.6	82.3	84.7	82.2	83.9
Financial assistance/support (money management, personal business)	72.8	73.5	66.5	64.7	67.9
Home/yard maintenance (housework, yard care)	73.2	66.1	62.3	56.7	63.2
Household chores (laundry, meals)	61.6	59.1	61.7	59.1	60.6
Personal care (toileting, feeding)	43.8	39.2	37.0	35.4	38.1
Nursing care (bathing, dressing, medications, bed transfer, wheelchair transfer)	40.1	34.4	33.1	30.6	33.9

the sample saying that they engage in each of these activities (per cent yes/no). Their responses are provided in table 2.2 and discussed below.

Caregiving is more about giving emotional support than "helping out"

Virtually everyone in the Caregiver Sample said that they provided emotional/moral support to the person they were caring for (emotional care) as well as general care (ran errands, drove them around). Approximately two-thirds of the employees in the sample said that they also provided financial assistance and helped with home and yard maintenance as well as household chores – activities that can be classified as "Instrumental Activities of Daily Living" (IADL). Finally, approximately a third of the respondents stated that they provided personal care (toileting, feeding) and nursing care (medications, bed transfer), activities that are typically categorized as "Activities of Daily Living" (ADL).

The data in table 2.2 show that the men in our sample were more likely than their female counterparts to provide financial assistance and yard work as part of their role as caregiver. They were also more likely to provide personal care and nursing care than their female counterparts – a finding that runs counter to what is reported in the literature. This is particularly true of men in the sandwich group. These gender differences are consistent with the research in this area (e.g., findings from the 2012 GSS).

Which of these activities demand the most time and energy from the caregiver?

The tasks and activities associated with caregiving can be conceptualized as falling along an "intensity" continuum, with some tasks demanding relatively little from the caregiver while others might consume a lot of time and energy. To increase our understanding of which caregiving activities demand the most from the caregiver, we calculated the percentage of the sample who indicated that each of the seven tasks in the measure was very demanding. The results of this analysis are provided in table 2.3

The provision of emotional support is the most intense aspect of caregiving

One in three employed caregivers in our sample (38%) felt that providing emotional/moral support to the person they were caring for was very demanding. One in five (21%) indicated that running errands and driving the person they were caring for around was very burdensome. The provision of financial assistance (15.9%), home maintenance (13%), and engaging in household chores were also identified as very demanding by an appreciable number of caregivers. The fact that relatively few people stated that the provision of nursing and personal care was very demanding probably has more to do with the fact that relatively few of the employees in our sample engaged in such activities than the actual demands such tasks place on caregivers.

The following important observations can be made from looking at the "role is very demanding" data. First, with one exception (home/yard maintenance) women were more likely than men to report that

Table 2.3 Caregiving Intensity by Caregiver Group:
Per Cent Saying Role Is Very Demanding (n = 7,966)

	Men		Women		Total
	Sandwich	Eldercare	Sandwich	Eldercare	
	Per cent of the sample saying that this role is very demanding				
Moral/emotional support	24.1	27.1	43.5	43.8	38.3
General care (transportation, running errands)	13.7	14.3	23.4	25.2	21.2
Financial assistance/support (money management, personal business)	12.2	14.9	17.2	17.0	15.9
Home/yard maintenance (housework, yard care)	12.1	15.9	12.3	13.5	13.0
Household chores (laundry, meals)	5.4	5.7	13.8	12.0	10.9
Nursing care (bathing, dressing, medications, bed transfer, wheelchair transfer)	2.8	3.4	8.5	8.5	7.2
Personal care (toileting, feeding)	2.9	4.8	8.5	4.2	5.7

they found all the caregiver roles examined in this study to be very demanding. The gender difference with respect to providing emotional support is particularly large. Second, while many people say they engage in these different roles, in most cases they do not find performance of the role to be demanding. Third, an over-focus on the strains facing caregivers who provide support with ADL (nursing, toileting, bathing) obscures the fact that it would appear to be the daily grinds and hassles of undertaking such high-frequency activities as offering emotional support, driving the dependent around, offering financial support, and helping with housework and yard work that take the greatest toll on caregivers over time.

Demands: Personal care (ADL) versus general care (IADL)

We undertook additional statistical analysis (i.e., factor analysis of the seven tasks) to determine if these seven tasks could be reduced to a smaller group of activities, as suggested in the research literature (see the discussion above of the caregiving activities framework). This analysis determined that the seven tasks fell into two groups:

- *Group One – Personal Care:* Personal care (e.g., feeding, toileting); Nursing care (e.g., bathing, dressing, medications, bed transfer, wheelchair transfer); Household chores (e.g., laundry, meal preparation)
- *Group Two – General Care:* Moral/emotional support (e.g., social support); General care (e.g., transportation, running errands, socializing); Financial assistance/support (e.g., money management, personal business); Home/yard maintenance (e.g., housework, yard care).

With one exception (household chores, which are typically categorized as IADL), the first group of activities seems to be a combination of tasks that researchers consider Health Care and Activities of Daily Living (ADL). Group two is very similar to what other researchers have referred to as Instrumental Activities of Daily Living (IADL). In the sections below we examine the implications for our respondents of engaging in these two different types of caregiving activities.

Women find caregiving to be more demanding than do men

Data on the demands these two sets of activities place on the caregivers in our sample are shown in table 2.4. Three conclusions can be drawn from these data. First, women find caregiving to be more demanding than do their male counterparts. This gender difference was apparent regardless of the type of activity being performed (ADL versus IADL) or life-cycle stage (sandwich versus eldercare). This gender difference is particularly interesting given the data showing that men were more likely than women to engage in many of the caregiving activities considered in this study, and it supports the importance of examining the impact engaging in the task has on the caregiver rather than assuming that all caregiving tasks are equally demanding. Second, having children at home does not seem to have an impact on perceived caregiving intensity

Table 2.4 Caregiving Intensity: Group Scores (n = 7,966) (percentages)

	Men		Women		Total
	Sandwich	Eldercare	Sandwich	Eldercare	
Personal Care (ADL):					
• Low demands	83.5	81.6	73.2	73.2	75.9
• Moderate demands	13.0	14.9	17.6	20.7	17.4
• High demands	3.5	3.5	9.2	6.1	6.7
General Care (IADL):					
• Low demands	43.3	41.0	27.7	27.4	31.9
• Moderate demands	39.1	39.2	42.0	41.4	41.0
• High demands	17.6	19.8	30.3	31.2	27.1

(there are no differences in demands between women in the sandwich group and the eldercare group). Third, regardless of gender, general care demands (i.e., IADL) seem to be more demanding than personal care demands (i.e., ADL) – a finding that runs counter to much of the research in this area. This may be because the caregiver is able to access more support from the community and the health-care system for activities that fit within the ADL bucket than for activities such as emotional support, which seems to be intrinsic to the role (i.e., caregivers take on the role of caregiver because they love their parents/in-laws, but this love then makes them more susceptible to worry, concerns, and anxiety). Alternatively, these findings might be due, in part, to how we measured the activities undertaken by the caregivers in our sample. Finally, these findings suggest that providing employed caregivers with emotional counselling and access to caregiver support networks may help them cope with the strains of taking on this role as much as (if not more than) the provision of support for concrete tasks.

Demands associated with the caregiving role

Finally, we calculated a summary measure of "caregiving demands" to give us a better understanding of the number of "high energy"

Table 2.5 The Demands of Caregiving: Summary (n = 7,966) (percentages)

	Men		Women		Total
Number of High Energy Roles	Sandwich	Eldercare	Sandwich	Eldercare	
Little to no energy: 1 or fewer	45.6	44.1	38.6	38.8	40.5
Moderate energy: 2–3	39.0	41.1	43.1	43.5	42.3
High energy: 4–5	12.0	11.7	14.3	14.9	13.8
Very high energy: 6–7	3.3	3.1	3.9	2.8	3.4

caregiving tasks typically accomplished by Canadian professional employees, as the research in the area (Sinah 2013) supports the idea that caregivers typically perform a variety of activities. We extended this work by looking not just at how many roles are undertaken by employed caregivers but also at how much energy is consumed by the performance of these roles. We did this by mapping what caregivers did to the amount of energy required by the role. We classified our caregivers into the following groups:

- Little to no energy spent in caregiving: respondent only engaged in 0 or 1 "high energy" caregiving tasks
- Moderate energy spent in caregiving: respondent engaged in 2 or 3 "high energy" caregiving tasks
- High energy spent in caregiving: respondent engaged in 4 or 5 "high energy" caregiving tasks, and
- Very high energy spent in caregiving: respondent engaged in 6 or more "high energy" caregiving tasks

The findings from this analysis are shown in table 2.5.

One in five employees finds the role of caregiver very demanding

According to our data, 40 per cent of employed caregivers perceive that the caregiving role consumes very little of their time and energy, 42 per cent say that it requires a moderate amount of time and energy, and

17 per cent say that the role requires a high or very high amount of their time and energy. Of note is the fact that the frequency with which the employees in our sample report low, moderate, and high levels of care-giving demands is not associated with either gender or life-cycle stage. These findings support the idea that it is the mix of caregiving activities undertaken as well as the amount of energy the person allocates to the role that is important in quantifying intensity – not just the likelihood that the employee will spend time in the task.

What do caregivers do? Answers from the interview study

We asked respondents two questions during the interviews to help us better understand the caregiver role: "What types of things (i.e., tasks, activities) do you do for the person that you provide care for?" and "What kinds of things does your spouse/partner do?" Responses given to these two questions are discussed below.

Caregivers have multiple demands on their time

Respondents identified ten different activities or tasks that they per-formed when engaged in caregiving. Quotations that illustrate what people were saying with respect to each of these activities are used in the section below to help the reader appreciate the complexity of the role. In many cases the quotations could have been used to exemplify more than one of the mentioned activities, as it was extremely rare for respondents to mention just one activity when they talked about what they did as a caregiver. The quotations themselves, therefore, provide a more illustrative example of the multiplicity of activities included un-der the caregiving umbrella than the statistics presented in the previous section. Taken together, these two sets of data do, however, show why employees can find caregiving overwhelming.

According to our respondents, the most common activity that they engage in as a caregiver (mentioned by an astounding 69 per cent of the caregivers in the sample) involves *offering emotional support* (rather than instrumental support) to the person they are caring for (typically a family member). Further analysis of the data determined that emotional support can take many forms but most often involves the caregiver sitting and talking to the dependent. Consider the following responses:

> There was a lot of emotional counselling going on, especially with my mother-in-law ... so I spend a lot of time talking with them. I often had to calm them down and stuff like that; sort of talk them off the ledge. You know what I mean?

> Whenever my mother would have an episode or a bad moment or would wander off or anything of that nature, I was the one my dad called. "Your mum's been missing for six hours; do you think you can go look for her?" "What do you mean, she's missing for six hours?" And the hunt would be on. At that time I really pretty much ignored my own family, my husband and my kids ... I'd be going to work, coming home, and running over to my mum and dad's to see what the latest fiasco was and trying to support my dad emotionally with what was happening.

As noted earlier, many of the caregivers in our sample (and likely in Canada in general) care for someone who does not live nearby. These individuals stated that they were engaged in caregiving when they provided *emotional support in the form of a long-distance phone call.* This is an important finding, as it suggests that caregiving cannot be restricted to activities that require physical presence. Those caregivers who lived a distance from the family member they cared for almost all considered that they were engaged in caregiving when they "touched base" with their dependent by phone (30 per cent of caregivers talked about this type of support). These phone calls seem to have two purposes: to provide emotional support to the elderly dependent and to reassure caregivers that "everything is all right" with their family member. For example:

> Never a day goes by that I don't talk to my mother ... about an hour on the phone a day.

> I spend a lot of time speaking to my parents on the phone and hearing for myself how they are doing – although you don't always get all the details on the phone. But they're pretty good at being honest.

Half of the caregivers we talked to stated that for them caregiving meant performing activities that involved *"a lot of running around,"* such as taking the person they were caring for to appointments (mostly medical) and/or running errands for them (e.g., picking up medications, doing grocery shopping). In most cases, the caregivers stated that they had to do the running around because the dependent either no longer had a driver's license or was too frail (mentally or physically) to take public transit. This first quotation speaks to the provision of support with getting to appointments as a form of caregiving:

Taking him to his doctor's appointments; visiting with him; helping with his meds; helping with meals; helping him at his residence; talking to him every day; going to do his errands, because he can't drive right now; and taking him to the hospital.

The next quotation illustrates that helping the care recipient with grocery shopping and running errands is also a form of activity performed by many employed caregivers:

It's usually helping her run errands, driving her around. What else do we do? I do all the maintenance of their place. I run her around when she has to do errands or anything because we don't like her to drive. She still thinks she can drive but, you know ..."

The interviews also showed that, for many (50%) of the employees we talked to, caregiving involves *helping with (or doing) the housework* for the person they are caring for. Most respondents who talked about doing housework said that they cooked, cleaned, and put out the garbage.

I'll help do the laundry or help cook or I'll do little things around the house, just to make life a little easier for them ... even running errands, too, sometimes ... I'll do shopping for them, too, and things like that.

One in four of those we talked to provided what can be considered to be *administrative support* or care management to their dependent. The number of activities we included within this group was quite large and included planning the person's medical appointments, organizing their meals, and scheduling activities. The following quotation illustrates the multiplicity of activities that this encompassed within the "administrative support" grouping:

> I just did little things, like putting the lawnmower away, arranging things in the house. In the wintertime, she needs to have some kind of railing, because she's got a really bad knee ... so I make some phone calls to some home care places to see if we can get a railing put in, so she can walk from her garage to her house by holding on to the railing. We don't actually do a lot.

One in five of the caregivers we spoke to (mostly men) helped with the physical tasks around the house (yard work, cutting the lawn, other household maintenance). For example:

> [My husband] takes on ... the larger house things, house maintenance things because he is a guy; so he takes on that traditional role.

The other two caregiving activities, the provision of physical care and financial support, were each mentioned by a smaller number (one in ten) of the respondents in the interview sample. The types of physical care mentioned by respondents correspond to what the literature talks about in terms of ADL activities:

> [S]he gets a catheter every day that I give to her ...

> [S]he wears diapers now – but she still wants to use the toilet so if I am there I help her with that ...

Financial support offered was more in the form of helping to pay bills rather than providing financial aid to the elderly family member. For example

> I pay all their bills. I have powers of attorney, so if there's a problem where they live – they contact me. I take care of all their banking and their investments – all that stuff.

Finally, although we analysed the data in a manner designed to highlight the various types of caregiving activities performed by the Canadian employees in this sample, we do not want the reader to think that the role is relatively simple. Rather, our analysis of the data determined that for many of the caregivers in our sample, caregiving involved "doing it all," as shown in the following quotation:

> *I do banking for her; I get groceries for her. I take her for clothes shopping; I take her for appointments. I clean up her apartment; I take her out for lunch or that kind of a thing the odd time. Or bring something in for her, like a supper or a lunch or something. I help her with her laundry, making her bed, and things like that because that's hard for her to do. The odd time I'll do laundry for her, but not on a regular basis, and just keeping her company, and that's what the phone calls are at night. And when I go there, sit down and have a cup of tea with her and that sort of thing ... just being a daughter.*

Many caregivers do not get any support from their partners

We also asked the respondents to tell us what caregiving activities were performed by their spouse/partner. Almost half of the sample (41%) indicated either that their partner did not engage in any caregiving activities or that they had no partner. With one exception (no one indicated that their partner provided any form of financial support), the types of caregiving activities engaged in by caregivers' partners were almost identical to those performed by the caregivers themselves. What is important, however, is to note that partners were less likely to provide each of these forms of care than were the employees who were the primary caregiver.

Men and women engage in a different mix of caregiving activities

Analysis of the data showed that men and women engaged in a somewhat different set of caregiver activities. The female caregivers in our sample were twice as likely as their male counterparts to say that they helped out by doing errands for the dependent and by talking to them on the phone. Surprisingly, it was the men in the sample who were more likely (17% versus 5%) to indicate that they took physical care of the dependent (feeding, bathing). This finding is opposite to what is reported in the literature and may be an artefact of the sample. It does indicate, however, that men provide physical care when there is no one else available to provide such support.

Analysis of our data also showed that the female caregivers in our sample were more likely than the men who engaged in the caregiving role to say that their partner did not provide any form of eldercare support (45% versus 30%). Those women who did receive support from their husband were more likely to note that their partner helped by doing yard work and gardening (i.e., traditional male tasks). The male caregivers in the sample, on the other hand, were more likely than their female counterparts to note that their partner helped them with their caregiving responsibilities by providing emotional support; taking the dependent to appointments; doing housework, groceries and errands; and providing physical care. Many of these tasks (cleaning, shopping, feeding, bathing) that their partners took on have traditionally been viewed as "women's work."

The sandwich group is more likely to engage in activities that involve a lot of "running around"

Life-cycle stage was also found to be associated with the types of caregiving activities performed. More specifically, employees in the sandwich group were more likely than those in the eldercare group to engage in four of the ten caregiving activities identified by the respondents: provide emotional support (55% versus 40%); take the dependent to appointments (47% versus 37%); shop and run errands for the dependent (55% versus 35%); and do housework for the dependent (45% versus 35%). Many of these activities are very time consuming. There were no cases where those in the eldercare group were more likely than those in the sandwich group to provide care.

Conclusions, Implications, and Recommendations

The answers to the questions reviewed in this chapter are of critical importance to those tasked with developing policies and programs to support employed caregivers in the delivery of the various activities they undertake in their role as caregiver. In the section below we summarize our key conclusions with respect to each of the questions addressed in this chapter, highlight a number of implications of these findings, and provide recommendations where possible or appropriate.

Conclusion: Prevalence of employed caregivers in Canada

Two estimates of the pervasiveness of employed caregivers in Canada can be derived from the 2012 Study. The first estimate, obtained by looking at our total sample of 25,021 Canadian employees, determined that 29 per cent of the men in our sample had no dependent care, 45 per cent had childcare, 17 per cent were in the sandwich generation, and 9 per cent spent time each week in eldercare. By comparison, 29 per cent of the women in the sample had no dependent care, 36 per cent had childcare, 20 per cent were in the sandwich generation, and 15 per cent spent time each week in eldercare. This would suggest that between 25 per cent and 35 per cent of Canadian knowledge workers are presently balancing work, caregiving, and possibly childcare

The second estimate was calculated using our sample of 7,966 employed caregivers. In this case, 60 per cent of the employees in the caregiving sample had multigenerational caregiving responsibilities (i.e., were in the sandwich generation), while 40 per cent were in the eldercare group.

In both samples, a higher proportion of employees were in the sandwich group of caregivers than in the eldercare-only group – a finding that is consistent with the fact that Canadian employees in professional positions are delaying parenting and are hence more likely to have both older parents and younger children at home.

Implications and recommendations for employers and policy makers

These data have several implications for Canadian employers. First, the high percentage of knowledge workers with caregiving responsibilities reinforces the need for Canadian companies who wish to attract and retain talent in a "seller's" market for labour to address the concerns of the employees in this group. Second, the high number of employees with both childcare and eldercare responsibilities reinforces the need for companies to address this issue. Finally, the data from the 2012 Study showing that many younger (i.e., Generation X) male employees are now involved in caregiving in the same numbers as younger women suggest that younger employees have more egalitarian attitudes towards who does what at home than do older Canadians. In the future, we would expect that an even higher percentage of males will be involved in caregiving as a result of the decline in family sizes in Canada (e.g., in one-child families, there will be no other family members available to care for aging parents). As such we recommend that employers and policy makers move beyond "gendered" solutions to this issue and recognize that balance of one form or another is now an issue for all.

Conclusion: Caregiving touches every segment of Canada's labour force

Our research indicates that caregiving does not conform to many of the stereotypes we unconsciously hold. Caregiving is not a transitory activity performed by older women. It is not just one person who is being cared for at a time. Many caregivers do it not just for love but also because there is no one else available. Those being cared for do not necessarily live in a "granny flat" in the garden – in fact, they often do not even live in the same country as the caregiver. Rather, our data indicate that caregivers are "typical" Canadians – the person next door, your best friend, you! – who provide care for a year or more to ill or disabled family members. Furthermore, our research shows that caregiving touches every segment of Canada's labour force: men and women; parents and non-parents; the married and the single; those who are employed, retired, or not in the labour market; individuals in the Generation Y, Generation X, and boomer/veteran cohorts. It is a "pan-Canadian" phenomenon. These findings are consistent with the data from the 2012 GSS, which indicate that no adult Canadian appears to be exempt or excluded from the caregiver role.

Conclusion: Caregiving is complicated

Employees in both the sandwich generation and the eldercare group feel responsible for the care of multiple elderly family members in their seventies who live within an hour's drive of their home. Most have been caring for these dependents for five to ten years. The fact that there are few differences between those in the eldercare and sandwich groups with respect to their caregiving situation is also very interesting, as it suggests that any differences in mental health and employment outcomes associated with family type can be attributed to the fact that those in the sandwich generation have to balance three roles (employment, childcare, and eldercare) – one more than their counterparts in the eldercare-only group.

Implications and recommendations for employers and policy makers

In summary, the Canadian employees in this sample feel responsible for the care of multiple family members in their seventies who live within an hour's drive of their home. Most have been caring for these dependents for five to ten years. What does this imply for employers? First, the fact that most employees care for one or more older family members increases the likelihood that they will feel torn between the need to care for their elderly family members and their work and also increases the relevance of issues associated with work and caregiving for employers and governments alike. Second, those employees who are caring for older family members (26% of the sample) can be expected to experience more and more challenges with balancing work and caregiving, given the research showing that caregiving intensity increases with the age of the care recipient. Third, the findings indicate that caregiving is not a transitory, end-of-life phenomenon but rather an activity that can impose challenges for a substantial period of time. Each of these caregiving situations is likely to come with its own set of challenges.

These findings provide support for our earlier observation that there is no one-size-fits-all solution to the caregiving issue and reinforces the need for governments and employers to provide a wide variety of supports that reflect the diversity in caregiving situations found in their workforce, and to be flexible with respect to their application and use. The demographic data presented in chapter 1, in combination with the data from this chapter outlining the ubiquity of caregiving in Canada's workforce, reinforce the necessity of developing such supports and services for caregivers now, while we still have time, rather than later when Canada is swamped by the tsunami of demographic change.

Conclusion: Women in the sandwich group have a unique set of challenges

While there are a number of similarities between caregivers in the eldercare and sandwich groups, there are also several key differences between these two groups that warrant attention, particularly by policy makers and employers. First, the data support the idea that employees in the sandwich group may find it difficult to make ends meet financially (i.e., be more likely to report that money is tight in their family) than those in the eldercare group. This finding is particularly interesting given the data showing that, when gender is taken into account, employment income is not associated with life-cycle stage. It may be that caregiving is more likely to impose a financial strain in families with children still living in the home.

Second, the data support the idea that it is the female partner in families with both childcare and eldercare demands who is more likely to have assumed primary responsibility for caregiving in the family. The data also show that mothers who are also involved in caregiving activities are more likely to live in a family where their partner is the primary breadwinner, suggesting that they are taking on this role because their partner has a secure income and/or that these individuals have reduced their commitment to their career as a way to manage their dual caregiving demands.

Implications and recommendations for employers and policy makers

The above findings imply that although women in Canada (and in our sample) are now more educated and share breadwinning responsibilities with their husbands or partners, traditional gender roles are still in place in many Canadian families. The fact that Canadian employees with mul tigenerational caregiving responsibilities are more likely to be financial-ly stressed is cause for concern, as most of the individuals in our sample had well-paid jobs. Policy makers need to explore this issue in more depth and determine how best to support Canadian employees who are struggling to support their children and their elderly family members. Suggestions offered by respondents on how this could best be done are given in chapter 8. Finally, the fact that both our study and the 2012 GSS show that many younger employees are in the sandwich group is of particular importance to employers, who will need to take this into consideration when addressing retention and succession-planning needs.

Conclusion: Caregivers engage in a multiplicity of activities

"Caregiving" is a very general term pertaining to a variety of care activities. Although researchers in the area have identified four main groups of caregiving activities (emotional support; assistance with health and daily living; organizational support, nursing, and personal care; and financial support), very few of the employees in our sample talked about providing nursing/physical care and financial support to elderly dependents. Rather, the 2012 Study supports the following conclusions with respect to the key components of the caregiving role:

- Caregiving is largely about the provision of emotional support. The most common caregiving activity by far provided by the employees in this sample involves offering emotional (rather than instrumental) support to the aging family member. Emotional support can take many forms but most often involves the caregiver in sitting and talking to the dependent. Caregivers who live at a distance provide similar support when they "touch base" with their dependent by phone. Phone calls are also done to reassure the caregiver that "everything is all right" with the dependent.
- Many employees also provide assistance with activities associated with health and daily living. They undertake caregiving activities that involve "running around," such as taking the person they are

caring for to appointments (mostly medical) and/or running errands for them. In most cases, this form of support is necessary because the dependent either lacks a driver's license or is too frail (mentally or physically) to take public transit. Doing housework for the dependent is also a common form of caregiving. Most respondents who talked about doing housework said that they cooked, cleaned, and put out the garbage.

- One in four provides organizational support to their family member by planning their medical appointments, organizing their meals, maintaining their calendar, and so on.

The data also show that the partners of these employees offer similar types of care, albeit less often than the employees themselves. Also noteworthy are the data showing that, with one exception (home/yard maintenance), women were more likely than men to report that they found all the caregiver roles examined in this study to be very demanding. The gender difference with respect to providing emotional support is particularly large.

Implications and recommendations for employers and policy makers

These findings have several important implications for employers. First, the group of employees who are attempting to balance work and caregiving is likely larger than our initial estimates, as employed partners of caregivers also provide care. Second, the fact that, for many employees, caregiving involves the performance of time-consuming activities such as home chores and "running around" reinforces the notion that employed caregivers could benefit from more flexible work arrangements. Third, caregiving intensity seems to be more strongly related to the mix of caregiving activities undertaken and the amount of energy allocated to the role than to task performance. These findings indicate that researchers should look beyond who does what with respect to caregiving to how much energy the caregiver perceives they spend in the role. Fourth, a primary focus on the strains facing caregivers who provide support with

ADL (nursing, toileting, bathing) obscures the fact that it would appear to be the daily grinds and hassles of undertaking high-frequency activities such as offering emotional support, driving the dependent around, offering support with financial management, and helping with housework and yard work that take the greatest toll on caregivers over time. Finally, increased flexibility at work is unlikely to offer much help to the majority of the employees in this sample who are providing emotional support to their family members. This type of emotionally draining activity is more likely to require empathy from managers and co-workers as well as support from employee assistance programs (EAP) and employee family assistance programs (EFAP).

The above data lead us to make the following recommendations with respect to addressing the needs of caregivers. First, employers should make sure that those with caregiving responsibilities have access to flexible work arrangements. Second, employers should expand their EAP offerings to include specific supports for employed caregivers (e.g., eldercare referral services, counselling). It may be useful to consider moving from EAP to EFAP in order to recognize the changing needs of the workforce with respect to support. Third, employers should engage in educational efforts within the workplace to increase awareness of this issue in their management cadre. Finally, all levels of government should increase the number and availability of mental health and counselling programs in the community.

These results also suggest that researchers and policy makers should look beyond who does what with respect to caregiving (the form of data typically collected in government surveys) to consider how much energy the caregiver spends in the role. They also suggest that researchers and practitioners should acknowledge the demands placed on caregivers by the more mundane (but still time consuming) aspects of caregiving. Finally, findings from the 2012 Study suggest that the provision of emotional support is part of high-intensity caregiving. The focus on ADL and IADL in the research literature means that this connection has not received the attention it deserves from governments, support services, and employers.

Conclusion: Canadians provide caregiving for a multiplicity of reasons

The advantages gained from talking to caregivers as well as surveying them can be seen by comparing the survey responses to the more detailed answers given during the interviews. While both sets of data tell a similar story (the decision to care is a combination of desire and necessity), the interview data provide us with a much greater appreciation of the complexity of this issue. Findings from the 2012 Study support the following conclusions with respect to why employed Canadians take on the caregiving role First, in many cases the reasons employees give for taking on this type of commitment are pragmatic (e.g., *"I am nearest"; "I am the only child"; "I am the only daughter"; "There is no one else"*). Second, it is apparent that many of the people we surveyed and interviewed felt that they had no choice but to provide care (e.g., *"I have no choice"; "There is no one else"; "Their partner cannot provide care"; "My siblings can't/won't provide care"; "They cannot look after themselves"*). Finally, it is interesting to note that very few people (only one in ten) talked about how they wanted to take on the role of caregiver (*"It is payback for the care they provided to me when I was young"; "My partner is providing care – and I do it to support them"; "I love them and want to care for them"*). In other words, *"Because I want to"* was not the top-of-mind response when employees were asked why they provide care.

Implications and recommendations for employers and policy makers

What do these findings mean for employers and policy makers? The fact that, for many of the highly educated knowledge workers in this sample, caregiving is something that they both want to do and have to do suggests that employers will have little choice but to address the issues faced by employees in this group if they want to recruit, retain, and motivate employees. Municipal governments will also need to address issues associated with caregiving if they want to attract people to their communities. For provincial and federal governments, supporting caregiving should be motivated by the need to be globally competitive.

As discussed in chapter 1, Canada counts on the fact that family members will engage in caregiving. The data in this chapter offer cautions with respect to these expectations. If governments have the expectation that Canadians will continue to do the heavy lifting with respect to caregiving, they need to increase their offerings of services to support employees in this task. Otherwise, we can expect the mental health of our workforce to suffer, as the research has shown that people who feel pushed into the caregiving role are more likely to experience challenges than their counterparts who elected to take on the role and felt supported by others in the role. As such, we recommend that both organizational and governmental policy makers view as a business imperative the task of developing policies and practices that address the needs of the caregivers in their workforce.

Chapter Three

Too Much to Do in Too Little Time: Balancing Caregiving, Employment, and (Perhaps) Childcare

The challenges ... I guess it's a time balancing, time management kind of thing. I have challenges at work where potentially I'm covering more than one team due to other issues that are occurring. And with the challenges that happen at work – doing more with less is what they're asking us to do – and doing it at different times of the day, the challenge is huge to try to balance work and all this family stuff ...

Caregiving requires a considerable amount of time and effort, as do paid employment and the rearing of children. Given that there are only twenty-four hours in the day, it can be expected that the demands imposed by employment and/or childcare will interfere with the kind of help that informal caregivers can offer to the elderly. So, if this is the case, why do people with heavy childcare and eldercare demands remain in the labour market? It's quite simple – caregiving and raising children require financial resources, and employment provides income that allows caregivers and parents to purchase needed goods and services (Brody 1990).

So, what impact does paid employment have on the amount of time people spend in caregiving? What impact does caregiving have on the amount of time employees can devote to their job? How do caregivers balance these conflicting time demands? Unfortunately, our attempt to find answers to these questions in the research literature revealed a lack of consensus on these points. This chapter addresses this gap in our understanding by using data from the 2012 Study to examine: (1) the amount of time employed knowledge workers in Canada spend each week in family labour, paid employment, and their total role set (i e., their objective work and family demands); (2) how overloaded these employees are at work and at home (subjective demands); and (3) these employees' ability to balance competing work and family demands. This focus on time, demands, and balance is relevant given that, when working parents and caregivers are asked to identify the biggest concern in their lives, they typically respond "time."

Chapter 3 is divided into four sections. The first three sections deal with objective demands (time in family labour, work, and total role demands), role overload (work-role overload, family-role overload, and total-role overload), and work-life conflict (work interferes with family and family interferes with work), respectively. All three of these sections begin with a brief review of key literature in the area ("Answers from academia"). This review is followed by the presentation and discussion of relevant data from the 2012 Study (quantitative and, if possible, qualitative). The chapter concludes in section four with a summary of key conclusions that can be drawn from the data presented, along with implications and recommendations for employers and policy makers alike, as appropriate.

Objective Demands

The situation isn't very complex, just time-consuming.

Three objective indicators of work and family role demands are discussed in the section below: time in family labour, time in paid employment, and total role demands.

Objective demands: Answers from academia

Before looking at the quantitative data from the 2012 Study which speak to time in family labour (defined as those tasks required to maintain a household and fulfil child and eldercare responsibilities), it is useful to first review the academic literature on this topic.

The amount of time spent per week in caregiving activities is often used as a measure of caregiving intensity, as research has established a positive association between time in caregiving and caregiver strain (Vitaliano, Young, and Russo 1991; Williams 2004). Research in the area suggests that the time caregivers spend in the caregiving role is impressive. In 2007, family caregivers aged 45 to 64 spent on average 5.4 years providing care; 10 per cent of these individuals had been providing care for at least thirteen years. The majority of this group were women, and more than half were employed (Cranswick and Dosman 2008). In one study of U.S. eldercare providers, an average of three hours each day was devoted to providing care, despite the fact that many were employed (Margolies 2004). Researchers have observed that caregivers often underestimate the time they will have to spend on providing care when they start helping out with small tasks. Over time, the increasing demands start conflicting with their work responsibilities (Mature Market Institute 1999).

Time devoted to caregiving also varies considerably depending on caregiver capacity. Using data from the 1996 GSS, Frederick and Fast (1999) showed that having responsibility for the care of more than one elderly dependent at a time, working full-time, and having been providing care for more than two years all reduced the hours spent per week on caring. The age of the care recipient as well as their suffering from one or more disabilities, on the other hand, significantly increased the care time. Another condition that increases amount of care (time spent and tasks performed) is living with the elderly in the same household (Dee and Peter 1992). This likely happens when the care recipient's health has significantly deteriorated so that constant care is required. Many caregivers have changed their living arrangements to live together with the care recipient when long-distance care becomes insufficient (Statistics Canada 2011a).

Autman and colleagues (2010) note that women spend more time in caregiving than men. On average, women spent 9.1 hours a week in providing care (an average of 6.4 hours providing in-person care and an average of 2.7 hours providing indirect care), while men spent 5.7 hours as caregivers (an average of 3.4 hours providing in-person care and an average of 2.2 hours providing indirect care).

*Academic evidence on the impact of employment
on time spent in providing care is contradictory*

A high proportion of caregivers also have paid jobs outside their home. There is conflicting evidence regarding how employment impacts the time people spend on providing care to the elderly. Several researchers have reported that neither work responsibilities nor work status (full-time versus part-time) significantly changes the intensity of caregiving provided by women (Armstrong 1994; Brody 1990; Kramer and Kipnis 1995; Rosenthal et al. 2004). This finding has been interpreted as suggesting that women feel strongly committed to their caregiving duties irrespective of the demands those duties place on their time and energy. Others note, however, that employment may affect the types of care women provide, as it is likely that working women have less time for personal care, housekeeping, and emotional support than their counterparts who are not in the labour market (Brody and Schoonover 1986; Mature Market Institute 2011).

Men's caregiving activities, on the other hand, seem to be more strongly impacted by their employment status, although even here the evidence is somewhat contradictory (Mature Market Institute 2011). While data from the 2002 GSS support the idea that having a job did not significantly affect the amount of time both men and women spent on caregiving tasks (Stobert and Cranswick 2004), earlier work by Stoller (1983) found that being employed decreased sons' caregiving activities by twenty hours per month, while the time daughters spent taking care of their parents was not affected by their employment status. This suggests that gender differences in time spent in caregiving may be diminishing over time.

Time in caregiving: The 2012 GSS

According to Sinah (2013), one-quarter of caregivers (26%) reported spending one hour or less per week caring for a family member or friend. Another 32 per cent reported spending an average of two to four hours per week, and 16 per cent spent five to nine hours per week on caregiving activities (Sinah 2013). Approximately one in ten caregivers were spending thirty or more hours a week providing some form of assistance to their ill family member or friend – making caregiving equivalent to a full-time job for these individuals, who were most likely caring for an ill spouse (31%) or child (29%). According to the GSS, caregivers in Canada in 2012 spent a median of three hours a week caring for an ill or disabled family member or friend, with most caregivers spending less than ten hours a week on caregiving activities. "Although the median number of caregiving hours was similar between men and women (between 3 and 4 hours per week, respectively), women were more likely than their male counterparts to spend 20 or more hours per week on caregiving tasks (17% versus 11%)" (Sinah 2013, 10).

Time at work

Time at work is the single largest block of time that most people owe to others outside their family. Consequently, it is often the cornerstone around which the other daily activities must be made to fit. As a fixed commodity, time allocated to employment is necessarily unavailable for other activities, including time with the family and time for leisure. Thus, time spent at work offers an important and concrete measure of one dimension of employment that affects individuals and their families (hours of work affect earnings) and society as a whole through its contribution to economic productivity. Higher work demands have been found to be positively associated with increased levels of stress and depressed mood as well as increased levels of work-life conflict, increased intent to turnover, and increased absenteeism (Duxbury and Higgins 2013a). Jacobs and Gerson (2001) determined that individuals in couples who worked more than 100 combined hours per week (i.e., total hours per week worked by the couple) were particularly pressed for time and were more likely to report increased levels of personal stress.

According to Statistics Canada,[1] in 2012 employed Canadians spent an average of 36.6 hours per week at work, with men spending more

---

1 Table 282-0028 - Labour force survey estimates (LFS). Available at: http://vanierinstitute.ca/families-work-canada/?print=print.

hours in employment per week (39.6 hours) than women (33.2 hours). It should be noted, however, that these estimates were calculated on a sample that included both full-time and part-time employees and as such do not speak to the amount of time spend in paid employment for those who work full time.

Additional data to inform this issue come from a report on family work (i.e., the total hours in paid employment worked by employed couples) produced by Statistics Canada (Marshall 2009), which showed that in 2008, 59 per cent of dual-earner couples spent between sixty-five and eighty "combined" hours per week in paid employment. Also note-worthy (particularly given the work done by Jacobs and Gerson [2001], which is cited above) are data showing that roughly one in four dual-earner families in Canada in 2008 worked more than eighty hours per week (Marshall 2009). Finally, Marshall (2009, 12) also presented data showing that the "average weekly hours of husbands and wives have converged over time from a difference of more than 9 hours per week in 1997 (43.3 and 33.8 respectively) to just over 7 hours per week in 2008 (42.0 and 34.7) placing two-thirds of couples in an equal work-hours category (their hours being within 10% of each other's)." Such informa-tion has relevance to the issue of work-life balance, which is addressed in the third section of this chapter.

Time in caregiving: Answers from the 2012 Survey

Research has found that, for full-time employees of both genders, an increased number of hours spent in dependent care per week places them at high risk for work-family conflict, role overload, and stress (Duxbury and Higgins 2013a). In the 2012 Study, time in family labour was quantified by looking at how many hours per week the employee and the employee's partner/spouse spent in two forms of dependent care: childcare (when relevant) and eldercare. In the section below we present and discuss two estimates of time spent in family labour. The first is calculated using the Total Sample (n = 25,021), while the second uses the Caregiver Sample (n = 7,966). Data on time in caregiving for those in the Interview Sample are less relevant to this discussion, given the fact that one of the criteria used to identify the Interview Sample was caregiving intensity, which is strongly associated with time spent in caregiving activities.

Time in caregiving per week: The Total Sample

The self-reported data on hours per week in child and/or eldercare (Total Sample) support the following conclusions with respect to the demands faced by employees in the sandwich generation. First, while the amount of time those in the sandwich generation devote to childcare and eldercare is highly variable, it is also quite considerable: approximately sixteen hours per week in childcare for men and nineteen hours per week for women, and around six hours per week in eldercare for both genders. Second, parents of younger children spend more time in childcare a week on average (approximately thirty hours per week) than do parents of older children, the majority of whom spend less than ten hours a week in such activities. Third, the majority of the men and women in the sandwich generation in our sample (over 80%) said that their partner also spends time each week in childcare and eldercare, a finding that has two important implications. First, it implies that caregiving is now a shared responsibility within most Canadian families. Second, it suggests that the number of employees balancing work and caregiving is larger than the study's initial estimates, which were calculated based on how many of the respondents to our survey indicated that they were caregivers. Finally, it is interesting to note that employees in the sandwich generation spend approximately three times more hours per week in childcare than in eldercare.

Gender norms with respect to who does what are still in place in many sandwiched families

As can be seen by looking at the data in figure 3.1, female employees spent more hours a week in childcare than their male colleagues – a finding that is consistent with much of the literature in the area and the fact that the women in our sample are more likely to have responsibility for

Figure 3.1: Hours in Dependent Care per Week: Gender by Life-Cycle Stage (n = 25,021)

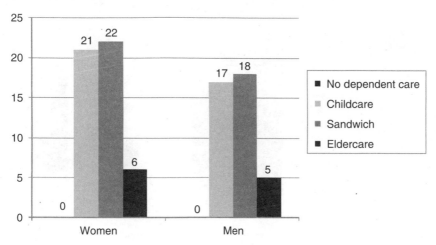

childcare in their family. There were, however, no substantive gender differences in the amount of time employees spent each week in eldercare. Also noteworthy are data showing that men and women with multigenerational caregiving responsibilities spent about the same amount of time per week in childcare as those in the childcare only group.

Time in caregiving per week: The Caregiver Sample

The responses from the employees who filled in the Caregiving section of the survey (i.e., Caregiver Sample) allow us to explore the caregiving demands of employees in the eldercare and sandwich groups in more detail. These data are shown in figure 3.2 (time in childcare by respondent and spouse), figure 3.3 (time in eldercare by respondent and spouse) and table 3.1. These data support a number of observations with respect to the amount of time Canadian employees spend in dependent care as well as the impact of gender and life-cycle stage on the demands associated with these two roles.

First, the data show that the amount of time parents and their partners in the caregiving group spend in childcare is highly variable (see

Figure 3.2: Hours per Week Employed Parents Spent in Childcare (n = 7,966)

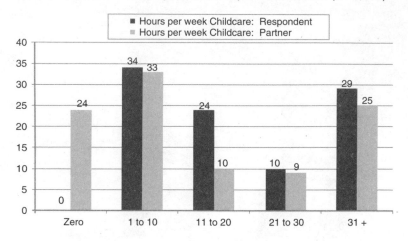

Figure 3.3: Hours per Week Employees Spent in Eldercare (n = 7,966)

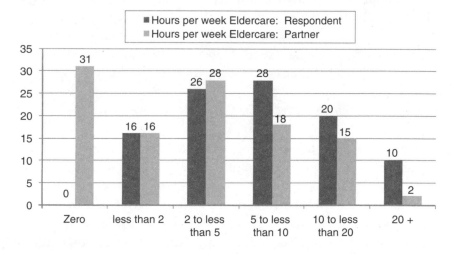

Table 3.1 Objective Work and Family Demands (n = 7,966)

Work and Family Demands	Men		Women	
	Sandwich	Eldercare	Sandwich	Eldercare
Respondent				
Hours per week in childcare	16.9	0	20.1	0
Hours per week in eldercare	6.1	7.1	6.4	7.9
Total hours in caregiving per week	23.0	7.1	26.5	7.9
Per cent saying that their partner spends no time per week in eldercare	18%	14%	28%	20%
Total hours in paid employment per week	52	50	48	47
Per cent performing supplemental work at home	71%	61%	57%	52%
Respondent's Partner				
Hours per week in childcare by spouse	24.6	0	17.4	0
Hours per week in eldercare by spouse	8.8	8.7	5.9	5.8
Total hours/week in caregiving by spouse	33.4	8.7	23.3	5.8
Total hours in paid employment per week	37.8	36.9	47.9	40.8

figure 3.2), with peaks at one to ten hours per week (parents of older children) and at more than thirty hours per week (parents of younger children). The amount of time employees and their partners in the caregiving group spend in eldercare is also highly variable (see figure 3.3) but in many cases substantial. Employees who filled in the Caregiver section of the 2012 Study survey spent between six and eight hours per week engaged in caregiving activities – essentially the equivalent of a full work day per week.

Second, the vast majority of the employees in this sample (over 80%) said that their partner also spent time each week in childcare and/or eldercare, a finding that supports our earlier observation that childcare and caregiving are now a shared responsibility in most Canadian families.

Third, analysis of data related to time in childcare and time in eldercare per week for respondents in the Caregiver Sample support the idea that while female employees spend more time per week in childcare than their male counterparts, time in eldercare does not appear to be related to gender. The following data support these conclusions. First, the female employees in the sample spent more hours per week in childcare than their male counterparts. Second, the men in the sample received more caregiving support from their partners than did the women, regardless of their life-cycle stage. Finally, the data from this study provide further evidence to support the idea that gender is not related to the amount of time per week employees spend in eldercare. Taken together, it would appear that gender role expectations with respect to being a parent are more intransigent to change than are expectations with respect to caregiving. This dynamic is most apparent in the sandwich group.

Fourth, the data suggest that dependent care demands are particularly onerous for those in the sandwich group, as employees who spend time each week in both childcare and eldercare (i.e., those in the sandwich group) spend significantly more time overall in family activities than their counterparts in the eldercare-only group (approximately triple the amount of time). This difference can be attributed to the fact that those in the sandwich group essentially spend as much time in childcare as those in the children-only group and as much time per week in caregiving as those in the eldercare group.

The women in our sample in the sandwich group, in particular, spent substantially more hours per week in caregiving than any other group of employees in our sample (on average, 26.5 hours per week – or the equivalent of three full work days!). This finding is consistent with the fact that the data from this study (see chapter 2) showed that these women reported receiving less support from their partner for caregiving (28% said their partner did not provide them with any support or help) than other respondents.

The following quotations from women in the sandwich group who participated in the interview study illustrate the challenges women with both childcare and eldercare face trying to balance all the demands on their time:

> *It's the balance of everything, and learning how to be that middle person in the middle of a teeter-totter and being able to balance your whole life with your whole*

work ... I think the only thing I can say is that all of this is all about time. When it comes right down to it, it has nothing to do with expense; it has to do with time and the emotional and the physical drain on the person that is caregiving.

I think the potential consequences of looking after my mom are just that I have less time left for myself, less time left to give to my kids ... I feel sort of pulled in multiple directions.

Time in paid employment: Answers from the 2012 Survey

My work role is very demanding ... I love it and enjoy it ... It's just the level of skill that I need to do my job is very demanding, and you need to be able to think. When you're preoccupied with all the something elses that come with looking after two families ... that's when it becomes touch-and-go.

We included two measures of objective work[2] demands in the survey used in the 2012 Study: hours spent in work per week, and hours spent per week in supplemental work at home (SWAH) – job-related work performed at home outside of work hours. We also asked respondents to estimate how many hours per week their partner spent in paid employment and SWAH, as stress and work-life conflict are positively associated with the total work demands within the couple. In the section below we first present and discuss estimates calculated using the Total Sample. This is followed by analysis done using the Caregiving Sample (table 3.1).

Time in work per week: The Total Sample

Canadian employees devote long hours to work each week. The average employee in the 2012 Study sample spends forty hours per week (39.8) performing work at the office, and two-thirds of our 25,000-plus employees work more than forty-five hours per week.

---

2 Note, in the discussion below the term "work" refers to time spent in paid employment.

Downsizing and restructuring have increased the work demands placed upon many Canadian employees who are now doing their own job as well as parts of jobs that used to be done by workers who are no longer with the organization. Employees with heavy work demands who cannot get their jobs done during regular work hours often have to work evenings and weekends (which have traditionally been viewed as family time) to keep "caught-up." More than half of the 25,000-plus employees in our sample (61% of the men and 50% of the women) offer a day's worth of SWAH to their organization each week. In other words, they donate a day's work of their personal time to their organization each week. All things considered, the "typical" respondent to the 2012 Study survey spends 50.2 hours in work-related activities per week.

On average, the men in the sample spend more time per week in employment-related activities (50.3 hours in work per week) than the women (46.9 hours in work per week). Part of this difference can be attributed to the fact that the men were more likely than the women to perform SWAH (61% of men versus 50% of women). That being said, gender is not related to either the amount of unpaid overtime performed per week for those engaged in such activities or the amount of time spent per week commuting to and from work.

As noted above, families where both the respondent and their partner report higher total time in paid employment per week are more likely to experience challenges with respect to work-life conflict and to report higher levels of stress than families where one if not both partners spend fewer hours per week in paid employment (Duxbury and Higgins 2013a; Jacobs and Gerson 2001). When we exclude from our calculations those respondents whose spouse does not work, just over half of the employees who responded to the 2012 Study survey (56%) had partners who worked more than 45 hours per week. Furthermore, a majority (62%) had partners who performed SWAH – spending approximately 8.1 hours in after-hours work per week.

The remainder of the men (31%) and women (14%) who completed the survey were the primary breadwinner in their family and had partners who worked significantly fewer hours per week than they did (less than 35 hours per week). Men were more likely to have a partner who worked fewer hours than they did (one in three were married to women who worked part time or not at all). Women, on the other hand, were more likely to be married to someone who also had very heavy work demands.

Having children at home impacts the amount of time in paid employment

The 2012 Study data support the following observations with respect to the relationship between time in dependent care, time in employment, and gender. For female employees, their partner's time in work is high- est when the family have children at home (i.e., in the childcare and sandwich stages of the life cycle). For male employees, on the other hand, their partner's time in work is lowest when the family is in the childcare stage of the life cycle (i.e., childcare needs are highest). More specifically, women in the childcare (46 hours per week) and sandwich (47 hours per week) groups spend significantly less time in work per week than their male partners, who spend fifty-one and fifty-two hours in work per week respectively. These data, when considered in tandem, suggest that families with children in the home (i.e., those in the child- care and sandwich stages of the life cycle) accommodate the increase in family demands by having the female partner reduce the amount of time she spends in paid employment. The male partners in these fami- lies, on the other hand, increase the amount of time they spend in paid employment – either to compensate for their spouse's reduction in work hours and/or because they can (i.e., their spouse is assuming re- sponsibility for childcare). These findings are similar to those reported by Marshall (2009).

Time in work per week: The Caregiver Sample

Analysis of the hours in work data for those in the Caregiver Sample (see table 3.1) gives further insights into how life-cycle stage impacts hours in work. More than half of the employees in this sample devoted more than forty-five hours per week to paid employment. While the men in the sandwich group spent the highest number of hours in paid employment per week (52 hours per week on average) and women in the eldercare group spent the least amount of time in this role (47 hours per week on average), all employees in the sample spent long hours in work per week. It should also be noted that, although the men spent more hours per week in paid employment than their female counterparts, both allocated a significant amount of time to their work role. In fact, caregiving responsibilities had no substantive impact on the amount of time spent in paid employment for the employees in our sample. This suggests that employees with dependent-care responsibilities will have less free time for leisure than those without such responsibilities.

Additional information can be gained from looking at the work demands of the respondent's spouse (table 3.1). The majority of the employed caregivers in this sample had a partner who also worked outside the home. The female partners of the men in the sample worked approximately thirty-seven hours per week. The amount of time the male partners of the female caregivers in the sample spent in employment-related activities depended on life-cycle stage, with the male partner in the sandwich group working significantly more hours per week on average (47.9) than the male partner in the eldercare-only group. The fact that the partners of the women in the sandwich group spend, on average, ten hours more per week in paid employment than the partners of the employees in the other three caregiver groups reinforces our earlier observation – that women in the sandwich group bear a higher caregiver load than either their male counterparts or women in the eldercare group.

Finally, it is interesting to note the data showing that men and women in the sandwich group are significantly more likely to take work home to complete in the evening and on weekends (SWAH) than are their counterparts in the eldercare group. Time in SWAH per week (approximately 7 hours per week) is not, however, associated with caregiver group for those who engage in such activities.

Total role demands: Answers from the 2012 Survey

> *It's just an overwhelming amount of time, like I said. If I had more than twenty-four hours in my day this wouldn't be an issue.*

Every day employed Canadians juggle the demands of multiple roles. They spend time and energy being a parent, a spouse, an employee, a volunteer, and/or a caregiver. They have hobbies; they exercise. Most individuals hold a variety of roles, which may change as they move through their career and life cycles. To get a better appreciation of the demands faced by Canadian employees we need to look beyond the amount of time spent in work and dependent care and examine these individuals' total role set. Total Life Roles were measured in the 2012 Study using a scale developed and tested by the authors in a study on role overload within the health-care sector. Respondents were given a list of twelve life roles (see table 3.2) and then asked to indicate, for each of these roles, the level of demands (i.e., time, energy) that the role places on them in a typical month: no time/energy in the role, almost no time/energy, a little time/energy, a moderate amount of time/energy, and a lot of time/energy. In the section below we first present and discuss estimates calculated using the Total Sample. This is followed by analysis done using the Caregiving Sample.

Total roles: The Total Sample

Canadians are busy people and balance more than work and family. Half of the 25,000-plus employees who responded to our survey were involved in four to six different roles. One in three (35%) participated in seven or more roles. While some of the roles employees participate in can be considered optional (exercise, sports, volunteer work) others are less so (employee, home maintenance, parenting, activities with spouse).

Not only do the caregivers in our sample engage in a number of different roles, they also expend a lot of energy performing these roles. A plurality of the caregivers in our sample juggled two to three (37%) or four to five (40%) high energy roles. Thirteen per cent were balancing six or more high energy roles!

The data in table 3.2 provide the following insights into what roles require higher energy from the role holder. The answer is quite simple: caregiving (parenting younger children, parenting older children, caregiving), paid employment (especially if one is managing the work of

Table 3.2 Per Cent of Respondents Engaged in Following Life Roles (n = 25,021)

	% Engaged in Role	% Saying Role Requires a lot of Energy
	Total	Total
Employee	100	50
Exercise, sports	94	7
Home maintainer	90	29
Spouse/Partner	82	23
Volunteer	52	9
Supervisor/Manager	50	26
Parent – children under 19	46	65
Parent – adult children	33	10
Grandparent	26	6
Caregiver to disabled, ill adult	17	25
Employed – second job	14	18
Divorced – shared responsibility	11	19

Shaded roles: Women significantly more likely than men to say role requires energy

others), being married, and maintaining ones' home. In other words, work and family roles require the most energy.

Two-thirds of the respondents indicated that the role of parent of children under the age of 19 required *a lot* of energy, while half stated that the role of employee required high energy. One in four indicated that maintaining their home, working in a management position, acting as a caregiver, and being a partner required *a lot* of energy. Given the above information, it is no surprise that many employed Canadians experience conflict between work and family, as roles in both domains require a moderate to high amount of energy for those who take on the role.

Also worthy of note are the findings that women are more likely than men to engage in a higher number of high-energy roles. Women were also more likely to say that the following roles require a lot of energy: parent to a child under the age of 19, caregiver, and maintaining their home. These findings are consistent with the data on time in dependent care and responsibility for dependent care presented earlier and indicate

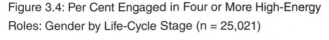

Figure 3.4: Per Cent Engaged in Four or More High-Energy
Roles: Gender by Life-Cycle Stage (n = 25,021)

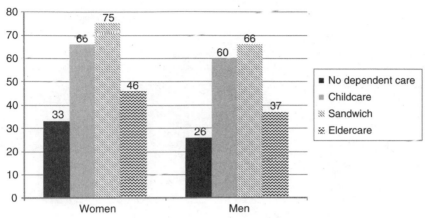

that many Canadian women are still working a "double shift" (i.e., they expend more energy at home than their male counterparts and almost the same amount of energy at work).

Figure 3.4 presents data for the total sample on the total amount of energy employees require for all the roles they are involved in by life-cycle stage and gender. These findings are very interesting and support the following conclusions:

- Men and women in the sandwich group engage in the highest number of high-energy roles.
- Men and women with children in the home engage in a higher number of high-energy roles than do their counterparts in the eldercare group.
- Those without any form of dependent care take part in fewer high-energy roles.

Total roles: The Caregiver Sample

More specific details on the total amount of time and energy male and female employees in the sandwich and eldercare stages of the life cycle

Figure 3.5: Number of High Energy Roles by Caregiver Group (n = 7,966)
(percentages)

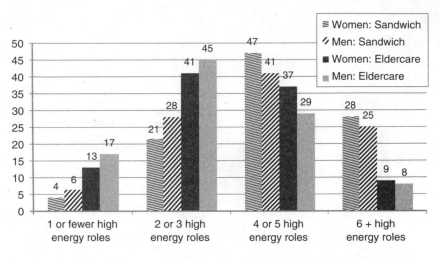

spend on the various roles they occupy can be obtained by looking at
the data collected from the 8,000 individuals who completed the
Caregiver section of the 2012 Study survey. Figure 3.5 provides a dra-
matic illustration of the total set of demands faced by employees in the
sandwich group – one in four of whom are engaged in six or more roles
that require the expenditure of high amounts of energy. While the wom-
en in the sandwich group take on more high-energy roles than their
male counterparts, this gender difference should not overshadow the
fact that both male and female employees in the sandwich group are
actively engaged in four or more roles that require a lot of their time and
energy. Given the link between role demands and physical and mental
health issues, these data are a wake-up call for governments and employers, as such a situation is unlikely to be sustainable in the long term.

Subjective Demands: Role Overload

You're tired physically; you're tired mentally thinking of what more you could do or
should do to alleviate the situation [mother's concerns and discomfort] *while at*
the same time trying to protect your own household and your job. It's overwhelming

and its self-imposed pressure but also external pressures because my mum's calling up at the same time, more often, saying, "I'm all alone here. What can I do?" I don't know what to do.

Life is a constant run from task to task. It seems that twenty-four hours is not enough.

Variants of the above comment were made by virtually all of the 111 caregivers we spoke to during the course of this study. These caregivers (and many others) are suffering from role overload, which can be defined quite simply as "having too much to do and not enough time in which to do it." Role overload means feeling rushed and time crunched, feeling physically and emotionally exhausted and drained, and not having enough time for oneself.

Formally, role overload is defined as "a type of role conflict that results from excessive demands on the time and energy supply of an individual such that satisfactory performance is improbable" (Duxbury, Lyons, and Higgins 2008). Measures of three types of overload were included in the 2012 Study survey: work-role overload, family-role overload, and total-role overload.

Work-role overload is a domain-specific overload that occurs when the total demands on time and energy associated with the prescribed activities of an employee's work role (e.g., assigned to work on several major projects at the same time, too many clients making competing demands) overwhelm the employee's ability to cope. The following quotation illustrates a situation where high levels of work-role overload are present:

They wanted me to work overtime. It was month-end, and I'm in accounting ... and you work like heck. I would get in around 7:00 in the morning and work right through, and then at the last minute, at 4:30, they said, well, could you work overtime? I said, well, I could work a little bit, but not too late; I've got to get home and do dinner. It's one of the new jobs that's been thrown on me, and so I phoned my wife to tell her that I have to work late. Well, she started to cry. She needed me right away. Meanwhile, you've got ... to get the stuff done at work for the next person. It's too much ... it's tough.

Most Canadians do more than engage in paid employment – they also spend time in family roles such as spouse, parent, sibling, and caregiver. Family-role overload (a second domain-specific form of overload) occurs when the sum of the expectations placed on employees by their family and society, as well as what they expect of themselves with respect to performance of their family roles, is too great for them to be able to fulfil all these roles adequately or comfortably. The following quotation illustrates family-role overload:

> We've had increased demands over the past year … there's been a tremendous change. My girls are now teenagers, and while they've always been good children – they are more demanding now. We've always spent a lot of time with my parents and his parents, but over the past year everyone's health took a turn for the worse. My mum passed away, and my husband's parents … their health has deteriorated tremendously. My father is very healthy, but being alone now, he's requiring a lot more care … and support. So the past year has been really busy, really bad. And then of course there is work …

Finally, total-role overload is a time-based form of role conflict in which an individual perceives that the collective demands imposed by all the roles they engage in (e.g., parent, spouse, employee, caregiver) are so great that time and energy resources are insufficient to adequately fulfil the requirements of the various roles to the satisfaction of self or others. For example:

> After the demands of work, after the demands of the kids, after the demands of my mom, I – and this is going to sound ridiculous – but I have two geriatric dogs that require some specialized needs as well … I just don't have the time, the energy or the patience…

> Time is so tight. It seems wherever I am I should really be somewhere else, because everything is such a rush.

In the section below we present and discuss two estimates of role overload. The first is calculated using the Total Sample (n = 25,021), while the second uses the Caregiver Sample (n = 7,966). While no specific questions on role overload were included in the interview script, most of our respondents made a number of comments in the interview that spoke directly to the issue of being overloaded. These quotations are included throughout the text to give the reader a better appreciation of the story behind the numbers (i.e., what it feels like to be overloaded).

Role overload: Answers from academia

Role overload was empirically defined and affirmed as an issue for employees in a 1964 U.S. study by Kahn, Wolfe, Quinn, Snoek, and Rosenthal. In their "theory of role dynamics" in industrial environments, Kahn and his colleagues identified role overload as a special, time-based form of either intra-role or inter-role stress (Kahn et al. 1964; Katz and Kahn 1966). While these researchers' main focus was on studying formal organizations, they also explicitly recognized that an individual's behaviour could be influenced by any or all of the groups and organizations to which that person belonged (e.g., company, union, church, and family). The goal of their research and theorizing was, therefore, to define a "common set of concepts for characterizing all roles in all these organizations" (Kahn et al. 1964, 12).

Consistent with Kahn and colleagues' (1964) argument that role stress can be problematic in a singular role and also across all the roles occupied by individuals, two primary sources for role overload have been identified: role-set diversity (i.e., too many demands from the complement of relationships within one role) and multiple roles. Conceptually speaking, therefore, role overload can potentially arise in the separate domains of work or family (i.e., domain-specific role overload) and/or may result from the accumulation of demands from several roles. Kahn and colleagues (1964) also argued that role overload in any single role (e.g., work) is not a necessary precondition for overload in the full complement of roles (total-role overload). Theoretically, therefore, they conceptualized that the combination of multiple roles can lead to perceived overload in total (i.e., total-role overload) even when specific roles (e.g., work, family) are not overly demanding when

considered in isolation. A complete review of the role-overload construct and how it has been studied is beyond the scope of this book. In
the section below we give the reader a brief description of the role-
overload construct and demonstrate its relevance to this topic. We refer
the interested reader to an extensive review of the extant research literature on role overload in Duxbury, Lyons, and Higgins (2008).

In the years since the concept of role overload was introduced, it has
sporadically been the subject of research in the occupational stress and
work and family literatures. Unfortunately, in these two significant
fields of research, few researchers have either differentiated the sources
of role overload and/or acknowledged that there may be a difference
between role overload within a single role (e.g., work, family) and the
total effects of too many demands across an individual's multiple roles
(total-role overload). Moreover, most of the studies undertaken have
focused only on the domain-based form of the construct, with overload
at work receiving more attention than overload within the family or
total-role overload (e.g., Duxbury, Lyons, and Higgins 2008; Glynn et
al. 2009). No empirical studies could be found that included all three
forms of role overload in one model. Nor could we identify any empirical studies that explored the link between these three forms of role
overload and the role of employed caregiver.

Others have noted the dearth of empirical research in this area. Eby
and colleagues (2005), for example, note the need for domain-specific
and cross-domain-effects research, while Glynn and colleagues (2009)
concluded their paper with the suggestion that the experience of multiple roles should in future be studied in a way that addresses their
interaction as well as their main effects. The lack of research in this area
is unfortunate, as the studies that have been done indicate that role
overload is both prevalent and consequential (Duxbury, Lyons, and
Higgins 2008). Work-role and/or family-role overload have, for example, been found to have a strong negative relationship with psychological health and a range of physical and psychological symptoms of
stress (see Duxbury, Lyons, and Higgins 2008 for a list of references).
They have also been linked to a host of negative organizational outcomes, including increased absenteeism, higher intent to turnover, and

reduced job performance (see Duxbury, Lyons, and Higgins 2008 for a list of references).

Role overload: Answers from the 2012 Survey

High levels of role overload have become systemic within the population of employees working for Canada's largest employers. Analysis of the 2012 Survey data (n = 25,021) reveal the following situation with respect to the role overload experienced by employees of Canada's larger organizations:

- A plurality of Canadian employees (40%) experience high levels of total overload, and only one in four (28%) report low total overload. These findings are not surprising, given the fact that total overload is a function of overload at work and at home.
- Work-role overload is symmetrically distributed, with the same number of employees reporting high overload (32%) as reporting low overload (32%).
- While a plurality of Canadian employees report moderate (37%) to low (37%) levels of family-role overload, one in four (26%) report high levels of overload at home.

These findings are a wake-up call for employers, given the link between high role overload and increased absenteeism, poorer physical and mental health, increased intent to turnover, and higher benefits costs. Employees who are overloaded are also less likely to agree to a promotion or attend career-relevant training, and often cut corners at work (Duxbury, Lyons, and Higgins 2008; Duxbury and Higgins 2013a).

Men and women in the sandwich generation are more overloaded

The data from the 2012 Study (Total Sample) show that the incidence of work-role overload is not associated with either gender or life-cycle stage, a finding that is consistent with the fact that demands at work are more likely to be associated with position and job requirements than

Figure 3.6: Per Cent Reporting High Levels of Total and Family-Role Overload (n = 25,021)

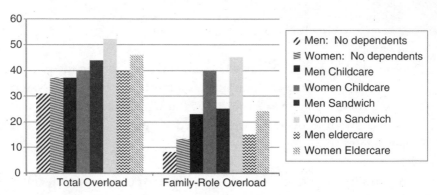

gender. Gender and life-cycle stage are, however, strongly associated with the occurrence of both total-role overload and family-role overload. The following conclusions with respect to total-role overload and family-role overload can be drawn from the data shown in figure 3.6. First, with one exception (childcare stage of life cycle) women report higher levels of total-role overload than men. These findings are consistent with the fact that women typically face heavier demands at home than their male counterparts but similar demands at work.

Second, employees in the sandwich generation report the highest levels of both total and family-role overload (if the comparison is done within gender), while employees with no dependent care responsibilities experience the lowest levels. These findings are not surprising given the very high role demands reported by employees with multigenerational caregiving responsibilities.

Third, eldercare demands are associated with higher levels of both total and family-role overload for women but not men. These findings can be explained by the higher levels of support men with caregiving responsibilities receive from their partner in comparison to the level of support women receive from their partner.

Fourth, women in the sandwich generation report very high levels of total and family-role overload. The high levels of family-role overload experienced by the women in this group are particularly striking and probably also account for the fact that these women also report higher levels of total-role overload. They are also consistent with the fact that the women in this group engage in a higher number of roles, have a partner who spends more time in paid employment, experience very high work demands, and receive less support from their partner for caregiving activities by comparison with men.

Finally, it would appear from our data that childcare is the main predictor of family-role overload – with men and women in the sandwich and childcare-only groups reporting higher levels of family-role overload than employees in the eldercare or no-dependent groups. The following quotation from a female employee in the sandwich group illustrates why this might be the case:

> *There were too many time-sensitive activities that needed to be accomplished ... all of which are important and urgent ... so it is a matter of trying to figure out how I was going to get all the deadlines met ... I'm constantly putting out fires. I'm never in a position to be proactive and catch up, or even get a little bit ahead around being organized in my home, and having everything done in terms of my obligations around my kids. They're five and six years old, so my daughters are at a very demanding age, and it's one of those situations where we'll just deal with today, and what doesn't get done backs up. I can't seem to get ahead of the putting out of fires.*

Subjective Demands: Work-Life Conflict

So I am pulled by work, pulled by my kids, pulled by my ex and pulled by my mother ...

It's a balancing act ... care of my children, care of my mother, and showing up for work ...

We all have many roles: employee, boss, subordinate, spouse, parent, child, sibling, friend, and community member. Each of these roles imposes demands on us that require time, energy, and commitment to fulfil. Work-family or work-life conflict occurs when the cumulative demands of these many work and non-work roles are incompatible in some respect, so that participation in one role is made more difficult by participation in another role.

At the present time, work-life conflict is conceptualized as having two major components: the perceptual aspect of feeling overwhelmed, overloaded, or stressed by the pressures of multiple roles (the topic of the preceding section); and the practical aspects associated with time crunches and scheduling conflicts. It is this second aspect of work-life conflict that is highlighted in the discussion that follows.

The 2012 Study examined two types of work-life conflict: *family interferes with work* (FIW) and *work interferes with family* (WIF). In the first case, interference occurs when family-role responsibilities hinder performance at work (e.g., a child's illness prevents attendance at work; conflict at home makes concentration at work difficult). The caregiver below is clearly experiencing this form of work-life conflict:

[My mom] *died of cancer in December, and it was particularly bad in November and December. She lives about an hour and a half drive away, and she needed someone with her all the time. I had a lot of problems trying to balance this with work because I didn't have enough time. I didn't want to just leave work, I had a responsibility there as well, so trying to balance work and her needs ... and of course, I just left my family, I just left my husband and my girls to look after themselves, really. You still think about them and you still worry ... but I tried to focus on Mum and dealing with medical personnel, and her ...*

In the second case, problems arise when work-role activities impede performance of family responsibilities (e.g., long hours in paid work prevent the performance of duties at home; preoccupation with the work role prevents an active enjoyment of family life; work stresses spill over into the home environment and increase conflict with the family). The following quotation from a respondent who works in a call centre illustrates this form of work-life conflict:

We're open for service from 7:30 in the morning until 6:00, 6:30 at night, and I have an issue where I have to rotate through the rest of the team leaders and do this night shift once every five weeks, and it's very hard to balance everything out based on that. My work's definitely a significant source of stress ... especially during the period of time where she [his mother] *was hospitalized.*

There is a vast academic literature dealing with the issue of work-life conflict. A complete review of this literature is beyond the purview of this book and counter to our primary objective, which is to get easily understood and relevant information on the challenges faced by employed caregivers into the hands of key stakeholders (governments, policy makers, employees, employers, unions). What follows, therefore, is a brief discussion of how work-life conflict is commonly conceptualized and information on why the reader should care about this issue. This is followed by an examination of data from the 2012 Study relating to work-life conflicts of employed caregivers.

Work-life conflict: Answers from academia

Research in the area (Duxbury and Higgins 2009; Duxbury and Gover 2011) has linked work-life conflict with a number of dysfunctional outcomes, including increased levels of stress, depression, absenteeism from work, thoughts of quitting one's job, poorer physical health, greater use of the health-care system, and greater resultant health-care costs. Given these far-reaching negative consequences, a better understanding of the relationship between gender, life-cycle stage, and work-family conflict is vital for academics, practitioners, and policy makers alike.

Research shows that men and women deal with high levels of work-life conflict very differently. Findings are quite consistent that for women, caregiving and employment interaction are unidirectional, and when an elderly family member, especially a parent, is in need of assistance, women provide it regardless of their employment status. They perform all of the tasks that are required, including helping with the more intensive activities of daily living – activities that contribute to higher levels of conflict (Kramer and Kipnis 1995; Johnson and Lo Sasso 2000).

Caregiving responsibilities may also hurt an employee's career advancement and promotional opportunities. Research in the area shows that employees involved in caregiving have had to decline training, challenging new assignments, and job transfers that involve relocation. These decisions severely hinder career advancement, as they limit an employee's ability to acquire new skills (Bumagin and Hirn 2001; Mature Market Institute 1999). Men seem to be somewhat more vulnerable to this risk than women (Frederick and Fast 1999).

Work-life conflict: Answers from the 2012 Survey

Despite all the talk about balance over the last several decades, data from the 2012 Study show that work-life conflict is still an issue for many Canadian employees. One in three of the 25,000-plus Canadian employees who filled in our survey experience high levels of work interferes with family (WIF). Another 30 per cent report moderate levels of this form of work-life conflict. The reverse trend is observed when one considers family interferes with work (FIW). Only 15 per cent of the employees we surveyed report high levels of FIW (met family demands at the expense of work), while 43 per cent report low levels of this form of work-life conflict. These data support the idea that Canadian employees are approximately twice as likely to let work interfere with family than the reverse – to put family first.

It's a balancing act – the more family roles one is juggling, the greater the WIF

The data from the 2012 Study (see figure 3.7) show that both forms of work-life conflict examined in this study are strongly associated with life-cycle stage. More specifically, both men and women in the sandwich stage of the life cycle experience the highest levels of WIF, while (not surprisingly) those with no dependent care responsibilities experience the lowest levels of this form of work-life conflict. Also interesting are the data showing that male employees in the childcare and sandwich groups experience higher levels of WIF than their female counterparts – a finding that suggests that having dependent children in the home is more problematic for male employees than for their female counterparts. These results may be due to the fact that many businesses subscribe to the "myth of separate worlds" for male managers and professionals (expect men to put work first) but are more understanding when their female employees have to stay home to care for their children (i.e., subscribe to traditional gender role-expectations). The following quotations from the interview study illustrate the conditions associated with *work interferes with family:*

> [Respondent felt overwhelmed daily]: *I felt stressed because I was worried about losing my parent ... and I wasn't able to be there as much as I wanted to be. I felt ... overwhelmed because I had things going on at work. I had to get back to work. I couldn't even deal full-time with the family crisis that was going on because I felt like I was needed in two places at once. I'm in a position at work where it's competitive. If you don't give 150 per cent you lose your position.*

> [My mother was dying of cancer] *...so I wanted to spend as much time with her as possible ... so just not being able to dedicate myself to that a hundred per cent was frustrating ... I'd have to say my biggest worry, though, was work because I didn't know how long Mum would be sick. I knew she was dying, but I didn't know how long it would take, and I couldn't just leave work ...*

"Family interferes with work" is more a function of childcare than gender or eldercare

When life-cycle stage is taken into account, "family interferes with work" (FIW) is not associated with gender (see figure 3.7). It is, however, highly associated with childcare, as men and women in the two life-cycle stages with children in the home (childcare, sandwich) experience higher levels of FIW than their counterparts without children (no dependents, eldercare only). As the following quotation from the interview study illustrates, employees talk quite differently about FIW than about WIF:

> *The challenge ... is, you're always trying to give each family* [his family, her family, their own family] *equal time ... So it's trying to find that balance between the families, and between finding your own personal time and not letting people down ...*

Figure 3.7: Work-Life Conflict (n = 25,021): Gender by Life-Cycle Stage

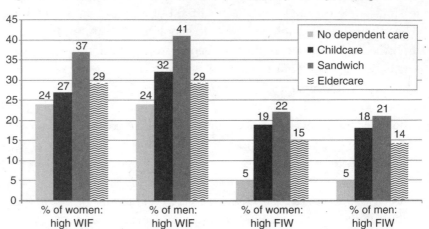

And so what? The consequences of high work-life conflict

As noted above, the 2012 Study data show that a substantive number of Canadian employees, especially those in the sandwich and childcare groups, experience high levels of WIF. Theoretically, the inability to cope with the dual demands of work and family can negatively impact employees as well as employers. In this next section, we use data from the 2012 Study to quantify the impact of high levels of WIF and FIW on the employed caregivers in our sample, as well as on their employers.

Findings from the 2012 Study: Total Sample

To quantify the impact of high work-life conflict on employees, we asked 2012 Study participants to think back over the past twelve months and indicate the extent to which challenges with respect to balancing work and family had caused them to reduce the amount of time they had to themselves, the amount of sleep they got, the amount of energy they had, and the amount of time they spent in personal activities (e.g., recreational, social, or leisure activities). Responses to these questions are summarized by gender and life-cycle stage in table 3.3.

Table 3.3 Impact of Work-Life Conflict on Employee Well-being (n = 25,021)

| | Life-cycle stage | Per cent who agree that work-life conflict has caused a reduction in· | | | |
		The amount of time they have for themselves	The amount of time they spend sleeping	Their personal energy	Time in personal activities
Women	No dependents	17	24	29	22
	Childcare	29	33	39	35
	Sandwich	37	42	48	43
	Eldercare	29	36	42	35
Men	No dependents	11	18	21	18
	Childcare	21	29	31	27
	Sandwich	27	34	37	33
	Eldercare	21	30	35	30
	Total Sample	27	24	31	36

While approximately half of the employees in the 2012 Study sample did not experience any of the negative impacts explored in this study, one in three had substantive challenges with engaging in personal activities such as sleep and exercise that are associated with good physical and mental health. More specifically, approximately one in four reported that work-life issues meant that they had less time for themselves and got less than the desired amount of sleep. Furthermore, one in three noted that work-life challenges had reduced the amount of time they were able to devote to social activities and recreation and meant that they had less energy overall – findings that are consistent with the higher levels of role overload reported by these employees.

What impact do gender and life-cycle stage have on the levels of work-life conflict reported by Canadian employees? A number of answers to these two questions can be drawn from the data presented in table 3.3. First, work-life issues are more likely to have a negative impact on women (less time for self, less time for sleep, loss of personal energy, reduction in their social life) than on men, regardless of life-cycle stage. Second, the data support the idea that many Canadian employees, regardless of

Table 3.4 Impact of Work-Life Conflict on an Organization's Bottom Line (n = 25,021)

	Life-cycle stage	Per cent who agree that work-life conflict has caused:		
		A reduction in work productivity	Them to be absent more often from work	Them to make greater use of employee benefits
Women	No dependents	17	17	17
	Childcare	23	29	23
	Sandwich	28	33	30
	Eldercare	22	26	24
Men	No dependents	15	14	11
	Childcare	21	22	16
	Sandwich	27	28	24
	Eldercare	22	24	20
	Total Sample	22	25	21

gender, give higher priority to meeting family and work-role responsibilities than they do to looking after themselves (e.g., getting enough sleep, socializing, exercising). The findings from this study also reinforce the idea that trying to "do it all" will negatively impact sleep and energy levels. Third, it is interesting to note that, no matter which personal outcome is being considered, people with no dependent care are "better off," while those in the sandwich group are worse off. Finally, men and women with eldercare responsibilities (those in the sandwich and eldercare groups) are more likely to say that work-life challenges are depleting their energy than are employees in other life-cycle stages.

Work-life conflict can also negatively impact employers when employees are not able to cope with the dual demands of work and family. The data shown in table 3.4 indicate that Canadian organizations are no exception to this rule.

Approximately one in four of the employees we surveyed stated that in the last twelve months they had experienced negative changes to their circumstances at work because of higher levels of work-life conflict. More specifically, a substantial number of the employees who participated in the 2012 Study (Total Sample) reported that work-life challenges had caused them to be absent from work more often (25%), reduce their work productivity (22%), make greater use of the benefits offered by the organization (21%), and reduce their work hours (19%).

Again, we can see from the data in table 3.4 that the extent to which work-life conflict negatively impacts the organization's bottom line is associated with both gender and life cycle. Women, for example, were significantly more likely than men to say that work-life challenges had caused them to be absent from work and to make greater use of employee benefits. That being said, it is important to note that gender is not associated with the likelihood that an employee will say that they cope with work-life issues by reducing productivity at work as well as their work hours. These findings indicate that inattention to work-life issues is problematic for many Canadian employees (and, by extension, the companies that employ them) and offers further motivation for addressing the issue of caregiving.

Further motivation to address balance issues for employed caregivers is provided by looking at the link between life-cycle stage, gender, and the likelihood that the employee will report any of the challenges examined in this study. The data in table 3.4 show that employees without dependents (regardless of gender) were less likely to report that work-life issues had impacted their ability to deliver at work. Also noteworthy are the data showing that the men and women in the sandwich group were more likely to say that work and family challenges had caused them to reduce their productivity at work, be absent from work more often, and make greater use of employee benefits such as employee assistance programs (EAP), prescription drugs, and counselling. These numbers are likely to increase as the percentage of caregivers in the labour market increases over the next several years and are likely to represent a significant cost to the employer. Taken as a whole, the data from this study indicate that Canadian organizations need to deal with work-life issues associated with caregiving or suffer the consequences to their bottom line revealed by this analysis.

Work-life conflict: Answers from the interview study

The following quotations from our interview respondents illustrate how complicated balance is for employees who are trying to combine paid employment, childcare, and eldercare. More specifically, the qualitative data show that, for employee caregivers, balance can involve the work and caregiver roles:

> *My work suffers. We can't afford mistakes on my job. Looking back, I should have just taken a couple of days off instead of trying to manage everything... Sometimes we try to juggle everything with our families, our work, and our parents. Our parents can't articulate, all the time, what's going on with them because they don't feel themselves slipping and it happens so fast ...*

As well, it can involve conflict between the family one creates and the ·family one was born into –

> *My spouse feels I should be at home more, and I have to balance it out so that they [my mother, my husband] don't get into an argument ... the whole thing is having a horribly negative impact on my children. So yes, the challenge is huge, and that's on a daily basis.*

– or conflict between one's work role, the need to keep two families happy, and meeting one's own personal expectations:

> *Overall, I'm very stressed out. I have a very short fuse because I'm feeling overwhelmed with the amount of work that I feel is necessary, so I usually have things slide at my house. I'll go over and help her [her mother] clean up her place and not vacuum mine ... We were in a high-pressure work situation, and I know that the work that I needed to get done was then redistributed to my other team members. I felt like I was dumping stuff on them. There was guilt, and not really feeling that I was pulling my weight ... and then I was also trying to look after my marriage. There's not really a whole lot of time for that. I've got to say that has probably suffered the most.*

> *It was very hard to try to even spend time with my son at his hockey games or, if I had to look after my children or take them to their activities at the same time as my husband had something else to do, it would create tension between my husband and myself. At work it was very hard to come to work when your head's not*

in the game wondering what's your mum doing? And phone calls during the day
... And taking my parents to all their appointments, to doctor appointments,
dentist appointments, eye doctors, you name it, every appointment, that was me.
I was exhausting all of [my] *vacation time, sick time, family-related time, at work*
... taking leave-without-pay time. It was a very trying time.

Two questions were included in the interview to help us better understand how caregiving impacts the accomplishment of other family-
role responsibilities. In this book we label the two forms of work-life
conflict we are looking at as *caregiving interferes with family* (CIF) and
caregiving interferes with an employee's ability to perform at work (CIW).

Caregiving interferes with family (CIF)

We began by first asking employees what impact their caregiving situation had on other members of their family. Six responses were given to
this question. One in four respondents felt that their *caregiving situation
had not impacted other members* of their family. The reasons they gave for
this opinion varied but in most cases reflected a lack of commitment
from the extended family to provide any form of caregiving support.

My sister ... she doesn't come by to visit; she doesn't phone ... she doesn't offer
any help ... So there really are no consequences ... they don't see it ... they dis-
tance themselves.

This group was in the minority. The rest of the sample noted a number of ways in which caregiving could potentially impact their family
– all negative. Most commonly (50%) they noted that their *family was
also stressed and overwhelmed* by their caregiving situation. For example:

If it's affecting me, it's obviously affecting her [respondent's wife]. *She worries
... she worries when I'm stressed out or I can't get something sorted out or fixed ...*

Half of the caregivers we talked to also said that the fact that their
time was taken up with caregiving duties meant that their *family*

(defined quite broadly) *had to pick up the slack at home* (i.e., contribute time and energy to getting things done that the respondent would typically do). The following quotation illustrates this form of spillover to the rest of the family.

> *Everybody has extra work to do … We all have to pitch in …*

> *Before this happened … I'm the one that looks after the dog and the kids, and did the grocery shopping … so these were extra tasks my husband had to take charge of while I was busy with my mum and dad.*

Just under one in five talked specifically about how their *immediate family* (spouse, children, siblings) *was negatively impacted by the situation.* For example:

> *I think it was extremely hard on … my kids … I just hope that's not how they remember him, but I think they will.*

Finally, one in ten said that the situation had *increased conflict within their family.* This increased conflict would be with their partner (e.g., *"it has put a strain on my relationship with my husband")* and/or their siblings (*"Yes … I think it has resulted in a lot of increased conflict and probably alienation in the family* [siblings])."

It should be noted that, when answering this question, respondents used a broad definition of family (mentioning their siblings, their partner, and their children), suggesting that all of these groups may be negatively impacted, either directly or indirectly, by CIF. These data imply, therefore, that caregiving is likely to have a much broader societal impact than is perhaps shown when we focus on caregivers only.

Follow-up analysis of the interview data determined that CIF varies with life-cycle stage (but not gender). More specifically, employees with multigenerational caregiving responsibilities were more than twice as likely as those in the eldercare-only group to indicate that challenges related to balancing work and caregiving had negatively impacted their spouse and children. Respondents in the eldercare group, on the other hand, were more likely to indicate that their caregiving situation had created conflict with other family members/siblings. By comparison, only one employee in the sandwich group gave this response.

Caregiving interferes with work (CIW)

We then asked the caregivers who had agreed to be interviewed to tell us how their caregiving situation had impacted their situation at work. Again, respondents gave us six different answers to this question. Just under half (40%) of the employees in our interview sample felt that their *caregiving situation did not impact their work*. Some employees (24%) attributed their ability to separate their family demands from their work to the fact that their boss was understanding.

> *In my situation it was pretty good because I had an understanding boss. In fact, in one way work was good because it took my mind off what was going on and gave me a place to get away from those other things, to focus on something else for a few hours.*

One in five felt that lack of negative spillover from home to work could be attributed to the way they personally coped with the situation:

> *Gosh. It's never been an issue because I keep vacation dates specifically so it will not …*

> *My work is my work. I keep that all separate. I'm a supervisor, so I keep it all separate.*

Also relevant to our discussion are the data showing that the other 60 per cent of the caregivers we talked to noted that their caregiving situation had *negatively impacted their productivity at work*. The following quotations provide insights into the link between high CIW and lower productivity.

> *Well, it's distracting. You go back to work, but you're thinking about it in the back of your mind … I was preoccupied. It was very hard to focus. So it definitely does impact your work.*

I was not nearly as productive as I had been in the past … my attendance was horrible; my frustration came out in really the wrong places. I would literally yell and swear at my boss … that's not the right thing to be doing. And I couldn't even see what was happening.

I was not really there, mentally … I spent more time trying to contact people, trying to do personal things at work. And occasionally I had to stay home from work because I was so stressed.

One in three noted that they had been *forced to miss work or take time off* because of challenges with balancing their work with the demands of caregiving. For example:

During peak times … I have to say – sorry, I have to take some time off – and then I get the looks … "How come she's allowed to take time off and I'm not?" It causes bad feelings at work.

It affects my work … I am absent from work … whenever my mother's needs go up.

Finally, while the numbers are small, it is troublesome that 7 of the 111 caregivers we interviewed reported that they had *lost their jobs* because they were unable to combine work and caregiving. For example:

I got … taken out of my position for a year, and when I did come back to work I was punished … And I had someone replace me in my duties … I fell apart … and I'm still trying to pick the pieces back up.

Again, follow-up analysis determined that the form of CIW experienced by our respondents could be linked to life-cycle stage. More specifically, those in the eldercare group were twice as likely to say that caregiving had no impact on their work situation because they were able to separate work and family. Employees in the sandwich group, on the other hand, were more likely to say that their caregiving situation had caused them to be absent from work more often. These differences are consistent with the survey data. There were, however, no gender differences in how CIW was manifested in our sample.

Conclusions, Implications, and Recommendations

The following conclusions are supported by the data reported in this chapter.

Canadian professional employees work long hours

The Canadian employees in this sample, as well as their partners, devote long hours to their job each week. Many also bring work home to complete during what is traditionally viewed as family time. These long work hours reduce the amount of time employees have available for other activities, including sleep, as well as time with the family and time for leisure.

Canadian employees also face heavy demands at home

The majority of Canadian employees and their partners also face heavy demands at home. While the amount of time employees spend in childcare and eldercare is highly variable, in many cases, it is considerable: around fifteen to twenty hours per week in childcare and six to eight hours per week in caregiving. Employees with younger children at home – mothers in particular – spend a lot of time in family-role activities.

Caregiving demands have little impact on the number of hours spent in paid employment

Caregiving responsibilities have no substantive impact on the amount of time spent in paid employment for the employees in our sample. This finding suggests that employees who care for elderly family members have less free time for leisure than those without such demands on their time. Having children at home, on the other hand, impacts the amount of time employees spend in paid employment. More specifically, mothers spend less time in paid employment and fathers spend more time in paid employment than their counterparts without children.

Canadians are busy people and balance more than work and family

While many of the roles employees participate in and devote their energy to can be considered optional (exercise, sports, volunteer work), others are less so (employment, home maintenance, parenting, engaging in activities with spouse). What roles require the most energy? The answer is clear: caregiving (parenting younger children, parenting older children, caregiving), paid employment, managing the work of others, being married, and maintaining one's home. Given these data it is no surprise that many employed Canadians experience high work-life conflict.

Many Canadian employees are overloaded by all they have to do at work and at home

Many of the employees in this study are physically and emotionally exhausted and drained from all they have to do at work and at home – outcomes that can be attributed to the fact that they are experiencing moderate to high levels of work-role overload, family-role overload, and total-role overload. In fact, the data from this study support the idea that high levels of role overload have become systemic within the population of employees working for Canada's largest employers. The incidence of work-role overload is not associated with either gender or life-cycle stage, a finding that is consistent with the fact that demands at work are more likely to be associated with position and job requirements than with gender. Gender and life-cycle stage are, however, strongly associated with the incidence of both total and family-role overload.

Balance is still unattainable for many Canadian employees

Despite all the talk about balance over the last several decades, data from the 2012 Study show that work-life conflict, in the form of work interferes with family (WIF), is still an issue for many Canadian employees. Particularly concerning are the data showing that employees who participated in the 2012 Study are approximately twice as likely to let work interfere with family than the reverse – put family first.

Balance is a very complex issue for those with caregiving responsibilities

The findings from this study show that balance is a very complex issue for those with caregiving responsibilities and can include balancing work and caregiving, balancing the amount of time and energy they give to the family they have created versus the family they were born into, and balancing work, keeping two families happy, and meeting personal expectations.

Work life challenges are problematic for employee and employer alike

Approximately one in three of the employees in this sample note that work-life issues have caused them to reduce the amount of time they spend in personal activities such as sleep, social activities, recreation, and exercise that are associated with higher levels of physical and mental health. Moreover, one in four of the employees in this sample also note that work-life challenges have caused them to be absent from work more often (25%), reduce their work productivity (22%), make greater use of the benefits offered by the organization (21%), and reduce their work hours (19%). The fact that there are no gender differences in the likelihood that an employee will cope with work-life issues by reducing work productivity and their work hours reinforces the idea that work-life issues are problematic for many Canadian employees (and, by extension, the companies that employ them) and offers further motivation for addressing the issue of caregiving.

Caregiving also results in increased levels of stress at home

The findings from this study show that in the majority of cases the employee's family (defined broadly as siblings, partner, children) is also stressed and overwhelmed by the caregiving situation. These data imply, therefore, that caregiving is likely to have a much broader societal impact than is perhaps shown by focusing on the caregiver only.

Employees in the sandwich group face a particularly onerous set of demands

Men and women with multigenerational caregiving demands spend approximately triple the amount of time overall in family activities as their counterparts in the eldercare group. This difference can be attributed to the fact that those in the sandwich group essentially spend as much time in childcare as those in the children-only group and as much time per week in caregiving as those in the eldercare group. Women in the sandwich group bear a particularly heavy load at home and spend substantially more hours per week in caregiving than any other group of employees in our sample (on average, 26.5 hours per week – or the equivalent of three full work days!) Despite these heavy family demands, employees in the sandwich group spend the same number of hours in work per week as other employees. They do this by being more likely to bring work home to complete in the evening and on weekends.

Employees with children at home are engaged in more high-energy roles

Employees with children at home (i.e., childcare only, sandwich group) take on more high-energy roles than those in the eldercare group, who, in turn, perform a higher number of high-energy roles than employees with no dependents. While the women in the sandwich group take on more high-energy roles than their male counterparts, this gender difference should not overshadow the fact that both male and female employees in the sandwich group are actively engaged in four or more work and life roles. Given the link between role demands and physical and mental health issues, these data are a wake-up call for governments and employers, as such a situation is unlikely to be sustainable in the long term.

Employed parents are more likely to report high levels of family-role overload and FIW

Childcare is strongly associated with higher levels of family-role overload – with men and women in the sandwich and childcare-only groups reporting higher levels of family-role overload than employees in the eldercare or no-dependent groups. Employees in the sandwich generation report the highest levels of total and family-role overload overall (if the comparison is done within gender), while employees with no dependent care experience the lowest levels. Family interferes with work (FIW), also seems to be more highly associated with having children at home, as men and women in the two life-cycle stages with children in the home (childcare, sandwich) experience higher levels of FIW than their counterparts without children.

The more family roles one juggles the greater the conflict between work and family

The data from this study show that the more family roles an employee is juggling, the more likely they are to experience WIF. Men and women in the sandwich stage of the life cycle experience the highest levels of WIF overall, while those with no dependent care experience the lowest levels of this form of work-life conflict. Those in the childcare and eldercare stages of the life cycle experience similar levels of this form of work-life conflict. Of note are the data showing that male employees in the childcare and sandwich groups experience higher levels of WIF than their female counterparts – a finding that suggests that having dependent children in the home is more problematic for male professionals than for their female counterparts – perhaps because work expectations are lowered for mothers but not fathers.

Work-life challenges contribute to reduced productivity for sandwiched employees

Men and women in the sandwich group were also more likely than any other group of employees to say that work and family challenges had caused them to reduce their productivity at work, be absent from work more often, and make greater use of employee benefits such as employee assistance programs, prescription drugs, and counselling. They were also twice as likely as those in the eldercare-only group to indicate that challenges related to balancing work and caregiving had spilt over into the home and negatively impacted their spouse and children. These numbers are likely to increase as the percentage of caregivers in the labour market increases over the next several years and are likely to represent a significant cost to the employer.

Gender differences in work and family demands are still apparent

Also noteworthy are the data showing that, despite the changes in Canadians' situations at work and at home, gender differences in work and family demands are still apparent. Gender differences of note observed in this study include the following: First, men spend more hours in paid employment per week than women. Second, women spend more time in childcare than men (although eldercare seems to be shared). Third, men were more likely to have a partner who worked fewer hours than they did (one in three were married to women who worked part time or not at all). Women, on the other hand, were more likely to be married to someone who also had very heavy work demands. Fourth, women engaged in a higher number of high-energy roles than men. Women were also more likely than men to say that the following roles require a lot of energy: parent to a child under the age of 19, caregiver, and maintaining their home. Fifth, women reported higher levels of total-role overload than men, a finding that can be explained by the fact that women typically face heavier demands at home than their male counterparts but similar demands at work.

Implications and recommendations

These data indicate that in Canada many employed caregivers try to do it all. They have added the demands associated with the caregiver role to the other demands they face at home (childcare) and work and cope by bringing work home to complete in the evening. For many knowledge workers, time for caregiving does not displace the time they devote to their work or their children. Rather, employees tend to cope with all they have to do by reducing the amount of time they spend in sleep, personal activities, and their social life. These strategies result in high levels of role overload, and many report being overwhelmed by all they have to do. Taken together, these three sets of data (high work and family demands, coping by "burning the candle at both ends," and high levels of role overload) support the idea that professionals with caregiving responsibilities are at higher risk of burnout and stress than other employees – a supposition that is also supported by the data from this study (see chapter 5). They also support the contention of Autman and colleagues (2010) that many employed Canadians are suffering from "a time famine."

These findings are a wake-up call for employers and government policy makers, given the link between high role overload and high work-life conflict and a number of dysfunctional outcomes, including increased levels of stress, depression, thoughts of quitting one's job and absenteeism from work, poorer physical and mental health, greater use of the health-care system, and greater resultant health-care costs. Employees who are overloaded are also less likely to agree to a promotion or attend career-relevant training, and are more likely to cut corners at work.

Taken as a whole, the data from this study indicate that Canadian organizations need to deal with work-life issues associated with caregiving or suffer the consequences to their bottom line. The data also reinforce the need for policy makers to address issues associated with caregiving, as it can be expected that, if something is not done, the high demands imposed by employment and/or childcare will ultimately limit the amount of care that informal caregivers are able to provide to the elderly. Finally, the findings from this study indicate that many Canadian women are still working a "double shift" (they expend more energy at home than their male counterparts and almost the same amount of energy at work). This dynamic is most apparent in the sandwich group. These findings suggest that men and women may need different forms of support for the caregiver role from their employer and the community. Greater details on how this might be done are provided at the end of chapters 7 and 8, which deal more specifically with how best to cope with the challenges associated with the caregiving role.

Chapter Four

And So? The Impact of Caregiving on Employees Who Provide Care

It's like having a gorilla or a five hundred pound weight on your shoulders; it's just there.

In the preceding chapters, we made the case that many employed caregivers in Canada are overloaded and overwhelmed by the dual demands of work and family and report difficulties balancing the demands they face at work (typically forty-five hours a week or more) with the demands they face at home (fifteen to twenty hours a week in childcare and seven hours a week in eldercare). On top of this, many Canadians try to "have a life" – that is, they try to find time to engage in social activities, volunteer, and have hobbies (albeit not as frequently as they would like). They also try to find time for themselves and for sleep – though the data show that, for many, a full night's sleep is more of an aspiration than a reality. As Turcotte (2013, 5) notes, "Having too many tasks and responsibilities when caring for a family member or friend can be a major source of stress, especially when caregivers feel they lack the resources to meet the needs of their care receiver." Most of the Canadian employees with families we surveyed report being time crunched and overwhelmed by all they have to do. This chapter uses quantitative and qualitative data from the 2012 National Study of Work, Family and Caregiving (the 2012 Study) to explore the consequences of caregiving for the large majority of employed Canadian knowledge workers who, either by choice or by necessity, have taken on this role.

Two questions are addressed: "What makes caregiving stressful?" and "What is the relationship between caregiving and employee well-being?" The answers to these two questions should help employers and policy makers identify policies and practices that can be put in place to reduce the challenges faced by employed caregivers in Canada, at this time and in the future. They can also help those who wish to make the business case for change with respect to how caregiving is managed, organizationally and nationally.

The chapter is divided into four sections. We begin, in section one, with a brief review of the academic literature linking caregiving and employee well-being. This section provides the reader with an appreciation of the issues under exploration in the rest of the chapter. Section two presents a myriad of data that speak to the question "What makes caregiving stressful?" We begin in section two by presenting and discussing data from the 2012 Study that were collected to help us better understand what makes caregiving stressful. Information on the following possible predictors of caregiver stress are included in this section of the chapter: subjective caregiver burden, objective caregiver burden, and caregiver strain. To further our understanding of the types of caregiver strain experienced by Canadian employees as well as our appreciation of the factors that make caregiving challenging and stressful, we then present qualitative data from the interview study that address these issues. The third section of this chapter uses information from the 2012 Study to answer the second question of importance to policy makers and employers who seek to make the case for change with respect to this issue: "What is the relationship between caregiving and employee well-being?" Our findings with respect to the following quantitative indicators of employee well-being are given first: perceived stress, depressed mood, perceived health. This is followed by the presentation of data from the interviews, which look more closely at the reasons why caregiving impacts employee well-being. Quotations from the interviews are used, as appropriate, to illustrate the realities behind the statistics presented in sections two and three. The chapter ends, in section four, with a summary of key findings and recommendations that are supported by the data.

The Impact of Caregiving on Employees: Answers from Academia

There is ample evidence in the literature to suggest that taking care of an elderly dependent may cause a variety of psychological and physical health problems (Schulz and Martire 2004; Schulz and Sherwood 2008; Turcotte 2013). First, providing personal care to severely disabled elderly individuals (e.g., bedridden or in a wheelchair) usually involves lifting and turning, which may cause muscle strain and back problems. Second, sleep deprivation can also occur, which leads to various physical and mental health problems, including fatigue, headaches, ulcers, inability to concentrate, and hypertension (MetLife 2003). Health can be further affected by the behaviours that employees engage in to cope with caregiver strain, such as smoking and alcohol use. Finally, employed caregivers tend to ignore preventive health check-ups and in general are neglectful of caring for their own health (Albert and Schulz 2010).

Caregiving not only affects people's physical health but may also affect their mental, psychological, and emotional well-being. Caregivers have to cope with the unpredictable nature of caregiving. They constantly worry about finances and the condition of the elderly dependent. They may often feel trapped and helpless. It has been reported that caregivers are more likely to suffer from depression (20% to 80% of caregivers), anxiety, fatigue, anger, resentment, hostility, and eating problems and, in some cases, to engage in abusive behaviours towards the care receiver (Abel 1991; Bumagin and Hirn 2001; Guberman 1999; Rajnovich, Keefe, and Fast 2005; Schulz and Martire 2004; Schulz and Sherwood 2008). Ultimately, the stress the caregiver experiences often spills over into their work life (Albert and Schulz 2010). The greater the intensity of the care, the greater the impact on the caregiver's health (Schulz and Sherwood 2008).

Findings from the 2012 GSS

The 2012 General Social Survey (GSS) on Caregiving and Care Receiving collected data from "regular caregivers" to help them identify the physical, psychological, and social consequences of providing care to someone with a long-term health problem, disability, or aging needs. Statistics Canada operationally defined "regular caregivers" to include Canadians who provided at least two hours of care per week to a child, their spouse, or an elderly family member with a disability or aging needs (Turcotte 2013). Not all individuals in this sample were employed in the labour market. Psychological distress was measured by asking respondents to indicate if they had experienced any or all of the following symptoms of psychological distress as a result of their caregiving responsibilities: tiredness, a feeling of being overwhelmed, isolation, irritability, unhappiness, depression, loss of appetite, and sleep problems. They were also asked if their overall health had suffered because of their caregiving responsibilities and if their personal health problems had required that they consult with a health-care professional. According to Turcotte (2013) one in three people who were providing care to an elderly family member reported multiple signs of psychological distress, and 15 per cent indicated that their physical health had suffered because of their caregiving responsibilities.

Why does caregiving negatively impact caregiver health?

A substantial amount of research has been devoted to discovering the reasons that caregiving may negatively impact caregiver health. What does this research tell us? First, there might be psychological and emotional aspects, such as guilt for not providing enough care, feelings of not being appreciated, role reversal, resurfacing of old wounds, closeness between the caregiver and the care recipient, increased awareness of their own aging, worries about the future, loneliness, grief at watching a parent deteriorate, isolation, regret at having to restrict social and family life activities, and so on (Abel 1991; Dee and Peter 1992; Fradkin and Heath 1992; Nolan, Grant, and Keady 1996). Second, the care recipient's condition may cause worries. Physical disability, old age, and the dependency of the care recipient were found to be strongly associated with stress (Dee and Peter 1992). Mental deficiencies of the disabled (accompanied by depression, difficulty bonding emotionally, and inappropriate behaviours in public places) may be an even stronger predictor of caregiver stress (Young 2006). Finally, stress levels may be increased by factors such as ambiguity, hours of caregiving, length of caregiving, number of persons cared for, low education and income, work-role conflict, and a lack of support from family and the workplace (Abel 1991; Dee and Peter 1992; Fradkin and Heath 1992; Neal et al. 1993). Living in the same household and living at a distance can both have negative consequences. Living in the same household has been found to increase stress (Dee and Peter 1992), while living at a distance reduces the amount and quality of caregiving and may cause "non-caregiver stress," especially when those in need are parents (Amirkhanyan and Wolf 2006). Economic downturns have also been shown to contribute to stress, as caregivers report being worried about their ability to continue providing care (Evercare Survey 2009).

Key factors contributing to declines in caregiver well-being – caregiver burden and strain

The terms used to denote the difficulties that caregivers experience in providing assistance to older adults are quite variable in the literature. The most frequently used terms are "burden" and "strain" or, less frequently, "stress." In many sources, some or all of these terms appear to be used interchangeably (Vitaliano, Young, and Russo 1991). Further complexity arises because the relationships among these terms are not well understood. For example, while some authors treat burden/strain as a form of stress, others have treated it as a stressor (Robinson 1983; Davey and Szinovacz 2008). There is, however, a consensus in the literature that high levels of caregiver burden and caregiver strain are associated with increased levels of depression, anxiety, fatigue, anger, family conflict, guilt, self-blame, emotional strain, psychosomatic disorders, health problems, feelings of isolation, and sleep loss.

Caregiver burden

The burden falls on me ...

Caregiver burden has been defined as the "the physical, psychological or emotional, social, and financial problems that can be experienced by family members caring for impaired older adults" (Vitaliano, Young, and Russo 1991, 67). Our review of the literature determined that caregiver burden is a multidimensional construct that may assume different meanings when used in different circumstances. As Vitaliano, Young, and Russo have pointed out, different conceptualizations of burden cause confusion and inconsistency in results, making it difficult to draw fair comparisons. In an attempt to clarify the definition and application of "burden," Montgomery, Borgatta, and Borgatta (2000) categorized the ways burden has been conceptualized in the literature into three groups: (1) workload and hours spent caregiving, (2) the distress or difficulty associated with care, and (3) the perceived impact of this workload on the caregiver's life.

"Perceived" as it is used in the third category is a very important distinction, as it underscores the subjective perspective of the caregiver on the objectively stated conditions of caregiving rather than the occurrence of these conditions. The authors indicated that this definition has been most commonly used in the literature. They note two types of perceived impact:

- *Subjective burden:* the emotional impact of caregiving, and
- *Objective burden:* the impact of caregiving on resources such as time, health, space, and finances, and restrictions on social and work activities.

Caregiver strain

It [caregiving] *definitely defines the boundaries of my schedule and my personal ambitions, and my home life and my social life ... which gets overwhelming.*

"Caregiver strain" is a multidimensional construct that is defined in terms of "burdens" or changes in a caregiver's day-to-day life that can be attributed to the need to provide physical, financial, or emotional support to an elderly dependent (George and Gwyther 1986). Research has linked high levels of caregiver strain to increased levels of depression, anxiety, fatigue, anger, family conflict, guilt, self-blame, emotional strain, and sleep loss. Caregivers experience *emotional strain* when they feel overwhelmed, obliged to provide care, or dissatisfied with life, or when they have to make emotional adjustments (e.g., engaging in arguments, role reversal, dealing with inappropriate behaviours) (Fradkin and Heath 1992; Hart et al. 2000; Robinson 1983). *Physical strain,* especially when dealing with bedridden seniors or those in wheelchairs, is associated with heavy lifting and turning. If intensive care is required, sleep deprivation is a common consequence of significant concentration on care tasks (Fradkin and Heath 1992; Guberman 1999; Robinson 1983). Caregivers suffer from *social strain* when they feel confined by their care duties and consequently do not have time to do things such as visiting friends, doing daily chores, or engaging in leisure activities. They have to juggle competing demands from other family members, change their personal plans, and make family and work adjustments (Montgomery, Borgatta, and Borgatta 2000; Robinson 1983). Caregivers experience *economic strain* when medical care, adaptive equipment, home modifications, or other purchases require extra financial resources. Women especially tend to reduce their hours of work or quit their job altogether to provide care, thus creating financial strain. When caregiving leads to poor caregiver health, extra expenses for their own health care impose additional financial strain. Caregivers also perceive situations where they have to reduce their regular spending and restrict savings as causes of strain (Bumagin and Hirn 2001; Fradkin and Heath 1992; Guberman 1999; Keefe and Medjuck 1997).

What Makes Caregiving Stressful?

Answers from the 2012 Survey: The Caregiver Sample

What makes caregiving so stressful? In this section of the book we shed light on this issue by reporting key findings obtained using three indicators that were included in the Caregiver section of the 2012 Study survey to address this issue: subjective caregiver burden, objective caregiver burden, and caregiver strain.

Subjective caregiver burden

The burden falls on me ...

Subjective burden was measured in the 2012 Study using the twelve-item measure of subjective caregiver burden developed by Montgomery, Gonyea, and Hooyman (1985). This measure asks respondents how often (rarely, some of the time, most of the time) they had experienced certain feelings, such as guilt, towards the person for whom they were providing care. We began our analysis of the subjective caregiver burden data by factor analysing the items included in the measure. This analysis revealed that subjective caregiver burden triggered the following three types of emotions in the caregiver: feeling strained/frustrated, feeling useful/needed, and feeling guilty/fearful. Data on the incidence of these three forms of subjective caregiver burden in our sample of employees with caregiving responsibilities (n = 7,966) are shown in table 4.1.

A number of observations can be made with respect to the prevalence of the different forms of subjective caregiver strain in our sample of employed caregivers. First, approximately two-thirds of the employees in the caregiving sample stated that they sometimes/often felt fearful for the person they were caring for and guilty that they were not doing enough. Second, one in four of the employees in the caregiving sample reported that they sometimes/often felt strained and frustrated with the person they were caring for. Third, women were more likely than men to report that caregiving left them feeling fearful and guilty as well as strained and frustrated. Finally, the vast majority of employees in the caregiver sample (93%) reported that caregiving made them feel useful and needed. Neither gender nor life-cycle stage impacted caregivers' perceptions that in providing caregiving they were doing something that was useful and needed.

Objective caregiver burden

Objective caregiver burden is the amount of observable disruptions or changes in various aspects of caregivers' life and household that can

Table 4.1 Subjective Caregiver Burden by Caregiver Group (n = 7,966)

Per cent who stated that they sometimes/often felt the following with respect to the person they were caring for:	Men		Women		Total
	Sandwich	Eldercare	Sandwich	Eldercare	
Factor One: Strained, frustrated	21.1	21.4	28.8	25.9	25.8
Strained in your relationship with them	36.4	36.4	42.0	39.6	39.6
That they seem to expect you to take care of them as if you were the only one they could depend on	29.7	30.6	38.0	36.8	35.3
That they try and manipulate you	21.8	22.2	30.9	28.1	27.5
That they don't appreciate what you do for them	23.2	22.0	28.1	26.0	26.2
That they make requests which are over and above what they need	20.7	22.0	25.4	22.1	23.2
That they are nervous and depressed about your relationship with them	17.7	19.3	22.4	21.9	21.0
Factor Two: Useful, needed	92.6	92.9	91.8	93.7	92.6
You are contributing to their well-being:	90.7	91.1	92.4	91.8	92.4
You feel useful in the relationship	88.6	88.0	89.3	91.5	89.7
You are pleased with your relationship	88.6	89.3	87.5	88.7	88.3
Factor Three: Fearful/guilty	67.9	64.8	76.7	77.5	64.0
It is painful to watch my relative age	68.6	70.2	78.4	79.5	76.1
I am afraid of what the future holds for my relative	67.1	66.7	75.7	75.8	73.3
I feel that I don't do as much for my relative as I could or should	64.3	58.8	68.6	68.8	66.9
I feel guilty over my relationship with my relative	27.4	24.9	35.3	33.0	32.1

be attributed to their caregiving responsibilities. Objective caregiver burden was measured in this study using the nine-item measure of objective caregiver burden developed by Montgomery, Gonyea, and Hooyman (1985). This measure asks respondents to look back over the last three months and indicate the extent to which challenges with respect to caregiving have caused a reduction in time for themselves, their personal freedom, their energy, and so on (little change, moderate change, substantial change). Generally speaking, the higher the percentage of the sample in the "little change" group, the better from the perspective of the individual and the family. Key findings with respect to the objective caregiver burden of the employees who completed the caregiving section of the survey are shown in table 4.2

The most commonly reported objective burdens of caregiving all relate to a lack of time and energy for the caregiver – a finding that is not at all surprising in light of the data presented in chapter 3! The extent to which time is an issue for employed caregivers can be better appreciated when one looks at the survey data showing that between 40 and 50 per cent of the caregivers in this sample reported that caregiving had substantially reduced the amount of time they had for themselves and for social and recreational activities. Similar numbers talked about how caregiving had reduced the amount of energy they had for other activities and had constrained their personal freedom. Also worrisome is the fact that approximately one in four of the employed caregivers in this sample reported that caregiving had substantially reduced the amount of money they had available to meet personal expenses and had resulted in a decline in their physical and/or mental health.

Which caregivers experience higher levels of objective caregiver burden? Examination of the data in table 4.2 provides the following answer to this question: women in the sandwich group. These women are more likely to report that caregiving has reduced their personal freedom and their energy levels. Which caregivers report lower levels of objective caregiver burden? Data from the 2012 Study support the idea that men in the eldercare group are substantially less likely to report any of the objective burdens examined in this study than are employees in the other three groups.

Table 4.2 Objective Caregiver Burden by Caregiver Group (n = 7,966)

Per cent who stated that caregiving has, to a moderate or substantial amount, ...	Men		Women		Total
	Sandwich	Eldercare	Sandwich	Eldercare	
Reduced the amount of time they have for themselves	45.9	34.0	51.7	47.7	47.5
Reduced their energy levels	39.6	28.0	51.3	44.1	44.1
Reduced the amount of personal freedom they have	39.6	34/4	45/9	40.6	41.7
Reduced the amount of time they spend in recreational and/or social activities	41.1	29.4	44.6	39.2	40.9
Reduced the amount of vacation activities and trips they take	36.2	27.5	36.6	22.5	35.0
Reduced the amount of privacy they have	34.6	27.6	32.2	27.2	30.3
Resulted in poorer mental health	25.6	14.7	31.4	29.2	27.8
Reduced the amount of money available to meet expenses	24.6	23.1	16.7	19.8	24.3
Resulted in poorer physical health	22.3	14.0	23.3	22.5	23.0

Table 4.3 Caregiver Strain by Caregiver Group (n = 7,966)

| | Per cent experiencing caregiver strain | | | | |
| | Men | | Women | | Total |
	Sandwich	Eldercare	Sandwich	Eldercare	
Physical caregiver strain:					
• Monthly	72.9	73.8	70.7	69.8	71.1
• Weekly	17.6	14.2	17.1	17.7	17.1
• Several times a week/daily	9.5	12.0	12.2	12.5	11.8
Financial caregiver strain:					
• Monthly	90.0	89.6	89.2	91.2	90.0
• Weekly	4.7	4.4	5.0	4.4	4.7
• Several times a week/daily	5.3	6.0	5.9	4.4	5.3
Emotional caregiver strain:					
• Monthly	84.0	83.9	76.7	77.6	79.1
• Weekly	9.0	8.0	12.2	10.7	10.7
• Several times a week/daily	6.9	8.1	11.1	11.7	10.2

Caregiver strain

It [caregiving] *definitely defines the boundaries of my schedule and my personal ambitions, and my home life and my social life … which gets overwhelming.*

Robinson's (1983) three-item measure was included in the optional Caregiver section of the 2012 Study survey to quantify caregiver strain. This measure asked employees with caregiving responsibilities (n = 7,966) to think back over the last twelve months and indicate (using a five-point scale) how often (never, monthly, weekly, several days per week, or daily) they had experienced physical, financial, or emotional strains that they attributed to their performance of the caregiving role. Table 4.3 summarizes key findings with respect to the extent to which the employees in our sample experience these three kinds of strain. The data in this table support a number of important conclusions that should have relevance for employers who seek to understand the burdens faced by their employees who provide care for one or more seniors. These conclusions are summarized below.

Physical caregiver strain

Physical strain due to caregiving is the most common form of caregiving strain reported by the employees in this sample. Just over one in ten (12%) of the caregivers in our sample reported that they experienced physical strain associated with their caregiving role and responsibilities on a daily basis. Another 17 per cent reported that they experienced such strain several times a week or more. The extent to which the employees in this sample reported moderate to high levels of physical caregiver strain does not appear to be associated with either gender or life-cycle stage – a finding that is somewhat unexpected given the fact that those in the sandwich group are younger and should, therefore, be less vulnerable to physical strain. The lack of gender differences in the incidence of physical caregiver strain is also interesting in that it runs counter to much of the literature on this topic. These findings support the idea that physical caregiver strain is associated with the type of tasks being done and that all employees who frequently perform these tasks are at risk, regardless of gender or age.

Emotional caregiver strain

One in five of the employees in our sample reported that they found eldercare to be emotionally overwhelming on either a weekly (11%) or a daily (10%) basis). While the incidence of emotional caregiver strain is not associated with life-cycle stage (sandwich and eldercare groups were equally at risk), it is linked to gender, with women reporting higher levels of emotional strain than men.

Financial caregiver strain

Only one in ten of the employees in this sample report moderate (5%) or high (5%) levels of financial caregiver strain. The relatively low

Figure 4.1: Incidence of Caregiver Strain: The Interview Data (n = 111) (percentages)

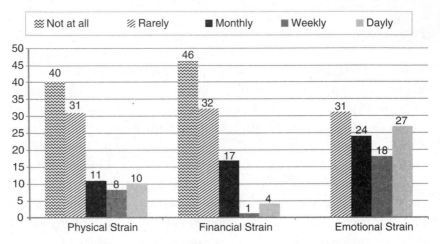

incidence of this form of strain is likely due to the fact that the employees in this sample are relatively well-paid professionals.

Caregiver strain: Answers from the interview study

During the interview we asked employees how often caregiving caused them physical, financial, and emotional strain. Responses to these questions are provided in figure 4.1.

The majority of the caregivers we talked to indicated that they rarely or never experienced either physical (72%) or financial (78%) caregiver strain – findings that are consistent with the survey data. By comparison, all of the caregivers in our interview sample reported experiencing some degree of emotional caregiver strain, with just over one-quarter of them stating that they experienced emotional strain daily. The differences in emotional strain between these two samples can be explained by the fact that the interview sample was theoretically selected to include a much higher proportion of employees reporting high caregiving intensity (50%) than was found in the caregiver sample (20%). These results indicate that there is a strong link between caregiving intensity and emotional caregiver strain.

What makes caregiving physically demanding?

Almost one in five of the people we interviewed had moderate to high levels of physical caregiver strain. To get more details on the link between caregiving and physical caregiver strain we asked respondents what physical challenges they had experienced because of their caregiving experiences. Exhaustion and tiredness (44%) were the most common physical manifestations of caregiver strain mentioned by these employees. Other complaints mentioned by approximately one in ten employees included headaches, nausea, insomnia, an increase in blood pressure, aches and pains, and tension in the shoulders and neck. The following responses typify what we heard:

My mother uses a walker. She moves very slowly. In winter it's almost impossible to take her out. It's very hard. I am afraid she's going to slip. I, myself, have problems with my back, and it's hard to support her. I am afraid I'm going to fall. I am afraid she's going to fall. There's ice or snow. Even if you pull up in front of the doctor's building, she still has to walk a few metres. So basically, it's physical strain – put the walker into the trunk; take the walker out of the trunk; support my mother, because she needs a lot of support – and I'm not strong enough. I'm doing it, but it's a real strain, physically.

Well, she can no longer walk and is wheelchair-bound and overweight. So physically we sometimes have to position her in the chair ... repositioning is a real physical act ... And it's a strain on your back and on your knees ... I have bad knees ... so pushing her around and taking her for appointments means that I'm physically under strain. After I leave her, I usually have to do something to alleviate it like icing and physiotherapy ...

What makes caregiving physically demanding? The above quotations show that in many cases those who provide caregiving are engaging in manual labour. Caregiving involves lifting and carrying, which are challenging for many Canadians with health problems of their own and which can be exacerbated by the care they provide their parents and/or in-laws. Given this list of symptoms, it is not surprising that employees with caregiving responsibilities are more likely to perceive that their health is poor and to seek care from their personal physician.

What contributes to financial strain?

The interview data give us a better understanding of why relatively few of the caregivers in our sample experience high levels of financial caregiver strain. Most respondents noted that their job made it easier for them to absorb the financial costs of caregiving. In fact, many of the respondents said that they continued to work so that caregiving would not contribute to financial hardship for their families (*"No* [financial strain] *... that's why I'm still working"*). Those who did report that the caregiver role contributed to financial strain attributed this issue to the fact that the multiple little expenses that they incurred when fulfilling their duties as a caregiver added up over time and were ultimately unsustainable financially. The following quotation illustrates this issue:

> *Yes ... every time you go to visit it's a lot of money, and gas is a lot of money. Covering some of her expenses while she's in the hospital, like her phone ... more money.*

Why is caregiving emotionally overwhelming?

The 2012 Study data support a strong link between caregiving and emotional strain. In fact, almost half the people we talked to reported experiencing this form of strain weekly or more. Examination of the interview data establishes a strong link between high levels of emotional caregiver strain and *worry about the dependent* (their health, their death, the quality of care they are receiving). Moreover, the emotional strain that caregivers are experiencing seems to be exacerbated by a lack of time for themselves and their families and the amount of work that has to be done. For example:

> *That feeling that you're not providing enough care for her* [his mother] *... she needs more care than I can provide ... but she doesn't want to go into a home, and I'm trying to keep her happy but she needs to be cared for and I can't do it. It's just*

that it can't be done anymore ... So it's been very, very stressful since probably
May, and it's an ongoing thing.

Also noteworthy is the fact that more than half of the people we talked
to with high levels of emotional strain specifically mentioned how emotionally draining it was *dealing with a family member with dementia and
Alzheimer's*. These feelings are captured in the following quotations:

Mostly emotional ... It has been difficult to see this happening [decline in mental health] *... It's your parent.*

*Depression would be the primary thing; watching them decline; knowing that
there was nothing I could do other than spend time with him. And Alzheimer's is
a horrible disease; it robs you of who they were.*

*I felt overwhelmed because I was worried about losing my parent ... You're losing
the person they were* [mother has dementia], *and a feeling of anxiety that you're
powerless over the ultimate end.*

Others attributed their emotional strain to their *relationship with the
person they were caring for*:

*Every minute that I spend with her is a minute of stress, absolutely ... that sounds
terrible, but she's a very demanding person and a very unhappy person. So I expend a lot of extra energy trying to keep her spirits up ... it's very, very tiring.*

Many identified *timing* (caregiving is unexpected, urgent, and requires a lot of time) as a factor contributing to their feelings of being
emotionally overwhelmed by their caregiving situation.

*It was conflicting demands on my time. So, not enough time to look after my kids,
work, and help this person.*

Many also linked their emotional reaction to their inability to make
plans or control the situation (feeling powerless, feeling trapped, "only
one available," "it all fell on me"):

This just goes on and on and on and on and on. It's not like I'll just take three months off and it'll be over. It's a very difficult thing to deal with – to plan around.

Never knowing when … and it's the uncertainty. You can't say, Monday he's going to fall. You don't know when. And that was mostly what was really stressful.

I guess it's the feeling that I didn't have a choice. I couldn't say no … I just feel that I have no control over what I do.

Very few respondents mentioned either distance or financial concerns as issues that made them feel overwhelmed.

The interviews also exposed how emotional caregiver strain seems to trigger a number of dysfunctional emotions and unhealthy responses in the caregiver. One in three said that the strain made them short-tempered and grumpy. Other emotional responses mentioned by respondents included becoming emotionally drained (18%); anxiety attacks (16%); crying (15%); feeling depressed, sad, lonely, and helpless (15%); anger and frustration (12%); feeling overwhelmed (11%); and wanting to be alone (11%). The following quotations illustrate the challenges faced by employed Canadians because of the emotional strains generated by caregiving:

So, she gets stressed and then I get stressed … My personal well-being has been extremely affected – there's no question. I've had anxiety. I've actually ended up in the hospital due to anxiety and stress.

For me? … There's the physical stress on my body, of the running around, and there's that feeling of failure, like you can't keep up with everything. The guilt.

What makes caregiving so challenging? Answers from the interview study

The above data show that caregiving imposes burdens and strains on those engaged in the role. The question remains, however, what in particular it is about the role that makes it stressful. To explore this issue we asked a number of questions in the interview portion of our study to increase our understanding of the mechanisms through which caregiving can impact employee well-being. The Cognitive Appraisal Model notes that stress may occur when people perceive their situation as challenging and threatening. Accordingly, we asked our caregivers the following series of questions: What are the challenges (if any) you currently face with respect to providing care for your elderly dependent? Are there any personal challenges? Any challenges with the dependent themselves? Any challenges at home? Any challenges at work? Any challenges within your community? What are the potential consequences of your current caregiving situation for you? What is it about caregiving itself that causes you to feel overwhelmed? What is it about caregiving itself that causes you to feel stressed? What are your overriding feelings about your current caregiving situation? Finally, as positive evaluations of the caregiving situation may somewhat mitigate the challenges faced by employed caregivers in the sample, we also asked respondents to identify the rewards they received from caregiving.

The personal challenges of caring for an elderly dependent

Eighty per cent of the caregivers we talked to were able to identify one or more challenges that they had personally experienced when caring for their elderly family member. Three challenges were identified by a substantial portion of our caregivers. The most common challenge, mentioned by 37 per cent of the employed caregivers in this sample, was *finding a "good" balance between work, life and their responsibilities to their elderly dependent*. For example:

> Yes. There are huge personal challenges. It takes time away from my leisure and from building relationships with other people. It takes time away from me building a career, and it takes time away from my son, having grandparents. Those are big personal challenges, and I worry about them [her parents].

> I would say ... just trying to fit all the people, friends, family into the time that is available, is definitely a challenge and definitely a difficulty. It can be a stressor as

well, too, just trying to find time to do everything that has to be done ... like even just making sure that you have the time in the day to ... look after the house, cook dinner. And where you fit in the work that you have brought home, as it has to be done for tomorrow. And then even just finding time for yourself to make sure that you have time to de-stress and not get too stressed, I find, can be a challenge, too.

One in five caregivers noted that they themselves had a *pre-existing medical condition* that made it difficult for them to do everything they needed to do, while 13 per cent noted challenges associated with *concern for their dependent* with respect to aging and their welfare *("They are a crisis waiting to happen")*.

Challenges with the dependents themselves

There was a fair degree of agreement within the group of caregivers whom we talked to on four characteristics of the care recipient(s) that made their situation more challenging and stressful. These challenges, along with quotations that provide the reader with a better picture of why the issue could be challenging, are presented below.

One in three stated that *declines in the dependent's mental or physical health* made their caregiving situation more challenging.

He's [his father] been depressed and that's part of why he stopped eating ... My mother is bipolar, so that's a huge challenge, with regard to her health as well ...

Physically ... if she comes out with us that's a great deal of work ...

One in three caregivers also talked about how the *personality of the care recipient* (being stubborn, being argumentative, wanting to remain independent) made the situation challenging.

They're both really stubborn ... We'll suggest things, like ... we can get this person in to help you, we can arrange meals on wheels, all this stuff. A lot of times, she, especially, will refuse ... She's hanging onto her independence, and she doesn't want to come to the end of her... it does made it harder, for sure, when you've researched things and you think you have a great solution to make their life more comfortable or their health better and they won't do it.

It would be easier if she went into a retirement facility … somewhere where she can have companionship, like people that are in the same boat and she has someone to talk to, or who has the same interests. But I'll tell you right now, that it'll never happen. She won't leave that house …

Other caregivers (22% of the sample) talked about how the fact that the person they cared for was *emotionally needy* (felt lonely and isolated) made things more challenging and stressful for them:

Oh, I know what they do that drives me crazy. They call us twenty times a day.

Well, she's not a very independent person. She never has been … she's very frustrating because there are things she could do on her own that she chooses not to do.

Challenges at home

While one in three of the employed caregivers we talked to indicated that they did not have any eldercare challenges that could be linked to their situation at home, this group was in the minority. Just over half of the employees in the sample stated that their caregiving situation had *negatively affected their home life* (left less time for family, had a negative impact on relationships at home, created tension, etc.).

There is a lot of tension with my wife … she has been helping out a little bit the last little while, but she makes it known that I somehow owe her for doing that. It's, like, you're walking on eggshells a lot of the time if you bring up anything to do with her [his mother].

As well, one in four said that caregiving had *decreased the amount of time and energy they had to fulfil the demands associated with being a mother, a father, or a spouse.*

Yes, we've been balancing that aspect of my life with work and childcare and all the activities … my son, for example, he had to miss a lot of sports activities, as I was going back and forth to City X … I just could not take him … it's just finding enough time in the week to do all the things I have to do. Lots of things that should get done don't.

It just means that there's things in my life that I haven't been able to do because of my responsibility to my parents …

Challenges at work

Employees identified three ways in which their work role conflicted with their role as a caregiver. One in four stated that being very busy at work made it *harder for them to find the time they needed for caregiving.*

The assignments don't stop just because your mom needs you …

A similar number of employees found *timing a challenge* (i.e., had difficulties scheduling caregiving activities around their work hours).

Well, the challenge is trying to establish a schedule where I can take care of the uncle-in-law and the kids … and do my job as well. I try to combine the three. Sometimes I have to take a lot of hours off … That's a big challenge, trying to find the right schedule.

Or they found it *challenging to get time off work for caregiving* (policies are just not there).

There are a lot of jobs that I have been offered [referring to promotions], *and I would have probably taken one if there had been fewer constraints on the work hours. I'm holding myself back …*

Finally, one in ten talked about how caregiving had *negatively impacted their career.*

I've had to take time off ... it's hurt my career ...

Challenges within their community

One in three of the caregivers we interviewed noted that the challenges associated with their caregiving situation were exacerbated by where they lived. These caregivers noted three challenges: (1) the bureaucracy in their community was very frustrating, and they just *could not find out where to get help;* (2) they *could not find any support for caregivers in their community* (lived in smaller communities); and (3) *there was a lack of programs* for seniors within their community. One respondent mentioned all three challenges during her interview with us:

> *We live in a rural area so there are no supports here ... not anything for her ... no programs at all that we can identify... but who would know, as social service staff here are just so unhelpful.*

Rewards from caregiving

During the interview process, we were struck by the fact that everyone talked about how caregiving had impacted or could impact them negatively. No one spontaneously talked about how caregiving had benefited them. Also interesting is how many people were able to identify a multiplicity of negative consequences of their current caregiving situation. For example:

> *I couldn't sleep ... it just left me absolutely drained. I felt sick, and I know my home life suffered because I couldn't really think about anything else except how to resolve this issue, how to make it happen ... it left me drained physically as well as mentally.*

This motivated us to ask the caregivers in our sample to try to identify benefits they had realized from taking on the role. Even with this prompt, one in four of the employees we talked to could not identify any aspect of caregiving that they felt was rewarding. Seven people told us, flat out, that they *"did not get any rewards at all from caregiving."* Just over one in five stated that *"we are not in it for the rewards"* but because they felt it was their moral responsibility to care for their parents/in-laws.

There was a high degree of consensus among the rest of the employees in the sample with respect to the rewards associated with this role. Half of the caregivers talked about how caregiving had *improved relationships within their family* and increased family bonding.

> I spend a lot of time with her, so I'm very privileged. I know her very well and I learn from her experiences. And I guess one of the greatest rewards … the relationship my kids have with their grandmother … The kids just love her.

One in three talked about how they *felt good knowing their family member was well cared for and safe.*

> I enjoyed having my mother live with me … I would feel guilty if she was in a long-term-care facility.

Others (12%) talked about the *sense of satisfaction* they got from helping someone they loved.

> I guess that sense of validation that you're around and you're helpful.

> Just, the satisfaction of hopefully giving back to them.

What Is the Relationship between Caregiving and Employee Well-being?

Answers from the 2012 Survey: The Total Sample

The 2012 Study survey included measures for three indicators of employee well-being: perceived stress, depressed mood, and perceived physical health.

Perceived stress

Perceived stress refers to the extent to which one perceives one's situation to be unpredictable, uncontrollable, and burdensome. Such conditions certainly seem to describe the circumstances of many employed caregivers. Individuals who report high levels of perceived stress are generally manifesting the symptoms we associate with "distress," including nervousness, frustration, irritability, and generalized anxiety (Cohen, Kamarck, and Mermelstein1983).

Approximately half of the employees who completed the 2012 Study survey reported high levels of perceived stress (Duxbury and Higgins 2013a). Furthermore, everyone who participated in the interviews associated with this study mentioned the word "stress" at least once during our discussions with them. In most cases they also linked the stresses of caregiving to declines in their physical health. For example:

> Well, you're always dealing with stress and anxiety … it has an impact on your health. You become hypertensive, you have difficulty sleeping … You don't eat as well, you don't sleep as well; you don't always take care of yourself as you should because you're involved with something that is very stressful.

Depressed mood

Depressed mood is a state characterized by low energy and persistent feelings of helplessness and hopelessness (Moos et al. 1988). Depression represents one of the most common psychological conditions seen by the family physician. Given the persistent, and often irreconcilable, time demands of the work and caregiving roles, it is not surprising that approximately one in three of the employees who responded to the 2012 Study survey reported high levels of depressed mood, almost the same proportion of interview respondents who mentioned they were depressed.

> Physically, when I get all stressed out then I don't eat properly and then I gain weight and then I get stressed and it's a vicious cycle. And I don't get the chance to go the gym and stuff because I'm busy running around … and I don't have time

for anything. So, that all contributes to gaining weight and getting depressed. From the emotional side, I just get frustrated, I get irritable, I end up crying on the couch talking to my husband, and then he has to support me ... it gets overwhelming at times.

I'm sleeping less ... I'm certainly stressed and maybe a little depressed ... Maybe a little bit of self-medicating with the drinking ... but no drugs.

Again, as illustrated by these quotations, respondents typically talked about a multitude of well-being issues at the same time (stress, depressed mood, and physical health problems), often in a way that suggests a cascade affect between the various conditions. For example, employees who are under stress sleep less and/or eat and drink more, all of which exacerbate the stress and contribute to a decline in their physical health.

What is the relationship between life-cycle stage, gender, and employee well-being?

The survey data in figure 4.2 support the following conclusions with respect to the relationship between life-cycle stage, gender, and employee well-being. First, women report higher levels of stress and depressed mood than men, regardless of life-cycle stage – a finding that is consistent with much of the research in this area. Second, dependent care, regardless of its form (i.e., childcare, eldercare) is associated with an increase in stress for both men and women. Third, eldercare care is associated with an increase in depressed mood for both men and women, regardless of whether or not the employee has children at home. Childcare, on the other hand, is not associated with levels of depressed mood when the comparison is done within gender. This finding is consistent with the literature reviewed earlier (Calvano 2013, 205), which notes the following differences between the two roles: "eldercare happens unexpectedly, increases over time, and entails role reversal of children caring for their parents." Or, as a female in the sandwich generation noted during our interview with her,

Figure 4.2: Perceptions of Mental Health: Gender by Life-Cycle Stage
(n = 25,021)

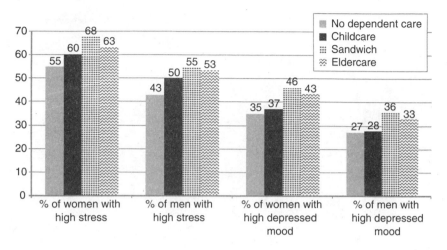

*Every new thing your child does is growth. With my mother it is loss; her person-
ality is dissolving before my eyes.*

Finally, men and women who spend time each week in paid employment, childcare, and eldercare (i.e., those in the sandwich group) report
the highest levels of perceived stress (68% of the women in this group
and 55% of the men) and depressed mood (46% of the women in this
group and 36% of the men) of any group in the sample. These levels of
stress and depressed mood are not sustainable over the long run and
provide solid evidence of the need to address issues around balancing
work and caregiving.

Physical health may also be impacted

Two measures were included in the 2012 Study survey to help us examine the relationship between caregiving and perceived physical health:
(1) Describe your usual state of physical health over the last year as
compared to that of other people your age (poor/fair; good; very good/
excellent); and (2) Have you visited your family physician in the past

Figure 4.3: Perceptions of Physical Health: Gender by Life-Cycle Stage
(n = 25,021)

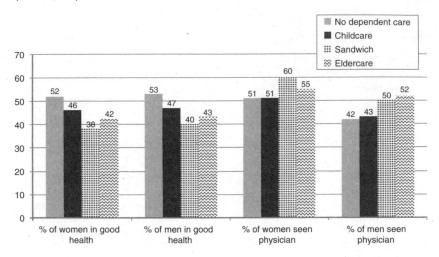

six months because of problems with your personal health? The higher the percentage of the sample in poor health, the greater the costs in terms of absenteeism, benefits costs, turnover, and early retirement.

Just under half (46%) of the 25,026 employees in our sample said that their health was very good to excellent, 38 per cent said that their health was okay, and 16 per cent said their health was poor/fair. Data showing the relationship between perceived physical health, gender, and life-cycle stage are shown in figure 4.3. The relationships between gender, perceived physical health, and life-cycle stage largely mirror what we observed for employee mental health. In both cases, (1) employees with dependent care are more likely to perceive a decline in their health, regardless of the type of care (i.e., childcare, eldercare) being provided, and (2) employees with multigenerational caregiving responsibilities (i.e., sandwich group) report the poorest levels of perceived health.

The idea that caregiving is associated with poorer physical health is further supported by data on visits to the physician (see figure 4.3). More specifically, men and women in the sandwich and eldercare life-cycle stages are more likely to have seen a physician in the past six months than are their counterparts in the no-dependent-care and childcare-only groups. Again, we note the higher number of visits by women in the sandwich generation – a finding that is consistent with the higher demands reported by these women.

Finally, quotations from the interviews also support a link between anxiety and stress and cardiovascular conditions for the caregivers in our study.

> *Pressure in my chest, sleeplessness, irritability, just all over not feeling great.*

> *My blood pressure goes up ... and I might get a headache and might get a bit dizzy, might be shaking a bit.*

Conclusions, Implications, and Recommendations

The following conclusions can be drawn from the data in this chapter.

A myriad of factors make the role of employed caregiver stressful and overwhelming

Not only is caregiving a physically demanding role that consumes a lot of the caregiver's time and energy, it also is emotionally impactful – a fact that is often not recognized by policy makers. What makes the role of caregiver overwhelming and stressful? The data from this study identify the following dimensions of the role as contributing to caregivers' feelings of being *both* stressed *and* overwhelmed:

- Overload (employed caregivers, particularly those in the sandwich group, have too many demands on their time).
- Role conflict (employed caregivers find it very difficult to balance work, life, and caregiving activities).
- Time and timing (caregiving is unexpected; it is urgent; it requires a lot of a person's time and has no defined timeline).
- The emotional burden of caregiving (feeling powerless, feeling helpless when the person being cared for is suffering from some form of dementia or is dying).

- Emotional attachment to the person being cared for (feeling concern for the well-being of the dependent).
- The nature of their interactions with the person being cared for (feeling frustrated that the person they are caring for will not listen to them, or generally acts in a way that makes it more difficult to provide care).
- Their lack of control over the situation (caregiving is unpredictable; caregivers are unable to make plans or control the situation; caregivers feel trapped).
- The amount of difficulty they have in getting help or support for the role (many have sole responsibility for the care of their dependent and cannot get support from their family, their community, the government, the health-care system, or their employer).
- A lack of personal choice/control (feeling powerless, feeling trapped, being the only one available, feeling that "it all falls on me)."

Emotional caregiver strain often triggers dysfunctional emotions and unhealthy responses

Emotional caregiver strain seems to trigger a number of dysfunctional emotions and unhealthy responses in caregivers. One in three said that the strain made them short-tempered and grumpy. Other emotional responses mentioned by respondents included becoming emotionally drained; having anxiety attacks; crying; feeling depressed, sad, lonely, and helpless; experiencing anger and frustration; feeling overwhelmed; and wanting to be alone. These responses are likely to impact how caregivers perform their roles at work and at home.

Caregiving takes a toll on those who care

The data from this study support a number of conclusions about the link between caregiving and caregiver health. First, caregiving can and does negatively affect employed caregivers' physical health (negatively impacts sleep; contributes to feelings of exhaustion and tiredness, headaches, nausea, increased blood pressure, joint and muscle problems, and tension in the shoulder and neck) as well as their mental, psychological, and emotional well-being (caregivers are more likely to report higher levels of stress and depressed mood). Second, caregiving triggers a strong emotional response from caregivers. While everyone who engages in the role states that it makes them feel useful and needed, many also say that caregiving triggers feelings of guilt, fear, strain, and frustration. Third, it is clear from the results highlighted in this and earlier chapters that caregiving reduces the amount of time and energy employees have for themselves, their work, and their families. It also consumes energy, leaving little for other important life activities. Fourth, the challenges of balancing work and caregiving demands are somewhat offset by the fact that having a job makes it easier for the caregiver to absorb the financial costs associated with the role. Many of the respondents said that they continued to work so that caregiving would not contribute to financial hardship for their families.

The role of caregiver is often physically demanding

Caregiving can be a physically demanding role that may require caregivers to engage in manual activities such as lifting and supporting the person they are caring for. In other words, it can be considered to be a form of manual labour that is performed by people who would not typically be engaged in a physically demanding job (e.g., older people, people with health problems of their own). The fact that the incidence of physical caregiver strain was not associated with either gender or life cycle leads us to conclude that the types of tasks being done by caregivers put people at risk regardless of gender or age! Also noteworthy are data showing that employees with caregiving responsibilities are more likely to perceive their health as poor and to seek care from their personal physician than are employees who are not caregivers.

Where you live matters

The results from the 2012 Study also showed that living in a community that lacked supports for seniors and caregivers increased the challenges facing caregivers. These caregivers noted three types of challenges: (1) the bureaucracy in their community was very frustrating and they just could not find out where to get help; (2) they could not find any support for caregivers in their community (lived in smaller communities); and (3) there was a lack of programs for seniors within their community.

The rewards realized by being a caregiver: What rewards?

None of the caregivers in our study talked about the rewards associated with caregiving unless prompted, and even then one in four could not identify any. Other caregivers noted that caregiving had improved relationships within their family, or increased bonding within their family, or that it made them feel good to know that their family member was well cared for and safe.

High levels of stress and depressed mood are endemic in Canadian workplaces

High levels of stress appear to be endemic in Canadian workplaces. Half of the employees who completed the 2012 Study survey reported high levels of perceived stress, and one in three reported high levels of depressed mood. Dependent care, regardless of its form (i.e., childcare, eldercare) is associated with an increased incidence of stress and declines in physical health for both men and women. Eldercare care was strongly associated with an increase in depressed mood, regardless of gender or whether or not the employee had children at home. Also noteworthy was the fact that the employees in our sample typically experienced a multitude of well-being issues at the same time (stress, depressed mood, physical health problems) often in a way that suggests a cascade affect resulting from the various conditions.

Employees with multigenerational caregiving responsibilities are in poorer health overall

Employees with multigenerational caregiving responsibilities (i.e., men and women in the sandwich group) reported the highest levels of stress and depressed mood and the poorest perceived health in the entire sample and were more likely to have seen a physician in the past six months than other employees. The findings are consistent with the data showing that the employees in this group reported very high levels of role overload and work-life conflict and had very high demands on their time, and are cause for concern given that the number of employees with multigenerational caregiver responsibilities is projected to increase. Failing to pay attention to this issue is likely to result in increased demands on Canada's health-care system and benefits plans and increased absenteeism costs for Canadian employers.

Implications and recommendations

The data reported in this chapter have a number of important implications for employers and policy makers alike. First, they further establish the need to deal with the challenges facing employed caregivers in the very near future. More specifically, policy makers at all levels (governments, organizations) need to identify ways to alleviate some of the frustrations, stresses, and physical challenges inherent in the caregiver role. Inattention to this issue is likely to result in a decline in the number of employees who are willing to take on the role (e.g., as a way of managing their stress, they may decide not to take on the role of caregiver) and/or who are able to do so (they may have mental and/or physical health concerns that make it impossible for them to continue as caregivers). It could also have implications for health-care costs and wait times (caregivers, particularly those in the sandwich group, are more likely to seek care from their family physician), succession planning (employees who are overburdened are less likely to consider a promotion), and benefits costs (caregivers make greater use of the company's benefits program).

Second, the data show a very strong link between the caregiver role and depression and emotional strain as employees support family members through the last stages of their life. This would suggest that the supports needed by caregivers are very different from those provided to parents. While increased flexibility in work hours might help employees accomplish necessary caregiving activities, it is unlikely to help them deal with the emotional consequences of caregiving. These findings lead us to recommend that employers who wish to ease this form of strain within their workforce consider the follow types of assistance: an employee family assistance program (EFAP), seminars on how to manage the emotional aspects of caregiving, and lobbying or taking responsibility for the provision of community centres with activities and programs for seniors in the communities where their employees live. If employers can offer support for childcare, they should also consider offering support for eldercare. Increased funding of mental-health initiatives and the provision of community support services, such as respite care and caregiving support networks, should also help employees who are feeling overwhelmed by all they have to do.

Finally, the findings suggest that having a job is a dual-edged sword for caregivers – employment income alleviates caregiver strain but adds to the employees' sense of overload and role conflict. Again, this finding emphasizes the need for government policy makers to seek solutions to the challenges expressed by those seeking to combine employment and caregiving.

Chapter Five

And So? The Impact of Caregiving on the Organizational "Bottom Line"

But I guess I'd have to say my bigger worry was work, and how do I manage it all – because I didn't know how long Mum would be sick. I knew she was dying, but I didn't know how long it would take, and I couldn't just leave my job ...

In the 1990s, eldercare was viewed as a responsibility that was no more intensive than childcare, and many employers and academics took the view that caregiving would have essentially the same impact on work-life conflict as looking after children (Abel 1991; Neal et al. 1990). More recently, however, researchers have noted that "eldercare can be so time consuming that it becomes an unexpected career" (Calvano 2013, 207). These researchers predict that the demands and complexity of the caregiving role, in combination with changes in family and work configurations, will place the burden of eldercare and the accomplishment of paid employment in direct competition (Calvano 2013; Airey, McKie, and Backett-Milburn 2007).

For the most part, the research in the area (see chapter 1) indicates that caregiving has and will continue to have a negative impact on labour-market participation. A number of industry-sponsored workplace surveys (MetLife 1997, 2006, and 2010) and observations by employers (Katz et al. 2011; McGowan 2009) can be found supporting this view (Calvano 2013). Some of the commentary on this issue is, in fact, quite alarmist (e.g., Cravey and Mitra 2011; Spillman and Pezzin 2000).

That being said, it is important to note that some of the scholarly research in the area is less definitive about the degree to which eldercare disrupts work. While most researchers agree that caregiving has the *potential* to interfere with employment, they disagree on the nature and extent of the disruption. While the uncertainty in the academic literature with respect to the relationship between eldercare and work is not surprising given the many methodological issues plaguing research in this area (Calvano 2013), it makes it challenging for employees and policy makers alike to make a defendable case for change. This is unfortunate, given the demographic data showing that the number of employees who provide care to elderly family members is likely to increase dramatically over the next several decades. This chapter presents data from the 2012 Study that speak to the relationship between caregiving and the organization's bottom line. Such information should help both employers and government policy makers understand how caregiving "threatens caregivers' employment and economic security and escalates employers' costs related to absenteeism and reduced productivity" (Fast et al. 2014, 1). It could also be used by employees and policy makers to spur key stakeholders, including organizations and governments, to take action with respect to this issue.

The chapter is divided into four main sections. Section one provides a short summary of what the academic literature has to say about the impact caregiving has on an organization's bottom line. Two key indicators of organizational performance, absenteeism and Statistics Canada's Employment Changes Index, were included in the survey component of the 2012 Study. Findings obtained from our analysis of these two indicators are presented and discussed in section two of this chapter. The third section of this chapter features key findings on this issue from the interviews we conducted with employed caregivers. More specifically, we look at the responses these employees gave to the following questions: "What challenges do you face at work because of your caregiving situation?", "How does your caregiving situation impact your productivity?", and "How does your caregiving situation impact how you deal with others at work?" Key findings are summarized and implications for employers and policy makers drawn in section four.

The Link between Caregiving and the Bottom Line

Answers from academia

In the brief review below we quote from a number of studies that have investigated the relationship between caregiving and paid employment. Also included in this section is a brief review of key findings on this issue reported by researchers using data from Statistics Canada's 2012 General Social Survey (GSS) on Care Giving and Care Receiving. Finally, it should be noted that the review of the research on the link between caregiving and the organizational bottom line provided in this chapter is intended to supplement the information included in the introductory chapter of the book.

How could caregiving impact an employer's bottom line? While many studies report that employees with caregiving responsibilities are more likely to be absent from work (Katz et al. 2011; Albert and Schulz 2010), other researchers found no such relationship (Keene and Prokos 2007). Also interesting are a study by Boise and Neal (1996), which concluded that employees with childcare responsibilities experience more absences than employees with eldercare responsibilities, and one by Hammer and Neal (2008), which found that sandwiched wives have much higher rates of absenteeism than their counterparts in the childcare-only or eldercare-only groups.

The data also support the idea that caregivers are more likely to come in to work late and/or leave early than are employees without such responsibilities. In the MetLife (2003) study, for example, taking time off, coming in late, and leaving early were common workplace practices for those with caregiving responsibilities. This trend appears to be on the rise. Mathew Greenwald and Associates (2009) reported that 65 per cent of employed caregivers engaged in these behaviours in 2009, up from 57 per cent in 2007.

Absenteeism aside, the research evidence also suggests that working caregivers often find it difficult to free up the time they need to engage in a number of work-related tasks that are linked to career advancement and job security. The 2003 Metlife study, for example, noted that

21 per cent of caregivers said that they often refused overtime, and 31 per cent said that they had forgone work-related travel. In addition, some respondents were considering quitting work altogether, with women being more likely to be contemplating this decision than men (20% vs 11%). As Fast and colleagues (2014, 5) note, "Missing days of paid work, working fewer hours or leaving work altogether because of caregiving translates into lost income and employment benefits for many. Some of these consequences will have long-term and cumulative effects over a caregiver's life course, threatening both their current and future financial security." Williams (2004) reports that these types of "work-related problems" increase with the amount of time an employee spends in caregiving. As well, Petrovich's (2008) commentary on her own experiences as a sandwiched caregiver provide a particularly poignant example of why employers need to be aware of what their employees are facing.

Employees' inability to balance work and caregiving is costly for employers

In summary, the academic literature in this area supports the idea that caregiving makes it harder for employees to perform both expected and discretionary aspects of their work. The increased absenteeism, reduced productivity, and higher turnover of employees with caregiver responsibilities have the potential to directly affect their employers' bottom line. Fast and colleagues (2014, 6) also note a number of indirect costs associated with work-caregiver conflict, including the need to pay extra to replace absent employees, the costs associated with the need to recruit and train replacements for employees who quit their jobs, and poorer customer relations. A study done in the United States in 2006 estimated that full-time employed eldercare providers cost U.S. employers $33 billion annually in 2006 (Met Life 2006). No comparable cost estimates are available for Canada (Fast et al. 2014). Also noteworthy are estimates from Fast's (2015) report for the Institute for Research on Public Policy showing that an inability to manage the conflicting demands of paid work and caregiving contributes to the loss of nearly 558,000 full-time employees from the Canadian workforce every year.

The impact of caregiving on the bottom line: The 2012 GSS

Fast and colleagues (2014) used data from Statistics Canada's 2012 General Social Survey (GSS) on Caregiving and Care Receiving to outline care-related employment consequences in Canada. They note the following:

- 44 per cent (2.4 million) of employed caregivers reported absenteeism, missing on average between 8 and 9 days in the past twelve months because of their care responsibilities. At the population level, this accounted for 9.7 million days of absenteeism per year (1, 3).
- 15 per cent (828,739) of employed caregivers reduced their paid work hours to provide care, cutting back their hours by 9 to 10 hours per week on average (1). As a result, employed caregivers worked 256 million fewer hours per year (3).
- 10 per cent (557,698) of employed caregivers left the paid labour force altogether to provide care (3).

These data from the 2012 GSS (9.7 million days of absenteeism, 256 million fewer hours of paid work, and the loss of 557,698 caregiver employees who left the paid labour force) lend credibility to the argument that caregiving contributes to an enormous "loss of productivity to employers, the labour market and the Canadian economy" (Fast et al. 2014, 3).

While the GSS data provide us with a tremendous amount of insight into how caregiving impacts the work behaviour of Canadian employees, there is still a lot we do not know. For example, the GSS does not provide comparison data for employees in other life-cycle stages. As such, we are missing key contextual information on how the work behaviour of employed caregivers compares to the behaviour of employees in other life-cycle stages. Our review of the literature determined, for example, that little attention has been given to the effects of multigenerational caregiving on workplace behaviours, and it is unclear if caregivers in the "sandwich generation" report higher levels of absenteeism and, consequently, reduced workplace productivity than employees who have only childcare or eldercare responsibilities. One key objective of this book is to address this gap in our knowledge by providing a comparison of key work-related outcomes by life-cycle stage and gender.

The Link between Caregiving and the Bottom Line

Findings from the 2012 Study

It had a huge impact on my productivity at work. I couldn't focus. I would have two pieces of paper to move off my desk; I would be literally staring at them, and I could not decide which one to do first. One could be a one-minute task, one could be a one-hour task, and I couldn't decide. I had no attention span; I would jump from one thing to another, to another, to another, to another. And never really finish anything. I wasn't able to do any follow-through – just couldn't do it. I would deliberately be away sick the day of an important meeting. I just, I couldn't do it. I didn't want to attend training; I didn't want to do anything. I didn't have an extra ounce of energy to do anything.

The above quotation from a 2012 Study participant articulates quite eloquently a number of possible links between caregiving and an organization's bottom line, both direct (absenteeism, missing meetings, reduced productivity) and indirect (lack of focus, reduced creativity). This section explores this issue using survey data from the 2012 Study. The link between caregiving and absenteeism is discussed first, followed by a discussion of how caregiving impacts employment more generally.

Absenteeism

Many organizations use absence from work as a measure of productivity (if workers are not on the job, the work is definitely not being done). While companies expect a certain amount of absenteeism and recognize that some absenteeism is even beneficial to the employee, too much absenteeism can be costly in terms of productivity and is often symptomatic of problems within the workplace. Statistics Canada has estimated that absenteeism costs the Canadian economy between $2.7 billion and $7.7 billion annually.

Figure 5.1: Per Cent of Sample (n = 25,021) Who Missed Work
in the Past Six Months as a Result of Four Identified Factors

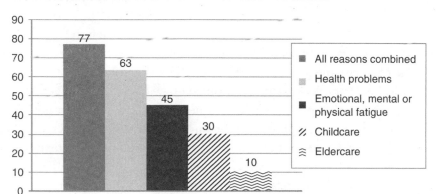

We included a comprehensive measure of absenteeism in our 2012 Study survey to allow us to examine the relationship between life-cycle stage and various types of absenteeism. More specifically, we asked respondents to think back over the past six months and indicate how many days of work they had missed because of: (1) health problems, (2) child-related problems, (3) problems concerning elderly relatives, and (4) emotional or mental fatigue. This question allowed us to calculate the percentage of employees who missed work as a result of each of these factors, as well as the mean number of days missed per year as a result of ill-health, childcare, eldercare, and emotional/physical fatigue.

As shown in figure 5.1 (Total Sample), just over three-quarters of the employees who answered our 2012 Study survey (77%) missed work in the six months prior to the study. The most common reasons for missing work included health problems (63%) and emotional, mental, or physical fatigue (45%). One in three missed work because of childcare issues, and one in ten missed work because of eldercare. Three per cent of respondents had experienced long-term absenteeism over the past year (operationally defined as missing more than thirty days of work in a year).

The measure that we used also enabled us to calculate the average number of days' absence per year for the various groups. On average the employees who participated in the 2012 Study missed twelve days of work per year. Approximately half of this absenteeism can be attributed to ill health (5.4 days absent per year as a result of ill health), but the absence due to emotional, physical, or mental fatigue (3.4 days per year) and childcare issues (3.4 days per year) is also substantive. Because only 10 per cent of the employees in the Total Sample missed work because of caregiving, the number of days off work attributed to eldercare for the Total Sample was quite low (an average of one day per year).

A very different picture emerges if one looks at the days absent per year for only those employees in the sample who missed work for each of the four factors (health, emotional/mental fatigue, childcare, eldercare) examined in the 2012 Study. In this case, those who took time off because of challenges related to eldercare missed almost ten days of work in the twelve months prior to the survey. This was approximately the same number of days absent per year because of ill health (9.2. days) and a greater number of days absent than was reported for the other potential contributors to time off work considered in this study: physical or mental fatigue (7.6 days), and childcare (7.8 days).

Absenteeism has increased over time

Statistics Canada reported that absenteeism rates were somewhat higher in 2011 than in 2001.[1] They attributed this to an increase in the first half of the 2000s in both the incidence and the number of days off work due to illness/disability and personal or family responsibilities. Our data (Duxbury and Higgins 2013a) show very similar trends. More specifically, the percentage of our sample who indicated that they missed work (all causes) increased by 7 percentage points between 2001 and 2012. In our case, much of this increase in absenteeism could be attributed to an increase in the number of people who missed work because of ill health (increased by 17 percentage points over time), challenges with respect to childcare (increased by 17 percentage points over time), and emotional and mental fatigue (increased by 12 percentage points over time). These data reinforce our claim that organizations that fail to

---

1 http://www.statcan.gc.ca/pub/75-001-x/2012002/article/11650-eng.htm.

Figure 5.2: Days Absent from Work per Year (n = 25,021):
By Gender and Life-Cycle Stage

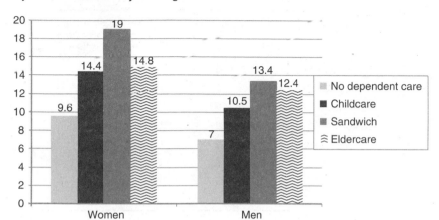

address work-life issues, particularly those associated with balancing work and eldercare, will pay a price in terms of increased absenteeism.

Absenteeism is strongly associated with life-cycle stage

Life-cycle stage is not associated with absenteeism due to health issues (Duxbury and Higgins 2013b). It is, however, associated with the other types of absenteeism examined in the analysis (see figure 5.2 and table 5.1). The data from the 2012 Study support the following conclusions on the association between life-cycle stage and absenteeism:

- With one exception (eldercare), women are more likely than men to be absent from work, regardless of life-cycle stage or reason for missing work.
- Men and women in the eldercare stage of the life cycle are equally likely to be absent from work because of issues with the elderly dependent they are caring for.
- Women miss more days of work per year than men when the comparison is done within life-cycle stage.

Table 5.1 Per Cent Absent Because of Ill-health, Childcare, Eldercare, and Emotional Fatigue (n = 25,021)

		Per cent who missed work in the last six months due to:			
		Ill Health	Childcare	Eldercare	Emotional Fatigue
Women	No dependents	63	0	0	48
	Childcare	66	58	0	47
	Sandwich	71	50	31	54
	Eldercare	68	0	30	51
Men	No dependents	51	0	0	37
	Childcare	56	46	0	34
	Sandwich	60	43	27	40
	Eldercare	59	0	30	45

- Employees with no dependent care responsibilities miss fewer days of work per year than their counterparts with childcare and/or eldercare responsibilities.
- Men and women with eldercare responsibilities (i.e., those in the sandwich and eldercare stages of the life cycle) are more likely to have to take time off work because of emotional or physical fatigue and ill health.
- Men (13.4 days) and women (19 days) in the sandwich group miss more days of work a year than do employees in the other three life-cycle stages.
- Women in the childcare and eldercare stages of the life cycle miss a similar number of days of work per year (14.4 and 14.8 days, respectively).
- Men in the eldercare stage of the life cycle miss more days of work per year (12.4 days) than their counterparts in the childcare-only stage of the life cycle (10.5 days).

Several other key conclusions can be drawn from the absenteeism data. First, having responsibilities related to care of a dependent increases the likelihood that an employee will miss work. Second, employees with multigenerational caregiving responsibilities miss more days of work than employees with responsibility for only one form of dependent care.

Table 5.2 Employment Changes Index (n = 7,966)

Per cent indicating that challenges with caregiving have caused them to:	Sandwich		Eldercare		
	Men	Women	Men	Women	Total
Reduce their work hours	23.1	25.0	19.8	22.6	22.5
Reduce their work productivity	26.9	27.6	22.1	22.6	25.4
Turn down a job offer or promotion	19.1	14.5	12.1	9.6	13.7
Suffer a reduction in their income	15.6	13.4	9.0	10.4	12.5
Be absent more often from work	26.7	33.6	23.9	26.3	28.7
Increase their use of the benefits offered by their organization	22.8	28.9	19.8	23.6	25.1

Third, eldercare is more likely than childcare to contribute to increased absenteeism for male employees. No such difference was observed for the females in the study.

There are other costs to organizations when employees cannot balance work and caregiving

In the 2002 GSS, Statistics Canada included a measure called "The Employment Changes Index" to assess the extent to which work and family issues contributed to a wide variety of negative work outcomes. This measure was included in the Caregiver section of the 2012 Study survey. Analysis of the data (see table 5.2) shows that a substantive number of the almost 8,000 knowledge workers in our Caregiver Sample indicated that challenges with caregiving had contributed to a moderate/substantial

- increase in the likelihood they would be absent from work (29%),
- increase in their use of employee benefits (25%),
- decrease in their work productivity (25%), and
- decrease in the number of hours they could devote to work (23%).

Also important are the data showing that 15 per cent of the sample indicated that challenges with caregiving had led to their turning down a promotion at work.

Table 5.3 Life Cycle and Employment Changes Index (n = 25,021)

		Per cent indicating that work-family challenges had caused them to:		
		Turn down a promotion	Be absent more from work	Increase use of employee benefits
Women	No dependents	17	17	17
	Childcare	23	29	23
	Sandwich	28	33	30
	Eldercare	22	26	24
Men	No dependents	15	14	11
	Childcare	21	22	16
	Sandwich	27	28	24
	Eldercare	22	24	20

More family roles equal more challenges in balancing work and family

The data in table 5.3 (Total Sample) allow us to examine in more detail the impact of life-cycle stage on the various indicators of reduced
work performance included in the Employment Changes Index. These
data support the following conclusions. First, employees in the sandwich group were, regardless of gender, more likely than those in the
eldercare-only group to say that challenges with caregiving had led
them to be absent more often from work and to turn down a promotion.
Second, women in the sandwich group were more likely than employees in the other three groups to say that caregiving had meant a moderate to substantial increase in their use of employee benefits and the
amount they were absent from work.

The Link between Caregiving and the Bottom Line

What do the interview data tell us?

In the interviews, we asked five questions to help us more completely
understand how an employee's caregiving situation could potentially
impact the organization's bottom line. More specifically, we asked our
111 employees the following five questions: "How has your caregiving

situation impacted your work?" "How has your caregiving situation impacted your productivity at work?" "How has your caregiving situation impacted how you deal with others at work?" "How has the role of caregiver helped you with respect to your performance at work?" "How has your role at work helped you manage your caregiver responsibilities?" These last two questions were included in the interview to determine the extent to which employed caregivers experience positive spillover between the work and caregiver roles, as recent research in the work-life area has suggested that combining work and family responsibilities need not always be detrimental. In the sections below, we present the answers employees gave to each of these questions. The questions relating to impacts on the bottom line are covered first. This is followed by the responses given to the questions addressing positive role spillover.

Challenges at work: Interview data

I have shaped my work around my situation with my mum. My mum's the priority, and my work sort of fits in around it.

How has your caregiving situation impacted your work?

Almost 40 per cent of the employees we talked to stated either that their caregiving situation had not impacted their situation at work at all (25%) or that the impact was minimal (16%). Of particular interest, however, are the reasons these employees gave as to why this was the case. All twenty-seven of the employees who stated that their *caregiving situation had not impacted them at work* were in the low-intensity caregiving group and had a supportive boss, colleagues, and/or family members. The following quotations help us understand why this group of caregivers were able to successfully balance their work with their caregiving situation.

Challenges at work? ... No, not really ... I have the best boss in the world, and the best team. I have such loyalty to them now because they were there for me when I was in a crisis... they supported me at that time, and it was a difficult time ... but I knew that they would pick up the pieces, the balls I was dropping, and I have so much gratitude to them for that, and respect … and I will do the same for them, because a hundred per cent, they were there for me during those difficult weeks.

No. It never has … what happened was, there was a whole bunch of appointments that whole year leading up to the actual surgery, and I was a little frustrated or worried because in order to go to an appointment with her, I'd have to take a personal day. But my sisters were able to work it out amongst themselves, so … I never actually did go to any appointments … it all worked out.

In the other cases (16%) where employees indicated that their work had only been minimally impacted by their caregiving situation, the respondents attributed their ability to balance these two competing demands to how they had personally managed their state of affairs (e.g., *I separate work and family*). For example:

Yes, there's times where you have some sleepless nights because you worry about things, but … once I'm here [work] *I usually can just get back into a routine.*

The rest of the sample noted three ways in which the caregiving situation had negatively impacted their productivity, their careers, and/or their job. Forty per cent of respondents (mainly employees in high-intensity caregiving situations) talked about how their caregiving situation had contributed to a *reduction of their productivity at work*. The reasons given for this reduction in productivity were quite varied as can be seen in the following quotations:

Oh, it was horrible. I was more reclusive; I was not nearly as productive as I had been in my work history. My attendance was horrible; my frustration came out in really the wrong places. I would literally yell and swear at my boss, which … that's not the right thing to be doing. And I couldn't even see what was happening.

Well, at work, I had difficulty concentrating and completing my work. I didn't have a lot of patience for the normal stupid situations that would arise … things that I would normally not be fazed by …

No. Well, they [his parents] *will phone me at work. I get an e-mail every day from them, and I get a phone call every day … and then they phone me up to say, we sent you an e-mail, and make me have to answer them, whether or not it's work time or not …*

These comments support the idea that the impact caregiving can have on productivity is often insidious and not highly visible to others. If not addressed, however, all of the above factors have the potential to hurt the organization's bottom line in the long run.

One in three tried to *minimize the impact of their caregiving situation on their employer* – but at a personal cost to themselves. The thirty-eight employees who gave this response found the time they needed to perform their caregiving role *by using their vacation days and by phoning in sick.* The following comments demonstrate this strategy:

And taking my parents to all their appointments, to doctor appointments, dentist appointments, eye doctors, you name it, every appointment – that was me. To do this I was exhausting all of my allowed time off work – be it vacation time, sick time, family-related time, everything time, taking-leave-without-pay time. It was a very trying time.

I would just take a personal day … but then that resulted in a financial loss …

Again, it should be noted that while the strategies used by this group of caregivers may minimize the impact caregiving has on the employer over the short term, our data showing high levels of caregiver stress and absenteeism indicate that these strategies are not sustainable over a longer time period. (Our data, as well as data from the 2012 GSS, indicate that many caregiving situations last for years!)

Finally, 5 per cent of the employees in our interview sample indicated that they had been told by their employer that if they did not give work a higher priority *their job was "at risk."*

It cost me a lot of credibility; I know my boss shared my performance issues with the rest of the management team … I was told that my job was at risk if my behaviour [left work early, missed work] *did not change.*

While such responses were not numerous, the link between caregiving and job loss in the minds of these employees (and likely others within these organizations) is distressing, as no employee should have to make a choice between having a job and caring for a loved one in the end stages of life.

How has your caregiving situation impacted your productivity at work?

You just can't do the work. You can't produce when you're thinking about your family. You're just not as strong. You're not as focused. You're not eating. You're not sleeping. And you're taking phone calls at work about personal matters. Instead of multi-tasking about work issues, because we're all multi-tasking about work, you're now working, and multi-tasking, about all those work issues plus personal issues. That's when mistakes get made ...

Not surprisingly the responses we got when we asked employees about the impact of their caregiving situation on their productivity at work and about how they deal with their colleagues at work in many ways mirrored the responses to the more general question that began this section of the interview ("How has your caregiving situation impacted your work?"). Just over half of the employees in our interview sample indicated that *the stress of caregiving negatively spilled over into the work environment*, either by having a negative impact on how they deal with their work colleagues or clients and/or by reducing their productivity. Examination of the responses indicates that, for many of the employees in this sample, the emotional turmoil of caregiving meant that they were less patient with their colleagues at work, less social with others, and less attentive to their work. The respondents also linked this lack of focus to a decline in their work productivity and increased absenteeism.

How has caregiving impacted productivity? One in three respondents talked specifically about being *less focused at work*.

Well, it's distracting ... hard to focus. You go back to work, but you're thinking about it in the back of your mind. So it definitely does impact your work.

One in four gave specific examples of how caregiving had decreased their work productivity in a *myriad of interconnected ways:*

You just can't do the work. You can't get to be in the field, and you can't be writing reports at the same level when you're thinking about your family.

A small number of respondents talked about how the stresses and strains of caregiving had contributed to a *reduction in their efficiency when at work* – either because they could not work as efficiently or because they were taking calls at work from the person they were caring for.

I would say in general I just don't work as efficiently ... as fast ... and probably my work in general isn't as sharp or quick as it would be when I'm doing a lot of extra things with my mum and for my mum.

And you're taking phone calls at work about personal matters.

How has your caregiving situation impacted how you deal with others at work?

Our data also showed that caregiving has the potential to cause friction within the workplace and have a negative impact on workplace relationships. One in three of the employed caregivers we talked to admitted that their caregiving situation had meant that they were less patient, cranky, and "short" with people at work:

I did not return calls, and when people asked me questions I'd snap at them ... just lose it.

One in ten admitted to being less sociable with their colleagues at work –

When work is really busy and there's stuff going on at home – when everything all comes at the same point, it's really, really hard. I think the work pressure combined with helping out my mum, when they hit at the same time, it's overloading. When this happens I just hide out in my office – I just have no energy to spare for anything or anyone else.

– or to being more scattered in their dealings with others.

I wasn't able to do any follow-through ... I couldn't do it – I would either do it and not say anything or not do it and hide from it.

Impacts of caregiving on work are largely negative

Finally, it is interesting to note that when asked "How has caregiving impacted your productivity at work?" and "How has caregiving impacted how you deal with others at work?" no employees talked about how caregiving had increased productivity or brought them closer to their colleagues. Instead, the data support the idea that caregiving had either no impact on their situation at work (in those cases where the caregiving requirements were less intense) or a negative impact (employees in the sandwich group). Particularly noteworthy are the data showing that employees with both childcare and eldercare (i.e., those in the sandwich group) were more likely than those in the eldercare group to indicate that their caregiving situation had negatively impacted their productivity at work, their relationships at work, and the amount of time they were away from work. These data reinforce the idea, put forward in many places in this book, that employers need to take action with respect to this issue.

Positive spillover between caregiving and work

One in three of the employees in the sample did not think that the caregiver role had produced any benefits for them at work. Nor did they think that their work role had helped them cope with their caregiving situation. The majority of employees, however, were able to identify ways in which being a caregiver had benefited them at work. One in three individuals talked about how *caregiving had helped them empathize with their colleagues and clients* who were in the same boat as they were:

If you don't have children and you don't have elderly parents you can't possibly understand, as a manager, why somebody would need to leave in the middle of the day and be able to give them that freedom to do that without making them go through hoops. Being there has helped me with that.

One in four felt that the caregiver role had *made them more diplomatic and patient* with others (e.g., able to "see the bigger picture"):

I think it broadens one's perspective. Especially when you do it for the first time, you suddenly realize, oh, there's more to this world than I had realized, and it broadens one's perspective. I think it makes, perhaps, one a little more tolerant of other people.

I would say, yes. It helps me, perhaps, think things through before acting, and consult with stakeholders, take into account the different opinions.

Just under one in ten talked about how the skills they had learnt at work and/or as a caregiver had transferred over and helped them in the opposite situation (i.e., *skills transfer*):

Oh, yes, there is a connection there, because sometimes clients and staff who depend on you, it's almost like they are a child or your mom ... and you've got to treat them ... well, not like a child, but there are some similar strategies you can use. To calm them down and things like that. I have learnt patience.

The final two responses were very similar ("*It helps me appreciate the difficulties the elderly face*" and "*I am more aware of people with health issues/ disabilities*"). Approximately 10 per cent of the caregivers we talked to mentioned these benefits.

How does your role at work help you manage your caregiver responsibilities?

Two thirds of the employees also felt that the *skills that they had acquired at work helped them fulfil their caregiving responsibilities*. In this case they talked about how the organizational and planning skills developed at work were the same skills that they needed to effectively provide care (25%).

> *I think probably my negotiation skills that I use at work carry over.*

> *The management skills that I'm learning at work definitely help. The big one is coaching. I'm working really hard on coaching my employees instead of giving them answers, and I'm able to do the same thing with my mum, and she gets less impatient because she doesn't feel like she's being told what to do all the time.*

Others (20%) talked about how their *work role had given them the coping skills* that they needed to deal effectively with the various crises that typified caregiving.

> *My work is pretty stressful as well … demanding … and I find that the things that help cope with stress at work also help me in dealing with my mom.*

One in ten appreciated the fact that there was a *social network within their workplace* that had made them aware of the challenges posed by caregiving prior to their taking on the role. One in ten also noted that they had acquired the *technical skills they needed to navigate the web* (a skill that they said was vital to their caregiving experience) at work. Also of note are the data showing that for a few people work provided an escape from the stress of caregiving.

Taken together these findings support the idea that a substantial number of employed caregivers experienced a positive transference from the skills learned as a caregiver to the skills they needed to deal with people at work and vice versa.

Employees in the eldercare group are more able to separate work and caregiving roles

The interview data also help us better appreciate the impact of life-cycle stage on the relationship between work and caregiving. More specifically, these data support the idea that employees in the eldercare group are more able to separate their work role from their caregiving role than are their younger colleagues in the sandwich generation. Those in the eldercare group were, for example, more than twice as likely as their counterparts with multigenerational care responsibilities to say that

- they did not experience any challenges at work that they could link to caregiving,
- caregiving had a minimal impact on their work because they separated work and family,
- the stress of caregiving did not impact either how they dealt with others at work or their productivity, and
- there was no positive spillover between the caregiver and work roles.

For those in the sandwich group, caregiving is both a curse and a blessing

While those in the sandwich group were more likely to report that caregiving had negatively impacted their productivity at work, they were also more likely to report positive spillover between the two roles. Many of the knowledge workers in the sandwich group talked about how the nature of their job (it is demanding, it never slows down, it is constantly changing, there are lots of deadlines) made it more difficult for them to balance work and caregiving. Others in this group specifically talked about the fact that their demands at work conflicted with their personal demands in terms of timing and available energy. Finally, it is important to note that virtually all of the employees in the sample who talked about how caregiving had negatively impacted their productivity at work were in this group.

The potential effects of caregiving on work identified by those in the sandwich group can be directly tied to the challenges they identified. In fact almost half of those in the sandwich group said that they had to either call in sick or use their vacation days to get the time off work they needed to deal with the unpredictable challenges of caregiving.

As noted earlier, those in the sandwich group were more likely to experience emotional caregiver strain. As such, it was not surprising to find that employees in this group were more likely to say that the stress of caregiving made them less patient with people at work. (They also admit to being less patient at home!) It would seem that those in the sandwich generation are getting worn down by all the demands on their time and lack the resilience to emotionally separate the two domains.

That being said, it is predominantly the employees in this group who also report positive spillover between their work and caregiving roles. More specifically, those in the sandwich generation are more likely to say that caregiving has made them more empathetic and able to see the "big picture" and that their work role has given them the organizational and planning skills needed to navigate the health and social service bureaucracies and get support for their family member.

The above findings support the idea that knowledge workers who have younger children at home and elderly family members requiring care living nearby, and who are also in their career ascendancy and working demanding jobs, will face more challenges in balancing the demands of work and caregiving than older employees with perhaps more seniority and fewer demands on their time from children.

Conclusions, Implications, and Recommendations

Evidence from the 2012 Study strongly supports the idea that the inability to balance employment and caregiving will negatively impact organizations' bottom line and make it more difficult for companies to manage their human capital. The following data support these conclusions and will help interested policy makers understand the mechanisms underlying this relationship. First, the knowledge workers who participated in the 2012 Study noted that caregiving demands had contributed to a moderate-to-substantial *increase* in the likelihood that they would be absent from work (29%), make greater use of employee benefits (25%), and turn down a promotion (15%), as well as a moderate-to-substantial *decrease* in their work productivity (25%) and the number of hours they could devote to work (23%).

Second, as noted earlier, many organizations use absence from work as a measure of productivity (if workers are not on the job, the work is definitely not being done). Men and women in the sandwich group miss almost twice as many days of work a year (13.4 for men and 19.4 for women) than do employees with no dependent care (7.0 for men and 10.6 for women). It should also be noted that there is no difference in absenteeism related to eldercare between those in the sandwich and eldercare stages of the life cycle when gender is taken into account.

Third, the majority of employees in the interview sample (60%) identified a number of ways in which their caregiving situation had negatively impacted their productivity (e.g., they were less productive, were distracted at work, missed more work time, found it hard to focus at work) and/or their career (e.g., they used vacation days to get time off, took sick days off work, feared that they might lose their job).

Fourth, the data from this study show that, while many employed caregivers make every effort to minimize the impact of caregiving on their work, the strategies they use (e.g., calling in sick, using vacation days) may come at a personal cost in terms of exhaustion, stress, and so on.

Fifth, it is interesting to note that approximately half of the employed caregivers in the interview sample indicated that the challenges they faced with respect to caregiving had negatively spilled over into the work environment, either by having an adverse effect on how they dealt with their work colleagues and clients and/or by reducing their productivity. More specifically, a plurality of the employees in the interview sample talked about how the emotional turmoil associated with caregiving meant that they were less patient/social with their colleagues at work and less attentive to their work. On a more positive note, a majority of this same group of employees saw a positive transference from the skills learned as a caregiver to the skills they needed to deal empathically, diplomatically, and patiently with colleagues and clients at work. They also noted that the organizational and planning skills, crisis management skills, and technical skills that they had acquired at work helped them in carrying out their caregiving responsibilities. Also important is the fact that one in ten appreciated the fact that there was a social network within their workplace that had made them aware of the challenges posed by caregiving prior to their taking on the role and that helped them cope with the challenges they faced.

Implications and recommendations for employers

The data from this study can be used by employers to make the business case for change in this area, as they demonstrate how inattention to the caregiving needs of employees will impact the bottom line (e.g., through increased absenteeism, increased use of employee benefits packages, challenges with respect to succession planning, declines in customer satisfaction, declines in productivity, increased conflict within the work group). The data linking multigenerational caregiving and decision making with respect to promotions are particularly concerning given the high number of baby boomers who are likely to retire in the next decade or so. Succession planning to replace this exodus of experience from the workplace will be problematic for organizations that do not address the work-caregiving issue. In view of the link between caregiving and the bottom line, the likely increase in the number of sandwich-generation employees within an organization's workforce in the near future increases the urgency of dealing with this issue for Canadian employers.

Data provided in this chapter also allow us to identify a number of things that concerned employers can do to help employees balance their caregiving needs with the needs of the employer. First, the employer needs to concretely recognize the challenges faced by caregivers by putting in place policies to address them, such as compassionate care leave, paid leave of absence, and unpaid leave of absence. Second, it would appear from this study that employers who offer their employees technical, crisis-management, and project-management training will not only create more skilled employees at work but will also help caregivers manage their situations outside of work. Third, the data indicate that employers will benefit by facilitating the creation of caregiving support networks within their workplace.

Chapter Six

Surviving (Even Thriving on) the "Rollercoaster Ride from Hell": Coping with Caregiver Strain

Well, a big thing is I do try to get my sleep and try to make sure that I am being healthy. That's been one thing which reduces the stress ... Another thing is just trying to put things in perspective when they do get stressful and just being appreciative for situations in life and what you have in life and what they are. So I really try to take that positive spin and find things to be thankful for ... For me, that definitely does help a lot ...

Your job is demanding and the meeting today is critical for your client and your career! Your partner just gained huge "best husband" points by making the lunches and taking the kids to school. Just as you are about to leave you get a call from your widowed mother who has Alzheimer's and lives alone. You are the primary caregiver, and your day just got off to a bad start. There have been other bad days – and you suspect that there will be many more in your future. How do you cope with this situation when there seems to be no end in sight? A good question – and one without a simple answer.

A book such as this, which looks at the challenges employees face in trying to balance work and caregiving, would be incomplete if it did not also talk about how employees can cope with such stresses. Coping refers to strategies that people use, either singly or in combination, in order to avoid being harmed by stressors (Pearlin and Schooler 1978). Coping is a necessary component of caregiving, as it is not possible to completely eliminate caregiver stress. In fact, psychotherapist Dr Denholm awarded caregiving the nickname of "rollercoaster ride from hell" because every day brings new challenges, new demands, and new adjustments (Brody 2012). *Caring for an aging loved one strains even the most resilient people.* While caregiving can be a rewarding and positive experience, the data presented in the previous chapters of the book have established, beyond a shadow of a doubt, that the role of caregiver can be extremely demanding, stressful, physically taxing, and anxiety producing.

There is considerable evidence that the role demands faced by employed caregivers burden them with significant stress and disruption of their own well-being and place them at risk for emotional and physical health problems. Studies indicate that caregivers are at increased risk for premature mortality due to coronary heart disease and stroke, particularly under conditions of high strain (Schulz and Beach 1999; Beach et al. 2005; Haley et al. 2010; Lee et al. 2003). Furthermore, the high demands on their time mean that caregivers are often less likely than non-caregivers to engage in healthy behaviours such as taking exercise, eating right, and getting enough sleep (Schulz et al. 1997). The health and well-being of family caregivers should be a government priority, as a decline in family caregiver health is one of the major risk factors for the institutionalization of a care recipient (Elliott and Pezent 2008) and the concomitant costs that such institutionalization entails.

Being able to deal with the inevitable stresses and strains of caregiving is part of the complex task of being a truly effective caregiver, as people who do not care for themselves may find it difficult to care for someone else.

Using data from the interview phase of the 2012 Study, this chapter, in combination with the material in chapter 7, offers concrete suggestions on what can be done to reduce the adverse consequences of caregiving for Canadian employees. More specifically, this chapter summarizes key findings from the "coping" section of the interview phase of the 2012 Study. In that section of the interview we asked our 111 caregivers to reflect on their own caregiving experiences and help us understand how their own behaviour impacted their ability to cope with their caregiving situation. For ease of reference, box 6.1 lists the questions asked. Also included in this chapter are the answers to the final interview question we asked of our employed caregivers: "What *one* piece of advice would you offer to a friend who has all of a sudden assumed care for an elderly dependent?" Responses to this question provide an indication of what those who are currently in the role think helps reduce the stresses that often accompany the role of caregiver. The information presented in this chapter, in combination with the material in chapter 7 (which looks at how the behaviour of other key stakeholders impacts the caregiver's ability to cope) should facilitate the identification of strategies, programs, and policies that could help caregivers cope more effectively with the stresses of caregiving.

Box 6.1: Coping with Caregiver Strain

1   What do you personally do to cope with the challenges associated with caregiving you identified earlier? Why did you cope this way? Did this strategy work to reduce your stress levels?
2   What did you do to cope with the emotional aspects of the situation?
3   Do you personally do anything that makes the situation worse (i.e., makes it more difficult for you to cope with the challenges you face combining employment and caregiving for an elderly dependent)?

This chapter is structured somewhat differently from the other chapters in this book, as it features only qualitative information collected from the 111 employees who participated in the interview study. The chapter is divided into seven sections. We begin in section one by providing a short review of the academic literature dealing with individual coping strategies. Sections two through six present key findings from the 2012 Study with respect to how Canadian employees cope with caregiver strain. Each section provides an analysis of a different question. Section two looks at how the caregivers we interviewed said that they coped with the myriad challenges inherent in the caregiving role. This is followed in section three by an exploration of how these caregivers coped specifically with the emotional strain that seems intrinsic to the caregiver role. Section four summarizes the responses given by the caregivers as they reflected on whether or not they had personally done anything to make their caregiving situation more challenging and/or stressful. In section five we switch our focus from discussing how employees cope with and react to caregiver stress to the strategies they said they used proactively to prevent caregiver strain from occurring in the first place. Section six looks more holistically at the issue of coping with caregiver strain by analysing the "one piece of advice on how to cope" that our caregivers would give to other caregivers. The final section of the chapter summarizes key findings from our analysis of the interview data relating to individual coping and makes a number of recommendations to those who are engaged in the role on how to cope effectively with their situation.

How do people cope with stress? Answers from academia

A review of the coping literature shows that, while literally hundreds of coping strategies and coping strategy typologies have been identified, there is no agreement as to which of these classification schemes is the more correct or has the greatest utility. The classification scheme used to guide the discussion of the results in this chapter is shown in table 6.1 and is based on the work of Lazarus and Folkman (1984). This scheme follows common practice by first dividing coping strategies into two main categories: problem-focused coping and emotion-focused coping. People using problem-focused strategies try to deal with (change, eliminate) the source of their stress. Emotion-focused coping strategies, on the other hand, are all oriented towards managing (minimizing, reducing, or preventing) the emotions that accompany the perception of stress. People typically use problem-based coping strategies when they feel they have control of the situation and perceive that they can manage the source of the problem. Alternatively, individuals usually use emotion-focused coping when they feel that they have little control over the situation and/or cannot control the source of the stress.

Both problem- and emotion-based coping strategies can be further classified as being either adaptive (constructive) or maladaptive (avoidance). Broadly speaking, adaptive coping methods lead to a reduction in stress as well as improved functioning and well-being. Maladaptive

Table 6.1 Ways of Coping with Caregiver Strain

Emotion Focused (Aimed at Regulating Emotions)	Problem Focused (Aimed at Regulating Behaviour)

Adaptive Coping

Seeking social support for emotional reasons (talking to someone about how they are feeling; asking a friend or relative for advice)

Cope (C, E): Talking/venting to a sympathetic other

Positive reinterpretation and growth (trying to see things in a more positive light)

Cope (C, P): Focusing on doing one's best, not worrying, being realistic

Cope (E) Engaging in introspection

Cope (P): Maintaining a positive outlook

Turning to religion (seeking God's help, finding comfort in religion)

Emotional restraint (trying to keep feelings from interfering with other things too much)

Cope (C, E): Engaging in an activity to take one's mind off of the situation

Cope (C): Carving out time to relax and take it easy

Confronting the problem (expressing frustration, etc., to the person causing the problem)

Cope (C, E, P): Sharing their concerns and expectations with the care recipient/using proactive communication

Calculated action (making a plan of action and following it; knowing what has to be done and just doing it)

Cope (C, P): Planning, organizing, and prioritizing

Cope (C): Doing the research / seeking constructive support (asking people in a similar situation how they dealt with it; getting advice from others on what do to)

Cope (C, P): Asking for help / delegating

Cope (C, E): Seeking help from a mental health professional

Behavioural restraint (avoiding making matters worse by acting too soon or without thinking)

Cope (C, P): Looking after themselves and their own health (taking exercise, getting enough sleep)

Maladaptive Coping (i.e., Avoidance)

Emotional evasion (making light of the situation; refusing to take the situation seriously)

Cope (W): Letting things go they shouldn't

Cope (W): Internalizing their problems

Denial (pretending/acting as if it has not really happened)

Cope (C, E): "Just getting on with it"

Emotional release (getting upset, letting one's feelings out)

Cope (W): Feeling guilty

Cope (W): Getting upset too easily

Cope (W): Taking out stress on the person being cared for

Making concessions (promising oneself it will be better or different next time)

Cope (W): Hanging on to responsibility

Behavioural evasion (trying to feel better by eating, drinking, smoking, using medication or drugs)

Cope (C, E): Turning to alcohol and comfort food

Key	C = use to cope with strain	E = use to cope with emotions	P = use to prevent strain	W = behaviour that makes things worse

coping strategies, on the other hand, are patterns of thinking and behaviour that cause and maintain emotional problems. While such techniques can reduce the symptoms of stress in the short term, they typically lead to increased dysfunction and a decline in well-being over the long run.

As shown in table 6.1, adaptive coping strategies, be they emotion-focused or problem-focused, involve activities that are oriented towards a threat (e.g., acceptance, problem solving, planning a response, getting ideas from others). Problem-focused adaptive coping strategies involve approaches directed either at identifying solutions to the situation or situation control (planning, research, prioritizing). Emotion-focused adaptive coping approaches, on the other hand, involve efforts to maintain hope, control emotions, and distract the individual from the stressful situation (e.g., cognitive restructuring, minimization, short-term avoidance). Seeking emotional support from one's partner or friends is also a positive form of emotion-focused coping. Finally, getting adequate nutrition, exercise, and sleep is a positive stress management strategy, as are physical fitness and relaxation techniques such as progressive muscle relaxation. These strategies make it easier for people to respond positively to stresses in their life.

Another adaptive, problem-oriented coping strategy known as anticipating a problem (or *proactive coping*) is also examined in this chapter. Anticipation is when one reduces the stress of some difficult challenge by anticipating what it will be like and preparing for how one is going to cope with it. Maladaptive proactive coping strategies include avoidance (avoiding anxiety-provoking situations at all costs), withdrawal, rumination, giving up/resignation, aggression, and escape (e.g., through self-medication). As shown in table 6.1, avoidance can be active or emotional.

What works to reduce stress?

While all these methods may reduce stress, at least temporarily, generally speaking research in the area suggests that people who use adaptive, problem-focused coping strategies will experience higher levels of well-being (Lazarus and Folkman 1984). Emotion-focused coping, on the other hand, helps in situations where the stressors are uncontrollable (e.g., a terminal illness diagnosis, or the loss of a loved one), which may be the case in some caregiving situations. Positive, emotion-focused mechanisms, such as seeking social support and positive re-appraisal, are associated with beneficial outcomes. Some forms of emotion-focused coping, such as distancing or avoidance, on the other hand, tend to be detrimental when used over an extended period of time.

Coping with the Challenges of Caregiving: A View from the Trenches

Coping with the challenges of caregiving

Respondents identified thirteen different strategies that they had used to cope with the stresses associated with an overwhelming caregiving situation. The eleven strategies used by a substantial number of caregivers (i.e., at least 10% of the sample) are described below, along with illustrative quotes.

Caregivers cope by talking/venting to a sympathetic other

The most common strategy the caregivers in our sample used to cope with caregiver strain (mentioned by 50 of the 111 caregivers we talked to) was to *talk or vent about their situation with a sympathetic other*. The other person could be a family member *("Talking with my children has helped me cope"; "I talk to my husband all the time about it")*, a friend *("I have a girlfriend who's also one of the prime caregivers for her mother, and so we share our irritations, periodically … so that helps, sharing the experience with other friends in the same situation")*, colleagues at work *("I also bent the ear of certain sympathetic people at work")*, a mental health professional *("I vent to my therapist")*, or a member of the person's social network.

> *[T]his might just be a phenomenon of our generation – even just reaching out and getting support virtually, on things like Facebook. When you're just frustrated*

and you need an outlet, you just post something like, "I'm having a rough look-after-mommy-day." Within half an hour or forty-five minutes you end up with thirty-five people saying, "I hear you. Yes, doesn't it suck?" So you don't feel alone that way. It's funny how much I've relied on that, because I wouldn't have been able to pick up the phone thirty-five times …

Analysis of the comments made by the caregivers in our sample showed that this "reaching out to others" coping strategy took many different forms. Many caregivers who used this strategy talked about how they just needed to "let off steam" and get rid of their frustrations with someone whom they trusted and who would empathize with their situation: *"I shut down; I ranted in my head and I bitched at my husband … It's good, because I just needed to vent, and he was somebody I could vent at … and he'll make comforting noises at the right time."* These individuals were not seeking solutions for their problems; rather, they used these discussions as an "emotional safety valve." For example, *"I cried. I vented. There was a whole gamut of emotions there and still are. It happens, and then it's over, and I just pick myself up and carry on."* Many talked about how this ability to vent with a sympathetic other made a difference and helped them "carry on." For example,

I'm really lucky. Both my children will listen to me rant and rave and whine and snivel about things, and that makes a big difference.

Others talked about how talking to someone else about their situation helped them either to put things into perspective (e.g., *"I talk about it with my colleagues here* [at work] *and friends as well … it really helps me to process stuff and put it into perspective when my frustration level is going up …"*) and/or to come up with suggestions on how to address the challenges they are facing. For example:

My partner – he's there to talk with me about it. He helps me come up with solutions …

The comments above suggest several ways in which talking and venting to others helps employees cope with caregiver strain: it helps them put things into perspective; it makes them feel less alone; it helps them get rid of their frustrations in a safe environment; and it helps them identify possible solutions to the challenges they face.

Caregivers cope by engaging in an activity to take their mind off their situation

While many caregivers coped by talking and venting to others, an equally large number (45% of all the employees we interviewed) said they coped by engaging in an activity that enabled them to forget, albeit for a limited amount of time, the challenges they faced in trying to balance employment, caregiving, and perhaps parenting *(engage in an activity to help them forget)*. Our caregivers identified a multitude of activities they used in this context. For many, the activity they used to cope (reading, TV, working on the computer) gave them time to themselves to recoup:

> *I watch a lot of TV. I just basically try and get away from the situation with my mind.*

> *I read novels, and I watch movies … it's a sanity thing …*

Some coped by "scheduling" time to do something with their partner –

> *We actually started scheduling a weekly date night just to get away from the stress. We try to do things outside of the house, away from the phone …*

– while others "escaped" the stress of the caregiver role by engaging in a social activity with friends.

> *I belong to a club, and every now and then my escape was to go to the social club. We would have supper together, or hike together, or do something. So that was my release. I don't know what I would have done if I had not been a member of that club.*

Many of the caregivers in the sample talked about how effective exercise was at relieving the anxiety and stress of their current situation.

Probably the biggest thing for me was exercise, physical activity ... doing something physical to burn off that anxiety or whatever ...

Others mentioned how helpful having a hobby – something that they felt passionate about – was to their ability to cope with the strains of caregiving:

I very often took weekend mornings and went bird watching. Yes, even though I had a million things to do and everything, I actually had to get right away from the house, from her, from demands from work, and I would go with a group and I would go for a walk in the woods and do something else that I love to do, because it helped ground me. It usually meant that I had to go over to her place in the evenings after work, or I would be there late in the afternoon on the weekends, but I needed that me time.

The above comments suggest that although many caregivers experienced a "time famine" (see chapter 3), they found that spending time in activities other than caregiving helped them to cope with the stress of caregiving by engaging them mentally in something that was not related to caregiving; by giving them a healthy way to decompress; and by taking them away (mentally and/or physically) from the situation that was contributing to their stress levels.

Planning, organizing, and prioritizing can help

Many caregivers (31% of those we interviewed) coped by spending time *planning and organizing* – an activity that was critical given the number of balls these employees were juggling at once! They made lists; they used day-timers, calendars, and Post-it notes; they pre-planned, planned, researched, and planned some more – all in an attempt to increase the amount of control they had over their situation. The following quotations typify what we heard from caregivers who use this strategy:

I research and pre-plan and think about how I am going to deal with the situation ... I prepare as much as I can.

So I got myself organised, basically, in my head, where did I have to go, what did I have to do. And then I started making notes so that I wouldn't forget things.

Many of the caregivers we talked to who used a prioritizing strategy to cope with caregiver strain spoke about how, in an effort to reduce the demands on their time to a manageable number, they forced themselves to give what they personally wanted or needed to do a higher a priority than what the person they were caring for wanted done. For example:

There are times when I will not answer the phone; I'll put it on voice-mail or whatever, and then I'll call her when I have the time.

I try just to simply relax and I keep saying to myself, you're doing the best you can and you can't be expected to do everything ... I have priorities. I have commitments to my work and my husband and my home and myself, and I can only do what I can do.

Many caregivers cope by "just getting on with it"

A quarter of the caregivers we talked to took a more action-oriented approach to coping with their work/caregiving situation. More specifically, employees who used this strategy focused their energy and attention on *"just getting through a difficult situation"* (i.e., *just get on with it*). In fact, many of the individuals who coped in this manner noted that they *"bit their tongue"* and elected not to *"verbalize their feelings,"* as past experience had taught them that prioritizing doing rather than verbalizing was most likely to reduce stress and anxiety:

I bit my tongue many times and just didn't say what I was thinking. I internalized a lot of my feelings ... speaking up would only make things worse ... and got on with it.

It should also be noted that many of the people who gave this response were resigned about their personal caregiving situation.

I do what I have to do, and I spend as much time as I can spend, but the challenge is ... I do it as a chore that needs to be done, not out of love anymore.

How do I cope with it? I don't ... I practise stoicism.

Many caregivers make a real effort to find time to relax and take it easy

One in five of the caregivers we talked to coped by making a *real* effort *to try and relax and take it easy,* though many also noted how difficult that was! The following comment illustrates the personal challenges many caregivers face in trying to carve out time to relax:

Sometimes instead of switching right into work mode when I go home from work, for example, cleaning my house or making supper, if I'm really tired now I will give myself a break. I don't know if that's the caregiver role, or just realizing that life's short and I'm getting older and why work all the time? I allow myself more time to relax than I used to. It's still not much, but when I have those moments I will grab them, whereas in the past I'd probably say, no, I can force myself to clean the kitchen or make a meal, if I'm really tired I just say, no, I'm not going to. I'm going to sit here ...

Also noteworthy is the fact that half of the people who gave this response talked specifically about how being with their pets facilitated their ability to *"relax and let it go."* The following response is typical of what we heard from our respondents:

Yes, I have a cat, he is a really good source of comfort ... and sometimes I will just go and shut down and do something absolutely mindless like pet the cat for hours, just because it shuts down the little voice in my head ...

Many caregivers turn to alcohol and comfort food

One in five caregivers *turned to alcohol and comfort food* to alleviate the symptoms of stress. The following were typical of what we heard:

I probably eat. It's funny but ... when I leave my dad I'll go and get a coffee and a doughnut at Tim Horton's, bring it home and just sit with my feet up and treat myself. It's almost like it's a reward. How else could I deal with it?

I drink just a bit more than usual. I relax with a couple of glasses of wine or some-thing ... It relaxes me ... gives me time to just sit and take a deep breath ... not every day but after events like [her scenario] *..."*

Caregivers also idiosyncratically use strategies to help them cope

There were also a number of coping strategies that were used by a rela-tively small number (one in ten) of individuals to cope with the chal-lenges of caregiving. Some coped by *making time for activities associated with good physical health* (e.g., eating healthy food, getting a good night's sleep). For example:

Well, one of the things that I recognized ... was that I wasn't eating properly and I had gained quite a bit of weight. So I joined Weight Watchers and I've lost twenty pounds ... it helped me cope better, because as soon as I start eating better it makes everything better.

The fact that relatively few of the employed caregivers in our sample use this strategy to cope is unfortunate but consistent with the fact that many of the caregivers in our sample experience physical health concerns.

It is also interesting to note that very few (one in ten) of the caregivers we talked to coped by *sharing their concerns and expectations* with the main source of their stress – the person they were caring for. Those who used this strategy talked about how they discussed issues pertaining to personal boundaries and what they were and were not willing and/or able to do for the person they were caring for. The following quotation describes this coping strategy:

So really it was just dealing with it head on, instead of not discussing it and let-ting it fester. So it's just talking about it and resolving it before it became a worse

*problem than it needed to be. I give her choices that are going to fit in better with
my schedule; I limit the amount of time that I give to her …*

*With my mom I try to set more boundaries and say, you need to give me forty-eight
hours' notice if you want me to do something, unless it's an actual emergency.*

Virtually all of the caregivers who used this coping strategy talked
about how difficult it was to have such conversations – which is perhaps why more people do not take this approach to coping with the
situation. The people who used this strategy were, however, unanimous in their belief that there were more benefits to such conversations
than to remaining silent.

Other caregivers employed a coping strategy that was a variant of
relying on planning and organizing coping strategies. More specifically, they spoke about *"doing the research"* and actively pursuing outside
support to help them with their caregiving situation. What made this
strategy unique was the single-minded focus this group of caregivers
had to "research and plan" their way out of their current caregiving
situation. Their goal was to identify appropriate external support networks for the person(s) they were caring for and then acquire the services of this resource. In other words, they were spending time
(researching) to save time (get outside support). For example:

*I made extra phone calls and did research about things that my mum could do,
services she could use without me being there. I then followed up – and followed up … and followed up. It took time but ended up saving me time in the
long term.*

A small number of people (all women in the sandwich life-cycle
stage!) coped by *asking a family member or a friend to help them out.* Friends
and neighbours were typically recruited to help with the caregiver's
own children *("I asked for the help of a neighbour … she helped me by driving
my kid to his activity"),* while family were asked to contribute to the care
of their parent *("I coordinate with other family members and get them to
pitch in …").*

Also noteworthy are data showing that one in ten of the caregivers we spoke to mentioned that they had *sought professional help* from a mental health counsellor *("Yes – I see a therapist")* to help them deal with the issues they faced and the symptoms of stress they experienced. All of these caregivers talked about how their discussions with their therapist had helped them *"learn how to step back from the situation and get perspective."*

Finally, it is interesting to note that virtually none of the caregivers we talked to coped by *taking time off work!* Examination of their comments showed that this was not a realistic option for many of the knowledge workers in the sample, either because they needed the income their job provided and/or because their career was an important source of satisfaction and intellectual stimulation.

Why did you cope this way?

We also asked the caregivers whom we spoke to why they selected the coping strategy they did. One in ten of the caregivers interviewed could not actually explain why they coped the way they did, saying *"It is just the way I do things,"* or *"That's just what I do when I am stressed"* *("Who knows?!")*.There was some consensus, however, within the rest of the group with respect to the motivations employees gave for selecting the coping strategy they did, with most mentioning one or more of the six reasons discussed below.

One in five caregivers thought about the person they were caring for when deciding how best to cope with their caregiving situation and selected strategies that they perceived would protect the interests of the care recipient – even if the use of these strategies came at a personal cost for the caregiver *("It's in the best interest of the person I am caring for").* The following comment typified what we heard from respondents with respect to why they coped the way they did:

> *[I]t's my mum, and I feel it's really important to try to give her a happy life. So for me to get all frustrated and annoyed and stomp my foot, whatever, it isn't going to help things. I do what I do to keep her happy and healthy … that's all one can do really …*

Many of the caregivers who coped by venting to their partner and/or by engaging in other activities to take their mind off their caregiving situation (one in five of the caregivers in the sample) did so in an effort to relieve the stress they were under (*"It helps me de-stress"*):

> [T]he venting and the crying ... Yes, it does work for me. It happens, and then it's over, and I just pick myself up and carry on ...

Many of the caregivers who coped by planning, organizing, and researching (one in five of the caregivers in the sample) stated that they did so based on the "logical and rational" assumption that these tactics would *increase the amount of control they had over a challenging situation*:

> My personality is one in which I need control over my environment and things around me, so an ability to control the situation helps me to organize my thoughts. And I had to step back from the emotional end of it.

One in ten of the caregivers we talked to stated that when figuring out how they could cope with their situation they followed a strategy of *keeping things as simple as possible* – which to these caregivers meant that they did not seek either opinions or help when deciding what to do but instead selected coping strategies that they could follow through on their own:

> When you don't expect anybody to help you, it becomes easier. Your expectations are lowered ... and you don't have to worry about ... things not going according to plan because someone isn't assisting when you thought they should ...

Others coped the way they did because they wanted to make the dependent person more aware of what was going on *(keeps the person they are caring for in the loop)*. For example:

> I needed her to know there were limits ... I pointed out that I wasn't going to be carrying all the load ... I tried to wean her from a total dependence on me and create some capacity; get her to be more independent, autonomous.

Finally one in ten of the caregivers we talked to indicated that the coping strategies they selected were chosen to *give themselves some breathing space*. The following quotation illustrates this response.

> *Like I said, the hobby, the bird watching took me away from the situation ... for four or five hours it wasn't in my head, and I didn't think about what the issue was until we were winding up and I knew I had to go ... but for that four hours it was my time, it was my learning, it was my needs I was dealing with.*

Did this strategy reduce your stress? Yes and no

We followed up on these two interview questions (i.e., how they coped with the challenges of caregiving and why they coped the way they did) with a third question designed to help us evaluate the effectiveness of the various coping strategies used by the employed caregivers in our sample: "Did this strategy work to reduce your stress levels?" While the vast majority (77%) of the sample of caregivers we talked to indicated that the coping strategy that they selected had helped them cope with the challenges they were facing (at least some of the time), one in four (23%) said that the approach they took did not typically work. Some (approximately one in four) of the respondents spoke unequivocally about how their *coping strategy had helped* –

> *Yes. It worked ... if there was one key reason it was realizing, at one point, that we weren't going to fix her; that we were not going to help her become a fully functioning person anymore; that that was just not in the cards. And once I was able to really accept that ... it changed my perspective ...*

– or *had not helped* (23% of the sample),

> *Do I have high blood pressure? Yes. Have I skipped the gym and gained weight? Yes. I would be healthier if I didn't have to look after my dad, but that's the way it is ...*

Others (half the sample) were more equivocal, noting that the *strategy worked sometimes but not others*.

Half and half. Sometimes they work and other times when I really want to do something … that's when it seems like they don't work.

How did you cope with the emotional aspects of your caregiving situation?

Emotions (i.e., affective states, feelings) are different from cognitive (i.e., rational and reasoned) and volitional (i.e., chosen) states of consciousness. Emotions can be defined as any strong agitation of the feelings in which joy, sorrow, fear, hate, or the like, are experienced. When a person experiences strong emotions they also typically experience certain physiological (e.g., increased heartbeat or respiration), and physical (e.g., crying, shaking) changes. The literature reviewed previously as well as the data from the 2012 Study established that caregiving often elicits a strong emotional response in the caregiver. We were therefore interested in determining how the employees in our sample coped with the emotions generated by their caregiving situation. Insights were gained by asking the employed caregivers we interviewed the following question: What did you do to cope with the emotional aspects of your caregiving situation?

The 100-plus caregivers we talked to used eight strategies to cope with the emotional aspects of caregiving. Five of these strategies (especially the most common ones) were also mentioned when the caregivers talked in a more general way about coping with the challenges of caregiving (i.e., talking/venting with partner; taking exercise/pursuing hobbies; seeking professional help; communicating with the person receiving care; drinking alcohol/eating comfort food). The other responses (doing nothing; engaging in reflection; focusing on the fact that they were doing their best) were, however, only mentioned in the section of the interview where the individual was talking about coping with the emotional strains associated with caregiving.

The most common approach (cited by almost half of the sample) to coping with the emotional strains triggered by caregiving was *to seek support from a sympathetic other*. The quotation below illustrates how hard it is for people to "let go" of their feelings:

I get sad and angry all at the same time; I don't like feeling it, I don't like thinking what I'm thinking, and I'm angry that I'm doing it, but I'm still angry at the whole situation. And sometimes I just feel so frustrated because I don't know where else to turn; I don't know whom to talk to. You can only babble at your husband so much, because he's going through the same thing.

One in four (26%) of caregivers stated they *just ignored the emotions* and *soldiered on*. In other words, they did nothing to cope with the emotional aspect of caregiving. Virtually all of the caregivers who gave this response seemed resigned to their situation (*"I just kept busy, I mean, I had no choice ... there was nothing I could do ..."*) and made a conscious effort to "put their emotions on hold" until some hypothetical period in the future:

I think you generally put it on hold until you have a chance to deal with it. I think at the time you just kick into what you need to do and then you just do it. And then afterwards, sometimes you can get emotional. But really right now in my life, anything that happens tends to be a crisis. So you just deal with it.

It is interesting to note that, while one in four of the caregivers in our sample talked about ignoring their emotions, none of these individuals neglected the practical or logistical challenges of caregiving.

In addition to the two strategies noted above, one in five caregivers coped with the emotions they were experiencing by *spending time on their hobbies* and in other activities that they enjoyed. They noted that this enabled them to relax and *"got their mind off"* the challenges they faced with respect to caregiving. What was striking was the number of caregivers (n = 14) who talked specifically about taking up yoga:

I did yoga and meditation that helped ... if I could find the time to do it ... and I got exercise. I went for long walks. I protected my sleep ... It's really basic things like getting enough to eat; getting enough sleep; not letting the stress get to you ...

One in ten coped with the emotional aspect of caregiving by thinking about the situation, engaging in reflection, and being introspective *(reflected on what was going on)*. They felt that this strategy allowed them to gain perspective on the issue and *"to step back from the situation"*:

> *Emotionally, I would say at a certain point in time … I was ready to hit the rubber room … but then I stepped back … I realized that I cannot be everything to everybody, and realized that emotionally I can't be there for her all the time.*

Finally, when analysing the data we identified three strategies that were used by relatively few (i.e., one in ten) of the caregivers in our sample. These individuals coped with the emotions of caregiving by *focusing on the fact that they were doing "their best"* –

> *I try my best and I hope that when it's all done I'm going to be able to say, I did my best. I don't want to end up saying, I should have done more. I don't want to be left with a feeling of guilt. I want to be left with a feeling of, I did my best, given the circumstances. It helps.*

– and/or by *seeking professional help ("I see a therapist regularly, so that's probably the main thing that I did")* and/or *speaking frankly to the person they were caring for* in an attempt to manage the situation *("I don't let her manipulate me anymore. I just say, Mom, I only have this much time and then I have to do this and I have to do that …")* and/or *drinking alcohol* and *eating comfort food*.

Is there anything you personally do that makes things worse?

The vast majority of the caregivers we talked to (80%) acknowledged that they personally did a number of things that made their caregiving situation worse. More specifically, they noted that they made things worse when they "hung on" to responsibility for the care of their family member (even when things got too much), got upset too easily, internalized their problems, took their stress out on the care recipient (were abrupt with the dependent, fought with the dependent) and/or themselves (self-guilt), and let things go that they shouldn't. Quotations illustrating each of these factors are provided in the section below.

One in three caregivers stated that they had made their caregiving situation more challenging by stepping up and assuming primary responsibility for the care of their family member (*engaged in the role even when it became too much*):

> I know I take on more than I need to. I do most of the housework for me and them ... most of the cooking, and so on. So I tend to take on more than I need to ...

Many of the caregivers who mentioned this particular challenge also noted that they had not wanted to "be the one in charge" but that fate and a lack of choice had intervened, with the result that they had, de facto, become the person who was responsible for caregiving:

> I did too much for too long ... put too much on myself ... I had to do a lot because she was in a really bad state and there was no choice ...

> I take it all on ... but I'm forced to ... there just isn't enough support out there to help.

Others acknowledged that they were in the position they were in because they did not like to ask for help and were too *"quick to volunteer"*:

> I'm very quick to offer, which does make it harder for me ... I mentioned my brother doesn't help, but I don't ask him, either. I offer a lot, so I am in a way my own worst enemy. I offer too quickly.

One in four described a vicious cycle where they made things worse for themselves by first *allowing the situation to upset them*, then acting quickly (and often irrationally) when they were feeling emotional, which led, in turn, to a further increase in their stress levels:

> Sometimes I allow myself to be caught up in the urgency, or the perceived urgency, of what needs to be done ... I rush out to solve a problem when, you know, it could be delayed ... and then I just feel worse.

Others noted that they let the situation *get to them*, which reduced their ability to deal with the situation in an effective manner:

> *I worry a lot. And I don't really have an outlet for my stress … so I worry and don't get enough sleep …*

One in four indicated that they made things worse by *giving in to the stress and taking it out on the person they were caring for*. This behaviour made them feel guilty, hurt their relationship with their family member, and reduced their ability to deal effectively with their caregiving situation:

> *I get very impatient with my dad … I let my frustration get the better of me and sometimes say things that are probably not the most helpful.*

> *Yes, probably when I get too pissed off! It doesn't help me, it doesn't let me sleep, it doesn't help me cope, it doesn't help my blood pressure; it's not a good thing … I often wonder why do I have to make things so complicated …?*

One in five noted that they made things worse when they *internalized the stress* and turned to alcohol (*"I do some alcohol therapy…"*) and medication to "deaden" the emotions they were feeling. For example:

> *I take medication. I've become very reliant on it, and my therapist says, you may want to consider if now is a good time to be lowering your dose. I go, "Hell, no. Are you out of your mind?" Because I don't want to face the situation without it. Right now … it's a very helpful tool, and I know if I don't take my medication I'm a mess. I'm ready to take everybody's head off at work and at home.*

A small number of respondents (one in ten, mostly women) said that they made the situation worse by *worrying and feeling guilty*:

> *By feeling guilty … they don't want me to feel guilty … I do that all by myself … that does make it harder.*

A similar number said that their *sense of apathy over their caregiving situation* had made things worse over time. The caregivers who gave this response all noted that they had not wanted to take on the caregiving role to begin with *("I didn't want to do this")* but were now *"resigned"* to it or had *"just given up."* Caregivers in this group stated that their tendency to not be proactive as a caregiver and *"to let things go that I shouldn't"* had aggravated their caregiving situation. For example:

> *What do I do? I'm avoiding. I'm running away from conflict, and the way I'm running away is, I'm not going to visit my mother as often as I should. When I go there, I feel I'm under duress. So I'm trying to avoid conflict, and I'm trying to avoid sadness and pain, but I am not. I am just changing the source of the sadness and pain.*

Preventing Caregiving Strain

Finally, we asked respondents to identify any strategies that they had found to be effective at preventing (or minimizing) the occurrence of caregiver strain. Almost one in five of the caregivers we talked to were *not able to think of anything that had worked to prevent or minimize caregiver strain.* As illustrated in the quotations below, the caregivers who gave this response were somewhat fatalistic in their approach to the situation:

> *No … there's nothing I could have done that would have prevented my mother from getting ill and my father from getting ill … a lot of what goes on just cannot be anticipated.*

> *No, because my dad falls at random, and I don't have any say over that. Or he gets into trouble randomly, and I have no say over that. It's hopelessness. I don't feel in control to change anything.*

> *Oh, there's no prevention … things are going to happen no matter what. It's almost a given.*

What prevents or minimizes the strains associated with caregiving? According to the employed caregivers in this sample the following strategies were important: planning and organization; better communication with the dependent and the family with respect to expectations;

being realistic about what you can and cannot do (*"accept that you cannot control everything"*); delegating work to others and getting help from other family members; maintaining a positive outlook and not getting angry; making time for oneself; and dealing with things as they come (*"worry about what might happen in the future doesn't really help anything"*). In other words, they cited many of the same strategies that caregivers identified when talking about coping with their current caregiver situation and the emotional stress they were under. Details on how each of these strategies can be used in a proactive fashion to prevent strain from taking root are provided below.

Planning and organization seem to be key strategies that caregivers can use to prevent or minimize caregiver strain. Reading the quotations below, it would appear that planning used in a prevention context seems to be more proactive in nature than the types of planning and organizing employees used to cope with existing caregiving strain, which seem to be more practical and hands on. Analysis of the data shows that one in three of the caregivers in this sample found *pre-mortem strategies* useful in preventing caregiver strain. The term "pre-mortem" is used in the management literature to describe a process in which a manager imagines that a project has failed and then works backward to determine what potentially could lead to the failure of the project or organization (Klein 2007). Management can then analyse the magnitude and likelihood of each threat, and take preventive actions to protect the project from encountering this problem. Caregivers apply a similar strategy when they imagine what could go wrong and then research and plan how to address these issues if they do in fact arise. For example:

> *Often, yes, you would just get your mind around it and say, okay, I'm going to go there and this is going to be the situation and I'm going to do A, B, C. So if I was prepared mentally and I had a plan then it wouldn't be so bad. Often we'd get there, and I knew exactly what I wanted to do or what I had to do or who I had to call and that worked out well. That really helped.*

> *Sometimes I will mentally rehearse how things are going to roll out, or how I'm going to explain something, so I'll plan out how I'm going to present it and figure*

out what she might say, and try and come up with the answers that way. I find
that does help.

One in four of the employees we talked to felt that the stresses associated with caregiving could be reduced by communicating with everyone involved in the situation in order to clearly establish expectations on who does what, and so on *(better communication with everyone involved to set expectations)*. Again, caregivers' comments show a strong overlap between this strategy to prevent caregiver strain and what management scholars refer to as a psychological contract. In the management literature, a psychological contract refers to the relationship between an employer and an employee. More specifically, a psychological contract concerns mutual beliefs, perceptions, and informal obligations between an employer and an employee. It sets the dynamics for the relationship and defines the practical details of the work to be done (Rousseau 1995). In an organizational setting, psychological contract violation is associated with higher levels of employee stress and exiting behaviour. The above quotations suggest that for many caregivers in this sample, anticipatory communication between the key stakeholders sets expectations and establishes the boundaries of the caregiving relationship in a manner similar to what has been described in the management literature on psychological contracts. The establishment of such a contract minimizes the likelihood of surprises, thereby reducing caregiving strain:

Well, I think communication and setting expectations is important; talking to my
sisters. We have a lot of plans – if this happens, then we do this ... which helps us
try to have some control over if my father keels over, what would we do with mum?
If my mother dies first, what will we do to support my dad? – that kind of thing.

Well, you have to talk to your parents and see what they would like. Try not to be
too prescriptive. Make them feel that it's their decision, not yours. So, you provide
information and options and ... It's a whole aging thing ... like "When are you
going to stop driving? Probably would be good to think about moving before
that."

One in ten felt that setting personal boundaries and having a realistic view of what aspects of the caregiving situation they could and could not control prior to taking on the role of caregiver (not after) helped them manage the situation in a manner that minimized the occurrence of caregiver strain (*be realistic about what you can and cannot do*). For example:

> *I focused on being realistic about what can be achieved in a day.*

Some (one in ten) of the caregivers in our sample stated that they used *delegation* in a proactive (rather than reactive) manner to reduce caregiver strain. More specifically, these individuals actively sought help for the caregiver role from other family members before the situation became a crisis, so that key relationships were already in place when things became really problematic. The following comment reflects this approach:

> *We all care about our family members, both my husband and my children and myself ... We're all supportive of each other. Anything that any of us does to help these elderly people in our lives, we value ... We care about each other, we communicate well, we're in a healthy place to be able to deal with these family crises that come up, because we all care about each other and about them, and that becomes the priority, making this work well. So being in that place, when we have a crisis, we can work through it because the relationships are there already ...*

A similar number of the caregivers in our sample (one in ten) talked about how *maintaining a positive attitude* – towards the situation and the person they were caring for – had helped them avoid caregiver stress ("*I just try to maintain a positive outlook ...*"). These individuals emphasized the importance of picking your battles (with the person you are caring for as well as other family members) and keeping on an even keel (i.e., trying not to get upset/angry). They also recommended that caregivers avoid making any decisions or taking action when tired, angry, and frustrated, as they had found that such actions often exacerbated feelings of stress.

> *Saying yes more often always works. Just shifting things around mentally.*

A lot of times now, when speaking with Mom, I just agree. Even if I don't agree with her, I'll agree with her on the phone. That's what my dad's told me to do. It does help a lot.

Finally, one in ten of the caregivers in our sample talked about the importance of making sure that they were rested *(Don't overload yourself – make time for you)*. These individuals noted that things *"always unravel"* when they are exhausted and felt that they were more able to roll with the punches when they reduced the demands on their time. This strategy is related to one discussed earlier (be realistic) but was slightly different in tone, with more of a focus on reducing demands.

Not overloading myself ... setting limits, calling every night rather than visiting, not answering the phone.

Coping with Caregiver Strain – Advice from Those Who Have Been There

Drink lots of wine. I'm kidding. Find some ways to incorporate your own self-care, like the physical fitness and the wellness, and make that time as important as cleaning their house and doing their grocery shopping, whether that means getting a babysitter for the kids, or just telling your husband, no, you're not going golfing, you're going to stay home because you need some down time. Don't be a doormat. Take charge and tell people what you need from them ... And above all else ... remember why you love them.

Well ... take some time to get all the public support systems in place that would be the first thing. Two, is to figure out how to have the heart-to-heart with the person you are caring for to see how they would like the next few years to go, given what the limitations on everybody are. Then, three, it's the administrative and financial details, get those in order: the power of attorney and wills up to date. All that stuff helps: touch base with the accountant, the financial adviser, so that you're part of the team and if someone becomes incapacitated or unable to manage their affairs, there's no big disruption there. You can transition and take over. And also, make sure you take care of yourself.

Wow. I guess my advice would be that you have to want to do that, like your heart has to be in it … If someone didn't have that emotional attachment and they're just doing it because they have to, it's not going to end well. I think as a child you have to pay them back at this stage in your life, but you don't want to ruin that relationship and be resentful, so find others to help so you are not forced to go beyond the point where you can.

We ended the interview by asking respondents, "What *one* piece of advice would you give to someone assuming care for an elderly dependent?" Responses to this question are incredibly rich (while we asked for one piece of advice only, many gave multiple pieces of advice, as illustrated by the quotations that begin this section), and, in essence, offer us another lens through which to examine how the employees we spoke to cope with the demands and strains inherent in the role of employed caregiver.

The most common piece of advice (mentioned by half of the 111 people we interviewed) was that the prospective caregiver should make sure that they *"get help, talk to other people – don't try to do this on your own"*:

Get some help. Don't do it all yourself. Go to a therapist, and don't feel guilty about it. Recognize that you have to take care of yourself, because too many other people are dependent on you …

Get help … navigating, tapping into the services that are available. Your doctor's probably your best person to talk to, to start with, because they would know of services that are available.

Make sure that they have somebody they can talk to, even if they can't help, they've got to have somebody to talk to and who will at least hear and be sympathetic.

One in four people recommended that caregivers make sure to take care of themselves and *make time for themselves*, as "What will they do if you get sick?"

Look after yourself, because if you can't look after yourself, you can't look after anybody else.

It's very important to find time for yourself. Sometimes, when it seems like you're too busy, you've got to stop and try to balance yourself out and find a bit of time to just do something you normally did before you ended up in this situation, like read a book ... it is a really hard thing to do because pretty much every minute that you have of your spare time ... But you really have to set aside time for yourself.

Approximately one in ten of the caregivers we talked to mentioned each of the following five pieces of advice for people just taking on the caregiving role. First, they stated that they would tell them to *connect with other people who are in a similar situation,* so that they could provide each other with support and advice:

One of the things that I really came across was that at one of the nursing homes they had a group for caregivers and they met once a month. I found it helpful to be able to sit down and talk to other family members about what I think some of the issues are ... there's nobody really to talk to unless it's somebody else who's looking after their parent ... it was run by a social worker, and I thought, this is really a good thing.

Second, they advised them to use adaptive, problem-focused coping strategies such as engaging in problem solving, developing a plan, and using the plan to organize and develop a routine *(plan, organize, and develop a routine):*

Get organized early, as soon as it takes place. Find out what's going on ... see what support there is out there ... start getting home-care in there ...

Third, they counselled them to *set boundaries on what they could and could not do:*

A piece of advice that I'd give? I would set the boundaries right from the beginning, and I would stick to them. I think this is one of the places that I went wrong ... So I think that you have to talk right up front about what the relationship is

*going to look like, and what the boundaries are going to be and what it is that you
can and can't offer.*

*Set limits. Set the parameters. Let them know that you are not available at certain
times. Tell them that you're doing things at certain times that cannot be changed,
so that you don't fall into the trap of being at their beck and call.*

Fourth, they warned new caregivers to *keep things in perspective*:

*Do not let it stress you too much because eventually they're not going to be
around, and that's far worse than the stress.*

*Stop working your tail off, because it's not going to get any better until they're
gone. It's sad but it's true. It's not going to get any better.*

Finally, they recommended that caregivers use an approach that falls
under the adaptive, problem-focused coping-strategy umbrella when
they stated that the way to cope was by *doing the research*:

*I would say, just … before you jump in and take it on, just think carefully about
what you're doing. Research what options are out there to support you and, I
guess, just be very clear with family members about your boundaries.*

Conclusions, Implications, and Recommendations

How can we relate the findings presented in this chapter on how employees cope with caregiver strain to the existing body of knowledge
on coping with stress? To answer this question we mapped our findings
on how the employed caregivers in our sample cope with caregiver
strain to the coping strategies identified in the literature (see table 6.1).
We used a similar strategy to classify the "one piece of advice" the caregivers in our sample gave new caregivers on how best to deal with the
role of caregiver, as shown in table 6.2.

We then use these findings to articulate a number of key conclusions,
as well as the implications of our findings. Recommendations are also
provided, as appropriate, in the section below.

Table 6.2 One Piece of Advice on How to Manage a Caregiving Situation

Emotion Focused (Aimed at Regulating Emotions)	Problem Focused (Aimed at Regulating Behaviour)
Adaptive Coping	
Seek social support for emotional reasons • Connect with others in similar situation as yourself – emotional support Practise emotional restraint • Keep things in perspective	Confront the problem • Set boundaries on what you can and cannot do Take calculated action • Plan, organize, and prioritize • Do the research Get constructive support • Connect with others in similar situation as yourself – practical support Practice behavioural restraint • Make time for yourself

Many caregivers are "their own worst enemy"

Employees use a lot of different strategies to cope with the challenges of caregiving. While many employees use adaptive, problem-focused, and emotion-focused strategies to cope with caregiver strain (see table 6.1), the use of maladaptive coping techniques is also relatively high. This would suggest that to some degree the high levels of stress and emotional strain experienced by the caregivers in this sample are caused not only by the situation they face but also by how they deal with these challenges. This is also consistent with the fact that one in four of the caregivers in our sample said that the coping strategies they used were not effective at alleviating their levels of stress.

The hows and whys of coping with caregiver strain are personal and varied

The following key conclusions on how caregivers cope with the stresses of this role are supported by the data provided in this chapter:

• The reasons people gave for using the coping strategies they did were quite varied and often quite personal and idiosyncratic.

- There is a high degree of overlap between the coping strategies people use to deal with the emotions elicited by their caregiving situation and the tactics they use to handle the more pragmatic and general aspects of caregiving.
- Many caregivers engage in anticipatory coping activities in an effort to reduce the occurrence of caregiver strain. As shown in table 6.1, virtually all proactive coping efforts involved the use of adaptive, problem-oriented coping techniques.
- Many caregivers cope by reaching out to a social support network that consists largely of family and friends. By talking and venting to others, these employees were more able to put their situation into perspective and to get rid of their frustrations in a safe environment.
- Many caregivers use emotion-focused positive coping techniques to help them cope. Caregivers who took this approach spent time in activities that provided them with the opportunity to decompress in a healthy way.
- One in three of the caregivers in this sample use adaptive, problem-focused strategies (i.e., planning, organizing, and prioritizing) either to cope with the stress or in an effort to prevent the strain from occurring. As noted earlier, such strategies are highly effective at reducing strain and improving well-being.
- Many of the caregivers in this sample use coping strategies that are likely to contribute to declines in their physical and/or mental health over time (e.g., drink alcohol, just try and do it all).
- Few caregivers cope by having the difficult conversations with the care recipient. Those who used this approach to coping with the situation were, however, unanimous in their belief that this approach had positive consequences for all involved and reduced their stress levels substantially.
- The vast majority of the caregivers we talked to (80%) acknowledged that they personally did a number of things that made their caregiving situation worse. Examination of the strategies summarized in table 6.1 supports their perceptions, as many of the behaviours that they talked about here were examples of maladaptive, emotion-focused coping strategies that involved avoidance and escape.

*Caregivers recognize the importance of dealing
with the emotional aspects of caregiving*

A couple of additional conclusions can be drawn from the recommendations in table 6.2. First, it is important to note that much of the advice the
experienced caregivers in our sample offered to others taking on the role
was likely to promote employee well-being. No one advised new caregivers to use any of the avoidance-type coping techniques listed in table
6.1 – even though many of these individuals used such coping strategies
themselves to manage their own situation. This would suggest that caregivers know what they should do but sometimes find it difficult to apply
these strategies to their own personal situation. Second, it should be
noted that a lot of the advice offered by experienced caregivers seems to
focus on how to deal with the emotional aspects of caregiving rather
than the logistical or physical elements of care. This is not surprising
given the data presented earlier showing that the emotional aspects of
caregiving are the main contributors to caregiver strain.

Implications and recommendations

The insights presented this chapter on coping with caregiver strain imply that policy makers and mental health practitioners need to identify
those mechanisms that will lead to an increase in the number of caregivers who use (1) adaptive, problem-focused coping strategies such as
planning and researching; (2) anticipatory, problem-focused coping
techniques (again, these revolve around planning, organizing, and researching); and (3) adaptive, emotion-focused strategies such as seeking social support. We also need to determine how best to reduce the
use of maladaptive strategies within the population. How we achieve
these goals might take many forms, including educational programs
within the community and workplace ("the dos and don'ts of caregiving"), the development of caregiver support networks within the community and the workplace, and the implementation of "caregiver
support hotlines" that provide information and resources to caregivers
who are seeking help. We would recommend further examination of

the utility of each of these approaches at enhancing employees' ability to cope with the challenges and emotional stresses inherent in the role of employed caregiver. Of course, none of these strategies will be effective if the caregiver does not have the time to spend in such activities. How this could be addressed is discussed, along with a fuller set of recommendations, in the next chapter, which addresses how others can help caregivers cope with the demands they face at work, at home, and in the community.

Chapter Seven

I'll Get By with a Little Help from My Friends: Coping with Caregiver Strain

They're starting to get used to the idea that people want to be parents and be able to work, it's ... progressing, say, from earlier in my career when maternity leaves were very short and women had to behave like they didn't have families. In terms of eldercare, it's after the fact you hear about how stressful it has been for a person who's been taking care of an elderly either parent or relative. It's one of those invisible things ... we need to make it visible ... it's a continuum of strain on people who are working.

Research on caregiver mental health suggests that, although caregiving can be stressful, taking on this role does not necessarily always lead to adverse mental health outcomes if caregivers make use of effective coping mechanisms and have access to supports in the community and the workplace. These findings imply that interested employers and policy makers might be able to minimize the extent to which the caregivers in their workforce and/or their community experience the downsides of taking on this role by implementing appropriate workplace and community supports.

In chapter 6 we made the case that employees who were more able to cope effectively with the inevitable stresses and strains of caregiving were more likely to be truly effective caregivers. While caregivers can and do use a number of strategies to cope with the demands this role places on their time and the emotional strain that seems to be part and parcel of caregiving, it is also important to recognize that caregivers are embedded within a number of social networks (e.g., family, work, community, Canadian society). Stakeholders from these various networks can (and often do) take actions that can either facilitate or make it more challenging for caregivers to execute their various roles: caregiver, parent, employee, partner/spouse. Using data from the interview phase of the 2012 Study, this chapter expands our examination of how employees cope with the demands and strains inherent in the employed caregiver role by including in the discussion the actions of other stakeholders in this relationship that can exacerbate as well as alleviate caregiver strain.

The chapter is divided into six sections. The first section provides a brief overview of the academic and practitioner literatures on strategies employers and communities can use to help employed caregivers cope with the demands and emotional strains associated with this role. This is followed, in sections two through five, by an examination of how the actions taken by four key stakeholders (family members, the employer, the community, the government) may make the caregiver's situation more or less manageable. The chapter ends with a summary of our findings with respect to how the actions of other key stakeholders impact employees' ability to effectively balance paid employment with caregiving; as well, it offers key recommendations that are supported by the data. This chapter, in combination with the material covered in chapter 6, should provide valuable assistance to those tasked with designing programs to support employees who are providing caregiving.

Coping with Caregiver Strain: Answers from Academia

A review of the literature on coping with caregiver strain identifies two main streams. The first stream is written by health-care practitioners (e.g., the American Psychological Association [APA], WebMD, the Mayo Clinic, the National Institute of Health) and advocacy groups (e.g., the American Association of Retired People [AARP], the Canadian Association of Retired People [CARP], the Alzheimer's Association). These practitioners and advocacy groups focus on offering practical tips to individual caregivers on how to cope with caregiver strain. For example, AARP offers the following suggestions on ways that caregivers can deal with the strain of their situation in a "healthy" fashion: get enough exercise; get enough sleep; eat proper food; make time for hobbies; ask for support from family, friends, or community resources; stop smoking; accept that there are events you cannot control; and set realistic goals and expectations. They also outline the causes and symptoms of caregiver burnout. Similarly, the APA provides on its website an excellent link to a number of key resources for caregivers.[1]

The second stream of literature on coping with caregiver stress is written by academics. Scanning the titles of the first several hundred of these articles leaves one with the impression that most research in this area is focused somewhat narrowly on caregivers caring for someone with a specific medical condition (e.g., Alzheimer's, dementia, terminal cancer, mental illness, a traumatic injury, a stroke). There were also a number of academic articles on elderly spouse caregivers and caregivers who cared for someone who was in a hospice, or caregivers in a particular socio-cultural group (e.g., African-American). Many of the more technical articles in the academic literature tested statistical models to determine if coping strategies were best viewed as a mediator or a moderator between some measure of caregiver demands and some measure of caregiver well-being.

The coping literature is extensive, and a complete review of the work in this field is beyond the scope of this chapter. Accordingly, we elected to focus our review at a more macro level and provide an overview of four approaches to the management of caregiver strain that seem to offer promise for those interested in addressing this issue: caregiver networks, employer support, community support, and public policy.

Caregiver network strategies

There are several ways that individual caregivers can cope with the strains associated with balancing eldercare and paid employment. To prepare for a caregiving role, a person may obtain information from the local library, health professionals, social workers, for-profit and

---

1 http://www.apa.org/pi/about/publications/caregivers/resources/key-websites.aspx.

not-for-profit care providers, family, friends, colleagues, other caregivers, aging or disease-specific organizations, government programs, or the Internet (De Graff 2002; Mathew Greenwald and Associates 2009). There may also be benefits to inquiring about training and skill-development options, respite services, help with day-to-day chores, and sources of emotional and financial support (Gahagan et al. 2004).

When caregivers were asked what assistance would be most useful to them, "occasional relief" was the most frequent response (Pyper 2006). Almost 70 per cent of caregivers reported that they needed a break from caregiving responsibilities either frequently (21%) or occasionally (47%) (Gahagan et al. 2004; Pyper 2006). While the desire for occasional relief was quite common among low-intensity caregivers, high-intensity caregivers (employees who combined longer hours of work with long hours of physically and emotionally taxing caregiving) reported an even greater need for relief. Occasional relief comes from a variety of sources, including family members, paid formal help, or government-arranged home care (Pyper 2006). Interestingly, in a Statistics Canada report, individuals in the "sandwich generation" were more likely than those caring for the elderly alone to feel as though they could do a better job if respite care were available (52% vs 46%) (Williams 2004).

Men and women seek support in different ways. Women have broader and more intimate networks of friends and colleagues; they attend support groups more often and consult therapists. Men, on the other hand, often avoid speaking about their eldercare issues at work and tend to limit discussions on the subject to their spouse. Men are also more likely to use online bulletin boards or establish phone-based caregiver networks (Abel 1991; Harris 1998; Henderson 2002; MetLife 2003).

The literature links access to informal networks to improved caregiver health. Female caregivers who share their care responsibilities with their informal network, for example, were found to report 30 per cent less stress than women who try to cope on their own. Reaching out for support is a strategy that women should be using more often, despite the fear of exposure or of being judged (Neufeld and Harrison 2000). The 2002 GSS reports that family offers the strongest caregiving network (Stobert and Cranswick 2004). Women most often turn to their sisters for help with caregiving tasks, while spouses and children are also frequently asked to help out. Women rarely seek help with basic care from their brothers, as brothers tend to engage in more sporadic assistance, financial support, and problem solving (Harris 1998; Montgomery 1992).

At work, caregivers may talk to their co-workers and supervisors and negotiate ways to adjust their work schedules to be able to meet their caregiving obligations (Mature Market Institute 1999). It is worth noting that work itself can serve as a respite from caregiving for both men and women. In fact, one study found that men who worked more hours suffered from less caregiving distress (Chumbler, Pienta, and Dwyer 2004).

Support offered by employers

Flexible scheduling, job sharing, telecommuting, family illness days, family leave, and similar policies have been consistently advocated in the literature to help reduce the conflict between work and caregiving responsibilities (Guberman 1999; Duxbury and Higgins 2003; Pyper 2006; Barr, Johnson, and Warshaw 1992). Neal and colleagues (1993), for example, found that flexible schedules and workplace policies supporting caregivers were linked to increased productivity due to stronger employee morale, reduced stress, and a feeling of loyalty to the employer. Similarly, "flexible work arrangements" (flexitime, compressed work weeks, irregular work hours, reduced hours of work, flexible location, and protected part-time status) were found to be associated with decreased work interference with caregiving (Scharlach 1994).

While the benefits of workplace support programs are commonly reported (Boddy, Cameron, and Moss 2006; Lechner and Gupta 1996; Neal et al. 1993), many such workplace programs are available to only a minority of Canadian workers (typically those working for large companies) and are provided in a discretionary manner. They also do not provide much assistance when workplace factors that contribute to difficulties balancing work and caregiving – such as heavy workloads; non-supportive management; unclear policies; continuous change; temporary, part-time, and contingent work; and non-supportive organizational cultures – are not addressed (Fredriksen and Scharlach 1999; Duxbury and Higgins 2003). Finally, policies do little good if the employee is working in an organization where cultural acceptance of eldercare responsibilities is low (Calvano 2013) – a state that, according to our research, describes many Canadian workplaces.

With the appropriate policies and supports in place, employment has the potential to offer significant advantages to caregivers. Employment provides caregivers with relief from their care responsibilities, greater financial and social resources, and additional support networks (Rosenthal et al. 2004).

Community support

Caregivers and their families rely on a variety of community supports to meet their needs. Some caregivers actively request support from the community in order to provide better care, while others are unaware of what supports exist and which ones will help them. Caregiver requests have included the development or expansion of educational, informational, and support programs that enable care providers to offer better care and successfully cope with the strains of caregiving (Keefe 2002). Counselling services that provide coping strategies, advice, and support have also been identified as necessary and helpful. Another important support is information and referral services to help caregivers navigate community services. Caregiving necessitates a continuum of services and supports, including training and education, respite, and other care services, in conjunction with workplace policies, job security, and income compensation programs (Rajnovich et al. 2005).

Public policy

The challenges that caregivers face when dealing with social policy are compounded by the "ambiguous status of caregivers" (Rajnovich, Keefe, and Fast 2005, 28) in our society. Since caregivers are not official clients of the health and social services systems, they are generally only entitled to services through the care receiver (Guberman 1999). Assessments tend to give little attention to caregivers' needs, despite research that supports the need to do so. Furthermore, when determining needs and entitlements, the underlying premise of many care programs is that families, often women, are responsible for providing care. Services are provided not to support or ease the burden of the caregiver but only as a last option to fill gaps not being met by family. This practice must be challenged, and public policy must look at the social and economic needs of caregivers.

Currently, there exists a fragmented array of supports. Tax credits, compensation programs, and workplace policies have been identified as critical to relieving and supporting caregivers. However, conditions for accessing such programs are often limiting and are cited as requiring re-examination (Eales, Keating, and Fast 2001).

In 2004 the Government of Canada introduced the Compassionate Care Benefits Employment Insurance (CCB)[2] program:

> Compassionate Care is a special benefit of Employment Insurance. It provides temporary income support for eligible workers who take leave to provide care or support for a family member who has a significant risk of death within six months. To be eligible, it will be necessary to submit a medical certificate from the attending physician of the family member who is ill.

The CCB is considered Canada's foremost workplace policy support for emergency caregiving situations and is a concrete recognition of the diversity and strain experienced by employed caregivers. In light of the increasing heterogeneity of families, in June 2006 the CCB expanded its definition of "family" to include a broader conceptualization of the term. While this represents a step in the right direction, critics of the CCB have noted several additional ways that this program could be improved. These suggestions include expanding eligibility (to include *all* who provide significant levels of care); increasing the benefit amounts (current benefits are inaccessible to some low-income workers); extending eligible caregiving relationships to include in-laws, aunts and uncles, friends, and neighbours; expanding the program to provide access to contract,

---

2 For a description of this program, see: http://www.hrsdc.gc.ca/en/ei/types/ compassionate_care.shtml.

temporary, self-employed, and part-time workers who are currently not eligible; and extending the amount of paid leave time.[3]

Coping with Caregiver Strain – Support from Family

My family does nothing, nothing ... I can't believe that I am shouldering all this responsibility and ... I'm really hurt that no one else is stepping up and it's all been dumped in my lap ...

As noted above, most caregivers rely on support from their family to help them cope with the strain of caregiving. Three questions were included in the interview study to help us better understand how family members can and do support their partners and/or relatives who are providing care: "What does your family do to help you cope with caregiver strain?" "What else could they do?" "Do they do anything that makes it harder for you to cope?" Responses to these three questions are discussed below.

What does your family do to help you cope with caregiver strain?

Just over one in four (28%) of the caregivers we spoke to indicated that they received no support at all from their family (*"Nothing – I am on my own"*). The following comments typify what we heard from this group of caregivers:

They avoid me ... they know if they stay away then they won't have to take on anything ... they don't hear of what she needs so therefore they don't have to offer to help.

My family? My siblings do nothing. Nothing. They don't phone, they don't ... they don't do anything.

The rest of the caregivers in our sample talked about two ways their family supported them. The vast majority of these (half of the caregivers

---

3 An excellent critique of this program can be found at: http://www.rapp.ualberta.ca/ en/Publications/~/media/rapp/Publications/Documents/Intl_Policy_Comparison_ of_Compassionate_Car_Benefit_2008Dec.pdf.

we spoke to, both male and female) spoke quite passionately about how their *partner provided both emotional and practical caregiving support.* Practically, their spouse helped the individual with caregiving duties:

> *When my dad was in the hospital last time we had to feed him. My husband did break-fast and lunch and then I did supper every day. And Dad was in the hospital for about three weeks. So my husband's incredible. The rest of my family ... not so much. They keep telling me I'm doing a wonderful job and just keep at it. But my husband is amaz-ing; he does the best he can ... I just do not know how I would do it without him ...*

Emotionally, caregivers' partners listened and took their side:

> *My partner ... has always been by my side, no matter what was going on, and helping me through the really emotional time where I realized my mother was basically gone.*

The importance of this form of support is underlined by the fact that virtually all of the interviewees who gave this response stated that they did not know how they would cope with all they had to do at work and at home without the kind of support they received from their signifi-cant other.

The data also show that *support from other family members* is also im-portant to the caregiver. Just over one in four (28%) of those in the inter-view sample talked about how much they appreciated the support they received from their own children and grandchildren:

> *Just having the kids keep going to see their grandma ... that is really good ... they pick up a little of the slack ... and by just letting you vent – they are being supportive.*

> *The grandkids really help ... they are just there for them ...*

Another one in five talked about support they received from their siblings:

> *We're [the three siblings] looking at seeing if we could, maybe, hire a house-keeper if all of us pool together ... that will really help.*

Analysis of the comments suggests that support offered by immediate family is somewhat different from the kinds of support offered by siblings. More specifically, respondents talked about receiving both emotional and instrumental support from their partner and children, while support from siblings more often involved listening and offering verbal support.

What else could your family do?

Half of the employees we talked to could not think of anything more that their family could do to help them cope with the stress of caregiving ("*Nothing – they are already doing all they can*"). They clarified this response by noting either that their family was already doing enough ("*No, they're wonderful*") or by recognizing that there were circumstances that made it hard for their family to do more ("*They do not live in the area*"; "*They are physically unable to assist*"). One respondent summed up this view as follows:

> *I'm not sure, I don't think that my family could do anything different other than live their lives the way they're living them.*

One in three of the caregivers we spoke to talked about how they would like their siblings to "*step up*" – to make more of an effort to visit with their parents; to offer more help to "Mom and Dad"; or to increase their involvement in the problem-solving process (i.e., offer more instrumental support). We grouped these responses in a category that we labelled *Siblings need to "step up."*

> *Sometimes when I say* [to my husband], *I have to stay home, he'll say to me, I think your brother or sister should look after it and you should come up to the cottage. And that sounds perfect, but to get them to look after it is another thing. He is right. They should participate more ... make more of an effort ... but they don't. So it is what it is, and I get tired of arguing that point.*

> *The only thing ... and this would be common, I think, in most families ... there's always adult children that help a lot and there's always adult children who do not.*

My brother, I'd have to say, does nothing to help ... you would like it if everyone could be counted on ... but that is just not going to happen.

It is also interesting to note that almost no one we talked to (only two people!) felt that their immediate family members (spouse, children) could do more than they already were.

Does your family do anything that makes things worse?

While half of the respondents indicated that their family did not do anything to make matters worse, the other half identified two main ways that their siblings made their caregiving situation more challenging: *they don't offer help ("they never offer help ... they just wait for me to ask for it. I hate always having to ask ... it is their father too ...")* and *they are not there for me ("They make false promises ... They say they're going to be there for me, then they don't show up ...").* Finally, none of the caregivers we talked to said that their partner and children did anything to make their caregiving situation worse.

Coping with Caregiver Strain – Support from Employers

My company has "Bring your kid to work"; imagine that was "Bring your mother to work" ... they need to rethink the whole thing – family leave days should not just be about kids.

Well ... I find accommodations at work to be quite interesting because it seems to me that people get work accommodations for flexitime and stuff ... when their kids are small, but for those of us whose kids are grown ... nothing.

The above comments represent the sentiments expressed by many of the caregivers we spoke to – that employers are willing to recognize the challenges faced by the parents in their workforce and to provide flexibility for parents of young children but do not recognize the needs of their employees with caregiving responsibility. How do employers facilitate and hinder the ability of employed caregivers to cope with the dual demands of work and caregiving? The responses our caregivers gave to our questions about this issue are discussed in the section below.

What does your employer do to help you cope with caregiver strain?

Almost one in three of the employees we talked to said that they received no support from their employer (*"Nothing – nothing at all"*) for the issues they faced balancing work and caregiving (*"No, no they don't. They really don't."*). Many, in fact, spoke at length about the lack of support for eldercare issues within their organization:

> *I felt very, very, very powerless there for a while. I just felt that they were completely not understanding of my situation ... if you take time off they treat you like you're a ne'er-do-well ... trying to cheat the system or something like that. That's ultimately how I felt like they perceived me; that I was taking advantage of the situation.*

> *When I asked to go part-time it was, like, if you can't cope, quit.*

More than one caregiver noted that in their opinion, the issues associated with eldercare were just symptomatic of what was going on the Canadian labour market in general. For example:

> *The social safety net for vulnerable people is shrinking in Canada, and that attitude of isolation and not worrying about other people and focusing on costs ... it sneaks into the workplace, and there is just no support for employees anymore ... if you have to take time off to look after an aging or ailing parent or child or whatever caregiving situation, it's like, okay, well, good luck,'bye ...*

This negative view was offset by the fact that half of the employees we talked to were able to identify things that their employer did that they found helped them cope with their caregiving situation. A substantial number of respondents (38%) appreciated the fact that their employer allowed them to *take time off / take a leave of absence* to cope with their caregiving situation:

I've never had a big problem getting time off when I need it ... they pretty well bend over backwards ... I don't really expect my employers to do any more than that.

Almost one in three talked very generally about how their *employer was supportive* but supplied few concrete details:

If I needed to go out, let's say, to go out for an emergency or something, they would just say go ... the underlying culture of the department is that family is important and you take care of that.

Well, they have all kinds of leaves. We've got a great employee services system if you need to take advantage of it; very good supportive management, so it's pretty good, as good as you can hope for.

They're very good. I work really long hours, but they're also very, very flexible with my ability to do workarounds. So that, more than anything, keeps me here.

One in five said that the fact that their employer allowed them to work *flexitime and/or telework arrangements* helped them cope with the uncertainties of caregiving:

My employer was very understanding ... they offered some flexibility in my work hours, and I was able to work at home for periods of time, so I could schedule visits to doctors and other people involved in my mother's care.

I have a lot of flexibility at work ... My manager says if I need to do something I can come in early, leave early, come in late and stay late, pretty much whatever hours I need to work, she totally trusts me. So I guess that's partly her personality and partly my work ethic, like she knows I'm not going to take advantage ...

One in five said it was not their organization that helped them. Rather they noted that it was the manager they reported to who helped them cope – not their employer *(immediate manager very supportive)*. They provided a number of examples of supportive management behaviours:

> *I need to be clear that when I say support from the employer, I mean from my manager as opposed to organizationally … I think in other circumstances … with, perhaps, a different manager, I might not have gotten that amount of flexibility. So I felt incredibly grateful for the type of manager that I have, who understood the circumstances and was flexible.*

> *My supervisors are both good … very understanding … very compassionate. If I need a couple of hours here or there, they let me go. I make up the time because I work hard … But no, I don't think my employer does anything.*

It is noteworthy that all the employees who felt their organization and/or their manager supported their caregiving demands also talked about how they, in turn, felt obligated to get their work done. This would suggest that employers who give their employees the flexibility and support they need to cope with the often unpredictable demands associated with caregiving realize higher levels of employee engagement and likely minimize the productivity declines identified in chapter 5.

Finally, relatively few of the caregivers we talked to (8%) mentioned that the employee assistance program (EAP) offered by their organization had really helped them cope with stress:

> *I see a therapist … and I'll give my employer credit … I do that through the EAP program, so I don't have to pay for it and then give time away to go to counselling.*

What else could your employer do?

> *What else could they do? Oh, nothing that I think is in their power to do. I just need more time.*

This sentiment, that there was *nothing else their employer could do* to help them cope with the stress of caregiving, was expressed by just over half of the employees we talked to. Most of the employees who gave this response noted that the problem boiled down to the fact that there were just not enough hours in the day to do everything that needed to be done:

I don't think so. It's just that when things happen, they happen … it's just a time factor.

One in four respondents made a passionate plea to their employer with respect to the need for *compassionate care leave*. Personal experience had taught all of these individuals that the leave policies in their place of work, generous though some of them might be, just did not provide enough support to caregivers who were caring for dependents who were nearing the end of their lives:

My employer lets me have five personal days related to my dad and that's really nice, but I don't really know when to take them … When he goes into the hospital, because of his age and his frailty, I need to be there all the time … and it's only five days … if there was anything, it would be more time to care for our elderly when we need to, because it's only short-term [and then they die].

I don't know if the workplace can make allowances for people who are, like me, in a special situation. I could go on sick leave, but I'm not sick. They have provisions for certain things, but they don't have a provision for something like this …

Others (one in ten) said that a *compressed work week schedule* would really help – much more than flexitime – as it would give them an extra day to take their parents to medical appointments that were scheduled during work hours:

It's like you wish that there was some sort of a program where, if you said, okay … I can only work four days a week … that would work out really well, but there's just no way.

As noted earlier, the academic literature in the area notes that "family-friendly" policies and programs alone, while necessary, are not sufficient if the organizational culture acts as a barrier to their use. One in ten of the caregivers we talked to spoke about this issue and said that organizations could do more by visibly embracing the issue of eldercare and focusing on *creating an organizational culture that supports* (rather than negatively stereotypes) caregivers:

Employers need to embrace the issue more visibly – that might change perceptions and attitudes ... but the culture in the office right now makes it hard to get access to any kind of flexible work arrangement ... If I could work from home then sometimes it would really help ... but we're not allowed.

In terms of my employer ... I think the problem is that there's a sense ... that if you ask for help, they'll be supportive at the time, but it's going to be held against you in the long run.

Finally, a small number of caregivers made suggestions on the types of workshops that they would like their employer to offer specifically for those who are caring for elderly dependents:

They might have a workshop on getting enough sleep, or they could have a workshop on caring for people with dementia or what your role is as executor.

Does your employer do anything that makes things worse?

Two-thirds of the employees in this sample indicated that while their employer did nothing to facilitate their efforts to balance work and caregiving, they also *did nothing to make it harder* for them to cope with eldercare demands. The rest of the caregivers we talked to did, however, identify three ways that their employer "made things worse."

One in ten of the caregivers we interviewed noted that their employer had very *high expectations with respect to workloads and deliverables.* This made caregiving more challenging, since their employer did not take into consideration the demands caregiving was placing on the employee's time:

The employer expects me to produce and perform at the level that people with no obligations do – evenings, weekends ...

Employees who gave this response talked in particular about the fact that their employer expected employees to be connected to work in the evening and on weekends and to work through their lunch hours, and did not recognize that this time now had to be spent in caregiving:

> You're expected to be there all of the time, all-in, twenty-four/seven for the period of a project, which even without eldercare is stressful … it becomes very all or nothing … just unforgiving, when there's a deadline.

Others talked about the challenges they faced when they took unpaid leave to deal with their caregiving situation, only to come back to work and find everything waiting for them (*work waiting when return from unpaid leave*):

> The other problem … is finding somebody to replace me … so what I often find is that I just come back to a pile of work, and even though I've used up leave time … I actually now have to do the work that I didn't do while I was on leave.

Others (10%) noted that the fact that their employer was *unsupportive of time off work for caregiving* made things more challenging and exacerbated their perceptions of stress:

> Yes, there's huge pressure to not take any time off …

Finally, one in ten caregivers felt that their employer made things worse by being *inflexible* with respect to work hours, work location, vacation time, and time even for lunch!

> Yes, I think that what the employer does that makes things worse is definitely giving a sense … that although options are available, like leave without pay, and support for leave, there's a general sense that it's not okay to use those options, and I really don't know why they have options that you then feel like you can't use.

> Yes, really no sympathy when I do need to take time off … they are just not willing to be flexible … And just making me feel like, oh, there she's going to have to take another day off, even though they know that I work many, many long hours. I do

a lot of overtime that I don't ask for time off, and so it's like, how can you possibly say anything bad about the fact that I need to take the occasional one or maybe two days a month … But anyway, that's the way it is.

Coping with Caregiver Strain – Support from the Community

We don't do anything that's targeted around our aging population; we might do park lunches for kids in the summer, but we never do anything that would be about providing some caring in a broad sense to seniors.

Three questions were included in the interview script to increase our understanding of how the community within which employed caregivers live helps and/or hinders their execution of the caregiving role. More specifically, we asked: "What does your community do to help you cope with caregiver strain?" "What else could they do?" "Do they do anything that makes it harder for you to cope?" Responses to these three questions are discussed below.

What does your community do to help you cope with caregiver strain?

The data from this study indicate that very few Canadian communities offer their citizens any form of support to help them provide care to elderly dependents. In fact just over half of the caregivers we talked to indicated that their community did *absolutely nothing* to help them cope with the stress of caregiving:

I don't see too much support from the community.

It seems like any community help costs money a lot of the time, and it's not really an option for me to shell out additional money … So I just cope as best I can …

Another 10 per cent of the employees we talked to indicated that they had *no idea* what their community offered, suggesting that, if resources are there, they are not well communicated to those in the at-risk group.

I've never really gone out to my community to find out what they could do to help me. I'm not sure what I need ... I don't know what I need to look for ... I don't even know where to begin my search.

Caregivers in rural communities also made the point that the lack of support for seniors was part of a much larger issue – a *systemic lack of services in smaller Canadian communities*:

I don't see what else they could do ... everybody in a small town has issues with how far away everything is, with getting services, period ... getting doctors to come up to the middle of nowhere. I don't know what more the community could do ...

While these data are quite damning, it is also important to note that virtually no one we talked to stated that their community did anything to make their caregiving situation worse. Rather, they felt that their community was just *"not there"* when it came to offering support for an issue that was of concern to many of their citizens.

The interview data do, however, show that when community services are available, they are seen as helpful and much appreciated. What does seem to help? *Community facilities* (e.g., church programs, recreational events, homecare programs):

Yes, we actually have a senior centre in the community, and I think that's really, really good. And one of the programs that the centre runs connects youth with the senior citizens and that, I think, is really beneficial ...

Meals on Wheels and *para-transport* were also both singled out by a substantial number of caregivers (20% mentioned each of these forms of support) as making a real difference:

[Our community] has Meals on Wheels and it has a seniors' bus. And it has homecare. Homecare does very light work, and the Meals on Wheels, she gets meals on Mondays, Wednesdays, and Fridays.

My mother ... She didn't have her license for a while, so she had people driving her. She has meals delivered. She's been offered resources that she doesn't always accept, but there are more resources out there for her.

Other respondents (15%) talked about a different community that supported them – *their church.* In fact, this voluntary service seemed to be the only source of support many received from their community:

She's a member of a church, and the people in the church are very kind and good about having various activities set up for the older people in the congregation ...

Well, I belong to the United Church ... and they're very supportive because a lot of them are going through the same thing.

What else could your community do?

While half the caregivers we talked to felt that community support for caregiving was *"just not there,"* virtually all of the caregivers in our sample were able to offer suggestions on what the community could do to help them cope with the demands caregiving places on them. Five of the six suggestions were offered by 20 to 30 per cent of the employees we talked to, demonstrating a high degree of agreement on what might help and a clear way forward for communities who wish to support the caregivers in their community.

Many of the employees we spoke to expressed a high level of frustration with the challenges that they had encountered in trying to "navigate" an overly complicated seniors' support system with multiple players and blurred lines of accountability and responsibility. These people asked their community to set up "one number that caregivers within the community could call to get advice and help" – to provide expert guidance, advice, and assistance for those with caregiving issues *(Give us guidance on how to find and access support services).* For example:

I guess there were times when I was looking for information, eldercare information, or even volunteer drivers or that sort of thing; I found information on that kind of thing really hard to find. It was not that it didn't exist, it was almost like it was too much and it was scattered, and I just needed a one-stop shop somewhere that I could go and say, okay, I need to deal with this question. And I didn't want to be pointed to every single volunteer organization or CCAC thing …

I suspect the information is there … but who has the time to navigate the systems and locate it? … I think it would just be nice … if there was somebody in the community who was an expert who could help …

A similar number of caregivers requested more seniors' community centres and *programming for seniors and caregivers in the community*. For example:

There's not a support group for caregivers in this area … it's needed. Every once in a while there's a workshop, and it tells you to take time for yourself and get your nails done, blah, blah, blah. It sounds really good, but …

I do think there should be more community centres for the aged, that people can go to … maybe go for a hot meal and some companionship once or twice a week …

I am totally frustrated that there's not more programs available for seniors …

An equally large number of the people we interviewed spoke quite passionately about how there were no facilities or supports in their community for elderly people who wanted (and were able) to live semi-independently. These caregivers felt that the community should address this issue by offering more *affordable accommodation options for semi-independent seniors*:

The problem is that she's living in a big house by herself … in the city where she lives, retirement homes are the only other option and they represent too much care. And it's that middle sort of graduated care step that's missing.

There could be more senior living spaces that are not nursing homes; that are places for people to live, that support people that are well and happy and want a good life, and want to live in a social environment. There's nothing really wrong with my mom. She just wants her independence. She wants her own little place, and there doesn't really seem to be much out there that doesn't cost a fortune. The private centres are really expensive, and the ones that provide government assistance aren't for her. There seems to be a huge gap in-between.

One in five of the employees in our sample felt that the solution was more high-quality and reliable *in-home care options* (e.g., cleaning, Meals on Wheels) for seniors who wanted to remain in their own homes. In fact, many of the caregivers we talked to requested the kinds of support that other Canadians living in other communities had noted made a difference:

If they do live independently, and you just want to buy a little help here and there … but nothing is available …

One in five also noted that *more transportation options for the elderly* (e.g., transportation for medical appointments, greater accessibility of public transportation) were needed in their communities:

Maybe transportation to and from the doctors' appointments, if that would be possible, and things like that. Transportation would be huge …

They could provide transportation for my parents to and from these medical appointments … this would really help with the stress.

Finally, a smaller number of those in our interview sample (10%) stated it would be helpful if the community *extended the opening hours for seniors' support services within the community* – a finding that is not surprising given the fact that all the caregivers in our sample were employed:

It's pretty silly, but everything has to be done during nine-to-five hours. That's when doctors' appointments are; that's when recycling places are open. And it's really a stupid thing, but that's what I find really stressful, because I have to try running around and doing it on my lunch hour, right?

Coping with Caregiver Strain – Support from the Government

I don't know of any programs … relief or assistance … that could be used. If they are out there, I think they need to promote them a little bit better. If they aren't out there, I think creating them would be a good idea, because I think a lot of people are facing the same issue. Eldercare is becoming more relevant.

They need to do a better job of just letting us know more about what is out there – what resources are available, how to access them, the cost … that kind of thing.

Three questions were included in the interview script to increase our understanding of how the actions of one final, key, external stakeholder – government (provincial and federal) – may help or hinder employed caregivers in balancing work and care for one or more elderly family members: "What does the government do to help you cope with caregiver strain?" "What else could they do?" "Do they do anything that makes it harder for you to cope?" Responses to these questions are provided below.

What does the government do to help you cope with caregiver strain?

Two-thirds of the employed caregivers we talked to were not aware of any policies or practices put in place by governments (provincial and federal) to support citizens who are looking after elderly dependents (*government does nothing to support employed caregivers*). This would suggest either that such supports are not readily available and/or that governments are not doing a good enough job of informing the public of what is available. The following comments typify what we heard from caregivers with respect to government support for caregiving:

I think from my perspective, there's a lot of lip service for support for these types of things from the government and not a lot of true support for it … I don't think our society is ready to deal with aging, let alone the government.

No service that I have tapped into. None that I'm aware of either ... Maybe I'm just naive ... but I'm not even aware of any assistance for people who are taking care of elderly dependents.

I have no idea what the federal government's done to help me cope ...

The only government support mentioned by a substantial number of respondents (20%) was related to services offered by the Community Care Access Centres (CCAC) that operate in Ontario:

What she does have right now is through the CCAC ... I guess that is the provincial government ... they do provide her with two baths a week. And they do provide her with a little bit of homecare to help her get dressed for the day and dressed for the evening and to make sure that she takes all her medications.

It is noteworthy, however, that even in those cases where the person mentioned a specific type of support there was a lot of confusion with respect to who did what and what services were available:

The province ... I guess they're the people that deal with CCAC, but I'm not sure; I'm not quite sure, really ...

One in ten acknowledged (and appreciated) the *old-age pension* provided by the federal government (*"Well, pensions are really helpful"*). The sentiment here, however, was that pensions, while an important form of support, offered only a limited degree of support:

He gets his Canadian Pension Plan and that's all he really has.

The rest of the respondents (20%) gave idiosyncratic answers that seemed to be specific to a particular community –

I think the early intervention in care makes a difference. One of the things that they're doing is the nurse practitioners in B.C., where the nurse can do a lot of the doctor's work, so it's taking a lot of the load off of the doctors ... any program that keeps them out of the hospital … is great … they recognize the importance of the social aspect of care.

– or a particular situation.

The federal government does offer some EI if your parent is, essentially, dying.

Veterans Affairs is very good. You can call them. It's a little bit tricky to know what he's eligible for, but one day I took an afternoon off and I thought, today I'm going to figure out what he's eligible for through Veterans Affairs. And I called them and finally, after being shuffled around, I finally got someone who could answer my questions … They're not quite as cheap as I thought they should be. But Veterans Affairs is very, very helpful.

What else could the government do?

Having a social safety net and more services available, and more flexibility and well-funded services definitely makes for a healthier environment in general.

While respondents had difficulty thinking of government supports currently available to them, they had no such problem identifying things that governments (provincial and federal) could do that they thought would help people in their situation. While there were a lot of idiosyncratic requests (one in four made suggestions that were very situation-dependent), many suggestions were given by an appreciable number of respondents. The most common request, offered by one in five of the people we talked to, was for the government to *provide more funding and support for programs to support caregivers and seniors,* such as homecare and the CCAC:

They've got to make the resources available to the end-user organizations to assist people. Not everybody has the cash to deal with it.

The [provincial] government needs to provide more specialists and programming within the local area.

Many of the people who gave this type of response noted that funding for necessary services for seniors had been slashed in recent years and expressed real dissatisfaction over this fact:

It's not because Canada doesn't have any money. It's what Canada spends money on. We don't need F35 jets. We need health care for our seniors ... there's so much more they could do...

Community support mechanisms ... that's what our seniors need ... but a lot of that has been cut back, unfortunately ... because they're deemed to be unnecessary. And it really troubles me that these services are being eroded, as these are the kinds of social programs that make a real difference.

One in five felt that the government (the federal government, in particular) should offer *tax credits* and/or *other forms of financial assistance for caregivers.* Such a tax break could take many forms, as noted by the suggestions below:

Put in some type of tax relief that's a little bit more robust than what's currently available.

Right now I'm getting very burdened by all the taxes that I'm paying. I'm just not getting a break ... We're middle-class and we're barely covering the bills. People with children get a child tax credit – people caring for their parents need the same kind of thing – a caregiving tax credit!

If I qualify for any type of tax benefits I would love to know. I don't know if there's anything out there ... it's tough.

A similar number felt quite strongly that the federal government should consider offering a new kind of *family care leave* – one that was modelled on and similar to parental leave. These employees all felt that such a program would be more useful to them than the compassionate care benefit currently in place:

I think that better eldercare benefits would help ... kind of like what they have for childcare ... I don't see that there's any difference, whether you're looking after your child or you're looking after your elderly parent or an elderly dependent ... it's exactly the same, right, and we seem to have it more on the childcare giving end ... we don't seem to have it synchronized at the elder stages of someone's life. Seems to be a little bit unbalanced ...

One in five caregivers implored the government (often quite emotionally) to *do a better job of communicating with caregivers* and to make the services easier to access (e.g., streamline, reduce the bureaucracy and red tape). The level of frustration experienced by caregivers who had tried to get information on care with the systems currently in place is palpable, as illustrated by the following quotations:

Communicate to caregivers – send them off in the right direction. We have to look for resources. We're all Internet-savvy but there's only so much Googling I can do, and some of it just hasn't helped me.

They give you so many darned forms to fill out. They could do things online with proper technology, it would be wonderful...

It seems that it's very difficult to get information from the government that will help families cope. If you don't go looking for it for yourself, you're never going to find it ... I've had to Google lots of things to even know what's going on. There is so much convoluted stuff on the provincial government website that I don't know how you'd even find out what to do. I think a coordinating body would really help.

One in ten said that the government could help by making it easier for seniors to access the *health-care system* and/or by increasing the availability within the community of *high-quality, long-term-care facilities for seniors*. Most who gave the first of these two responses talked about the need for more doctors and more health-care services for seniors and the need to reduce wait times in hospitals:

We need more doctors and nurses ... the wait times in the emergency rooms and health care and clinics and stuff are unbelievable – hours.

Well, there's a whole issue around just enough health care and medical care and hospice care and senior care ... there's not enough of that to go around right now.

Respondents who discussed the need for more high-quality, long-term eldercare facilities expressed their need for such a service as follows:

I think that that's something that the provincial government could offer; some respite care even in a care-home setting, because they don't have enough health-care aides to sit with every resident, and not every resident requires it ...

They could step up and make more long-term-care facilities. It's just a huge void.

One in ten also wanted the federal government to consider ways to make it more feasible for employees who are engaged in end-of-life caregiving situations to reduce their work hours *(protect the jobs of caregivers)*. They offered a number of suggestions, such as tax credits and/or pro-rated benefits for employees who reduce their work hours because of their caregiving situation, as well as income averaging and changes to EI benefits:

It probably would help some if the government were to offer a tax credit that helped people who were working a reduced work week ... that kind of thing ... I still work my full work schedule, because if I go to 0.8 or 0.6 you take a financial hit. But if there was a tax credit to make up for it? Or partly make up for it? Well, that would be good. You just look at where you spend tons of your time. Eldercare is going to eat up a ton of people's time.

Finally, as noted earlier, a number of people responded with idiosyncratic requests and suggestions that related to where they lived and what their parents needed. Suggestions here included *"physiotherapy and occupational therapy"; "make transferring Health Insurance between provinces a bit more seamless"; "provide seniors' benefits like eye-care"; "They don't cover a lot of his prescriptions."*

What does the government do to make things worse?

> *I think that the big frustration is ... I don't think that the system is really set up*
> *to help you ... that or they're overwhelmed with the amount of requests for help*
> *they get ... I really hated when the Home Care case coordinator said they were not*
> *a babysitting service, because I'm not asking anybody to babysit my mom. What I*
> *am asking for is help me care for her ... because it is far more economical for some-*
> *one to stay in the community under the care of a relative, as opposed to putting*
> *them in a home.*

Two-thirds of the employees in this sample identified things the government did that made it more difficult for them to balance work and
caregiving – the same proportion of the sample that stated that the government offered no support at all for caregivers. Many of the answers
given in this section echo the requests for support that caregivers gave
earlier. Most commonly (30%), caregivers felt that the *services provided*
for seniors are inadequate, under-resourced, and insufficient in number – deficiencies that made it harder for them to balance their job with the demands of the caregiving role:

> *You really have this feeling that the system is there to discourage you from using*
> *it, really, really, really. You can get a certain number of hours of health care. You*
> *can have this ... you can have that ... but it never happens. She's had social work-*
> *ers come in and talk to her a couple of times, and as helpful and friendly as they*
> *are – and they do provide information – it's all about giving either lists of busi-*
> *nesses that you can get on your own, or that a family member who uses a com-*
> *puter can help you to get on your own ... or just trying to make sure that you're*
> *not abusing or using any social services that are publicly funded any longer than*
> *you absolutely, positively have to ... It hurts more than it helps, because you feel*
> *like these services really aren't there to be used ... except in a crisis, which you*
> *wouldn't get to if the system was set up more for prevention instead of just dealing*
> *with crisis.*

One in four talked, again quite emotionally, about the challenges
they faced finding appropriate information on and support for their
caregiving situation (*they make it hard to find information and/or support*):

I feel that the system needs a complete revamp when it comes to the elderly ... to make sure that they'll get help ... I called the federal government, provincial government, the city of [city name] to see how can I get that care, and despite all this I was unable to find anything ... they make it much too difficult – virtually impossible, really – to really find what the information could be or where it could come from.

Looking after my grandmother came about very suddenly, and it was unexpected. And I had no idea how to even begin to undertake that, and it is virtually impossible to get any kind of assistance or even sympathetic understanding ... or guidance or a booklet or something that points you in the right direction or tells you what call to make. It's just a series of websites with dead links and forms that have nothing to do with your particular case. And, when you talk to somebody on the phone, if they decide to be gracious at that particular moment, they're unlikely to have a clue how to help you and generally shuffle you off to somebody else.

A similar number expressed frustration at the *sheer amount of paperwork required to get any form of support*:

On a related note, and it goes back to money, unfortunately, is the amount of paperwork that we've had to do to get any type of support. There's a provincial grant you can get, and then a federal caregiver tax credit. These things aren't coordinated, and you don't really know about it unless you know to ask. And every time you go back to the doctor, your doctor charges $125 to fill out one of those forms. If they're offering these kinds of things, make it easier for us to access them. And I don't think doctors should be allowed to charge $125 to fill out a form. I think that's just wrong.

Finally, one in five explicitly stated that the government had exacerbated their stress levels by *cutting funding to needed services*:

I'd say the very tight purse strings of the provincial government ... I don't know if it's the way that resources are allocated or a lack of money, or a combination of both, but it definitely doesn't help at all ... there have been major cutbacks in seniors' care ... virtually impossible to get any form of support ...

In terms of the federal government ... the fact that this government is taking away infrastructure and focusing on user fees ... makes it scarier ... it definitely makes the so-called playing field more uneven, and it offloads all of the care even more onto individuals, instead of having community or collective support in areas that would make things better.

Conclusions, Implications, and Recommendations

A number of conclusions can be drawn from the data reviewed in this chapter. These conclusions, along with the implications they might have for how best to move forward on this issue, are outlined in the section below.

Support from family

How do other stakeholders in the employed caregiver relationship help employees cope with the strains and demands of caregiving? Unfortunately, one in three of the caregivers in this sample said that *no one* provided them with any form of help or support for their caregiving role. While many caregivers mentioned that they received emotional support from their partners (they listen, give good advice), their friends, and their extended family, very few received tangible help from any of these stakeholders. A lack of support from family members was often an issue for the caregivers, with many mentioning that they would like their siblings (1) to make more of an effort to visit with and offer concrete help to "mom and dad," and (2) to increase their involvement in the problem-solving process (i.e., offer more instrumental support).

Support from employers

The data from this study suggest that very few employers are providing any form of support for the knowledge workers with caregiving responsibilities in their workforce. A quarter of the interview respondents stated that they received *no* support whatever from their employer for the issues that they faced in balancing work and caregiving. Others noted a number of things that their employer did that they found helped them cope, including allowing the employee to take time off work and/or take a leave of absence and/or use flexitime or telework work schedules. One in ten indicated that the EAP offered by their organization had really helped them cope with stress. When asked what the employer could do to help them manage this issue, the employees in this sample expressed a desire for their employer to recognize eldercare as a legitimate work issue by allowing them to take compassionate leave and/or to work a four-day week.

Implications and recommendations for employers

These data not only show that more needs to be done to support the needs of employed caregivers, but also point to several concrete things that might be helpful. Accordingly, we recommend that employers who wish to address the needs of the employed caregivers in their workforce consider formal policies and practices with respect to paid time off work for eldercare, formal leave of absence for those experiencing high levels of caregiver strain, compassionate care leave, compressed work weeks, and enhanced EAP/EFAP.[4] A formal policy framework in each of these areas would also communicate to management and staff that caregiving is a legitimate work issue. It should be noted, however, that the data from this study are consistent with academic work in this area showing that the development of caregiver-friendly policies and practices, on its own, is unlikely to make much of a difference to caregivers if the culture of the organization "punishes" those who use them. As such, we recommend that employers also focus on implementing these policies in a fair and transparent manner and link their use to managers' performance pay so that their use does not depend on job type or whom employees report to.

Support from municipal, provincial, and federal governments

One in three employed caregivers in the 2012 Study sample noted that they could not find any support for caregivers or programs for seniors within their community. Many caregivers also stated that they found the lack of provincial and federal government support for the caregiving

---

4 Employee family assistance program (EFAP).

role challenging. They felt that the services provided for the aged were inadequate and insufficient in number, that the bureaucracy made it very difficult for someone in need to find help and information, and that budget cuts had reduced the amount of support available.

Municipal governments: Data from the 2012 Study support the idea that very few Canadian communities offer their citizens any form of support to help them provide care to an elderly dependent. Only three community supports were identified as being helpful in this study: community seniors' centres, Meals on Wheels, and para-transport. That being said, virtually all of the caregivers in our sample had suggestions for how their community could help them cope with the demands caregiving places on them. Many spoke about how they would like their community to (1) provide expert guidance, advice, and assistance on caregiving issues ("one number to call to get advice and help"), (2) build more seniors' community centres, (3) offer more in-home care options (e.g., cleaning, meals), and (4) increase the number of transportation options for the elderly (e.g., transportation for medical appointments, greater accessibility of public transportation).

Provincial and federal governments: Almost two-thirds of the employed caregivers in this sample were not aware of any policies or practices put in place by provincial or federal governments to support citizens who were looking after elderly dependents. This suggests that either such supports are not readily available or that governments are not doing a good job of informing the public about what is available. The only government support mentioned as useful by a substantial number of respondents (20%) were services offered by the CCAC.

Implications and recommendations for governments and policy makers

What could governments do to help support employed caregivers? The information from this study recommends that governments take the following actions: (1) provide more funding for programs such as those offered by the CCAC; (2) give tax credits and/or other forms of financial assistance for those providing elderly care; (3) provide funding for more high-quality, long-term eldercare facilities in communities across

Canada (rural areas in particular); (4) introduce some form of family care leave (e.g., replace compassionate care leave with a leave that is modelled after parental leave); (5) provide expert guidance, advice, and assistance for caregiving issues ("one number to call to get advice and help"); (6) build more seniors' community centres; (7) offer more in-home care options (e.g., cleaning, meal preparation); (8) increase the number of transportation options for the elderly (e.g., transportation for medical appointments, greater accessibility of public transportation); and (9) streamline the bureaucracy so that people are more aware of what support is available and more able to obtain help.

Finally, it should be noted that, within the past year, the federal government has started to act as a "caregiver information clearing house" (see http://www.seniors.gc.ca/eng/index.shtml) by bringing together in one place a summary of supports available at the federal level (e.g., the Canadian Revenue Agency) and the provincial level (Community Care Access Centres). This initiative, while a step in the right direction, constitutes only a baby step until funding and service delivery issues are resolved. As noted earlier, family caregivers save the government a lot of money. Canadians need to see some of these savings passed along to those who assume the burdens and costs of caregiving.

Chapter Eight

A Call to Action

The data from this study suggest that families, employers, and governments at all levels are ill-prepared to deal with the tsunami of population aging that is about to sweep the country. Despite the fact that we have known about the population aging crisis for several decades now, findings from the 2012 Study show that there are few systems and processes in place to deal with this issue. As a result, most of the employed caregivers we surveyed or spoke to in the course of our research feel stressed, unsupported, frustrated, and often unappreciated. The strong links between caregiving and employee well-being, the organizational bottom line, and government expenditures on health care indicate that the current system is unsustainable over time. The data presented in this book provide a wake-up call for change. It is hoped that governments and employers will heed this call sooner rather than later.

The recent implementation of more progressive national policies around childcare in Canada, while commendable, may not be sufficient to help the growing group of employees who are caring for aging dependents. In fact, as can be observed, the findings from the 2012 Study support the idea that the more attention governments give to issues associated with childcare, the more likely it is that employees engaged in eldercare will feel inequitably treated and invisible. This reinforces the need for employers and governments to put tangible policies and programs (e.g., tax credits, leave policies) in place to help those engaged in caregiving.

It is also important to note the paradoxes apparent in our data. Many elderly dependents want independence. Many caregivers want to facilitate this sense of independence in a way that ensures that their mother or father is safe and healthy within the community but require supports from the various layers of government involved to make this happen. Governments, particularly those at the provincial level, will likely be able to realize health-care cost reductions if they provide enhanced supports for caregivers within the community. Finally, high levels of caregiver strain negatively impact employee productivity and employee well-being, resulting in increased health-care costs and poorer economic performance at the national level. It would seem, therefore, that all stakeholders would benefit if governments and employers put specific programs in place to support Canadians in their desire to care for their parents in the end stages of life. Unfortunately, the data from this study reveal a huge gap between common sense and common practice when it comes to this issue. The central problem, as our data indicate, is that funding and policy development with respect to eldercare and caregiving are falling through the cracks, with all the key players appearing to place the onus on different levels of government to pay for solutions. This issue needs to be addressed urgently to prevent the problems that we have outlined from taking further hold within an increasingly grey Canada.

The urgency of addressing caregiving issues is underlined by the data from this study showing that knowledge workers in the sandwich group are particularly vulnerable to caregiver strain and all that that entails. These employees tend to have younger children at home and elderly family members requiring care living nearby. They are in their career ascendancy and working demanding jobs, and they face significantly more challenges in balancing work and caregiving demands than older employees with perhaps more seniority and fewer demands on their time from children. Moreover, the findings from this study show that, regardless of gender, employees in the sandwich generation are getting worn down by all the demands on their time and lack the resilience to emotionally separate the two domains. The fact that most feel that their employer does not acknowledge the problem or has not put strategies in place to address it exacerbates the challenge for those in this group, many of whom attempt to cope by meeting family and work-role responsibilities at the expense of looking after themselves. This is unfortunate, in light of the data showing that trying to "do it all" will likely have a negative impact on employees' sleep, energy levels, physical and mental health, and productivity levels.

These findings are a wake-up call to employers, given that the proportion of Canada's workforce with dual caregiving demands is likely to increase in the next decade as our population ages and knowledge workers continue to have their children in their thirties. The age distribution of the employees in our sample within the sandwich generation (half are younger employees within the Generation X cohort) also helps dispel the myth that older employees are the only ones likely to engage in caregiving activities. Taken together, these data emphasize the need for employers and governments to deal with this issue in order to remain competitive. What can concerned employers do? While we closed each chapter with recommendations on ways forward, we feel it appropriate to summarize in the section below a number of the key recommendations for employers arising from this comprehensive empirical study of employed caregivers.

Summary of the recommendations for employers arising from this study

This book provided key recommendations at the end of each chapter. Key recommendations for employers and governments who wish to address the needs of the employed caregivers in their workforce are summarized here for ease of reference. Moving forward we recommend that employers take the following actions:

1 implement formal policies and practices with respect to paid time off work for eldercare, formal leave of absence for those experiencing high levels of caregiver strain, as well as compassionate care leave, compressed work weeks, and enhanced EAP/EFAP. Having in place a formal policy framework in each of these areas will also communicate to management and staff that caregiving is a legitimate work issue. It should be noted, however, that the development

of policies is, on its own, unlikely to make much of a difference. As such, we recommend that employers also focus on implementing these policies in a fair and transparent manner and link the use of these policies to managers' performance pay so that their use does not depend on job type or on whom employees report to.

2   move beyond a "gendered" solution to this issue, as caregiving negatively impacts employees of both genders.

3   develop a flexible set of policies with respect to caregiving to reflect the diversity in caregiving situations to be found in their workforce.

4   expand their EAP/EFAP offerings to include specific supports for employed caregivers (e.g., eldercare referral services, counselling).

5   engage in educational efforts within the workplace and within communities to increase awareness of this issue in their management cadre.

6   offer seminars on how to manage the emotional aspects of caregiving within the workplace and the community.

7   either lobby for or take responsibility for the provision of community centres in areas where their employees live. These centres should offer activities and programs for seniors.

8   offer their employees technical, crisis management, and project management training. Such training is likely to benefit all employees, not just those with caregiving responsibilities.

9   facilitate the creation of caregiving support networks within their workplace.

The interested reader is referred to a recent (2010) report produced by the Family Caregivers' Network Society in British Columbia. This report includes an excellent set of recommendations as well as a comprehensive set of references to programs to help caregivers.[1]

---

1   The report can be found at following website: http://www.familycaregiversbc.ca/wp-content/uploads/2010/10/Updated-Supporting-Family-Caregivers_Action-Plan-for-British-Columbia-May-31_2010.pdf.

Employed caregivers in other economies

It has been reported that Canada lags behind other industrialized countries in its patchwork of caregiving policies (Canadian Healthcare Association 2009). This raises the following question: "What can Canada learn by looking at how other industrialized nations are addressing issues associated with caregiving?" To answer this question we began by undertaking a web search using the keywords "caregivers," "support/policies," and "industrialized nations." This search uncovered an overwhelming number (2,160,000) of books, reports, and scholarly articles. While the amount of material uncovered when the search criteria were narrowed to the OECD was smaller (385,000), a review of even a fraction of these documents was considered beyond the scope of this book. The search did, however, identify a potential way forward, as it uncovered several key sets of studies on caregiving in the OECD nations. The first is summarized in a book on this topic published by the OECD in 2011 entitled *Help Wanted? Providing and Paying for Long-Term Care.*[2]

The second set of key resources uncovered by our search was produced by a research consortium called EUROFAMCARE, which has explored the situation of "family carers of older people" in twenty-three European countries. This study was multifaceted and included a review of statistics describing family caregiving in all twenty-three countries and in-depth studies in six countries: Germany, Greece, Italy, Poland, Sweden, and the United Kingdom.[3] The in-depth case studies include three stages, only the first of which is completed at this time. This first stage is impressive, however, as it involves face-to-face interviews with 1,000 caregivers in each of these six countries, where caregivers were defined as individuals who provided four or more hours of care/support per week to an elderly relative (aged 65 or over). The second two stages of the study involve a twelve-month follow-up

---

2 The full report can be accessed at: https://www.oecd.org/els/health-systems/47836116.pdf.

3 The home page of the consortium can be found at: http://cordis.europa.eu/project/rcn/67322_en.html. Included on this site is a list of all the reports produced by the EUROFAMCARE.Table 1.1. SCA 2015 Report

study of the caregivers who participated in the first set of interviews to monitor changes over time, as well as semi-structured interviews with between thirty and fifty service providers per country. An excellent summary of the EUROFAMCARE initiative can be found in Lamura and colleagues (2008).

The third key resource uncovered was produced by the Institute for the Study of Labor (Bauer and Sousa-Poza 2015) and is an up-to-date overview of the impacts of informal caregiving on key stakeholders within the OECD, including caregivers and employers.

In the sections below we provide a brief summary of how countries within the OECD approach caregiving, with the hope that some of the policies implemented within other industrialized economies may be transferable to Canada. Finally, it should be noted that there is a lot written specifically on caregiving in the United States and Australia that may also have relevance to the readers of this book. We refer them to the report written by the Family Caregivers' Network Society (2010). Included in this report is a table outlining caregiving policies in several European countries as well as in Canada, the United States, and Australia.

Implications for governments: What can we learn from the OECD?

The OECD (2011) drew the following conclusions with respect to family caregiving in OECD countries: (1) Family caregivers are the backbone of any long-term care system; (2) Support for family caregivers is often "tokenistic"; and (3) Supporting family caregivers effectively is a win-win solution.

The report identifies a number of ways in which governments can (and should) support family caregivers, including: (1) the provision of cash support to caregivers; (2) mandating the use of more flexible work arrangements; (3) the establishment of support services such as respite care, training, and counselling; (4) increased coordination between formal and informal care systems; (5) the introduction of universal long-term-care (LTC) benefits; and (6) the increased availability of formal support for caregivers. Details on several of these recommendations are provided below.

Financial support of family caregivers

While the report concluded that governments should provide cash to family caregivers, it noted that efforts in this area should be approached with caution, as such policies, if badly designed, can become counter-productive (OECD 2011). Two forms of financial support were identified in the report: an allowance for the caregiver or cash benefits paid to the care recipients. The pros and cons of each approach were noted both within the OECD report and by Bauer and Sousa-Poza (2015). In their excellent discussion of this issue, Bauer and Sousa-Poza note that at this time entitlement to financial benefits paid to the caregiver differs across the various OECD countries and that, even when the financial support is fairly generous, "the regulations for granting such compensation are very restrictive to minimize disincentives to work among certain low-wage earners" (6). Three-quarters of the OECD countries provide some form of cash benefits directly to the care receiver. There is concern, however, that "introducing such financial incentives into an altruistically motivated care relationship could promote monetary dependency by caregivers and thus decrease intrinsic motivation" (7). In summary, while on the surface the provision of financial supports for caregivers seems like a win-win approach, the research in the area has identified a number of challenges, including the fact that caregivers "risk being trapped into low-paid roles in a largely unregulated part of the economy, with few incentives for participating in the formal labor market ..." (14). These caregivers may also find it difficult to re-enter the labour market at the end of their "caring spell."

Flexible work arrangements

The report notes that working caregivers experience a number of negative outcomes associated with their caregiving demands and recommends that flexible working arrangements be promoted within the OECD. Bauer and Sousa-Poza (2015, 6) talk about the fact that, although many caregivers need to take a leave of absence from their job to provide care for an elderly family member, there are drawbacks associated with the provision of such a benefit. More specifically, they note that "in most OECD countries, caregivers are entitled to leave work for a limited amount of time, but the absence granted from work varies and only some countries provide paid leave." They also note that even when paid leave is provided, it tends to be short (usually less than a month), and the amount of financial compensation varies widely.

Support services for caregivers

The OECD report notes a number of support services that may be of value for caregivers. For caregivers who temporarily leave the workforce for caring purposes, they recommend training and employment support programs to facilitate their transition back into the workforce. They also suggest a number of policies and programs that they perceive can help alleviate the negative impact of caring on mental health, including respite care and physiological support.

Long-term care (LTC)

While most OECD governments have set up collectively financed schemes for personal and nursing-care costs (e.g., formal LTC coverage arrangements), there is wide variability within the OECD in terms of how these benefits are provided and how much support is in fact available. As noted in the report:

> One third of the countries have universal coverage either as part of a tax-funded social-care system, as in Nordic countries, or through dedicated social insurance schemes, as in Germany, Japan, Korea, Netherlands and Luxembourg, or by arranging for LTC coverage mostly within the health system, as in Belgium. While not having a dedicated "LTC system," several countries have universal personal-care benefits, whether in cash (e.g., Austria, France, Italy) or in kind (e.g., Australia, New Zealand). Finally, two countries have "safety-net" or means-tested schemes for long-term-care costs, namely the United Kingdom (excluding Scotland, which has a universal system) and the United States. (OECD 2011, 15)

The report ends by expressing concern over the costs of LTC services and stating that, to maintain cost control, it will be important to target care benefits where needs are the highest, move towards forward-looking financing policies, and facilitate the development of financial instruments to pay for the board and lodging costs of LTC in institutions.

Greater availability of formal care

The report notes that while promoting options to combine care and work and the provision of counselling and training to support caregivers is crucial, the availability of formal care is also important, and it recommends that governments make it easier for caregivers to gain access to formal care services. Along with this recommendation, it points to the need for greater coordination between formal sources of care and informal support networks.

Implications for governments: What can we learn from Europe?

The EUROFAMCARE study (Lamura et al. 2008) drew the following conclusions with respect to family caregiving in Europe: (1) family caregivers are the backbone of caregiving in most of Europe; (2) the economic value of family caregiving is enormous; (3) support for family caregiving makes sense both socially and economically; (4) most caregivers in the twenty-three countries included in the EUROFAMCARE study do not access caregiving support services, either because they are too expensive or because they are not available; and (5) a lack of information and advice for caregivers (especially about diseases, the availability of various services, and access to services) is still a problem across Europe and remains a key factor preventing many European caregivers from adequately gaining access to support services. It is also interesting to note that, although this study focuses on caregivers in general, 41 per cent of all the caregivers in their sample are employed individuals who experience real difficulties in combining paid work and caring responsibilities.

It is also interesting to note that the six countries included in the in-depth pilot studies were selected to represent the different care regimes currently in place in Europe. Lamura and colleagues (2008) describe these regimes as follows (753–4):

- The Scandinavian model (represented by Sweden), which is "characterized by high public investments in home/residential care and a residual family role";
- The liberal, means-tested model (represented by the United Kingdom), which focuses on the "public provision of care to the economically more dependent population, thus implying a broader role for private care providers for remaining users";
- The subsidiarity model (represented by Germany) which allocates "primary responsibility to families, backed up, however, by a long-term-care insurance scheme funding care services provided by religious and nongovernmental organizations";
- The family-based model (represented by Greece and Italy) "with limited public responsibilities and formal service provision, a central role being played by kinship networks, in connection with low female employment"; and
- The transition model of post-socialist societies (represented by Poland), which is very similar to the family-based model but "with much more severe financial constraints following recent economic restructuring and care decentralization/pluralization processes."

Lamura and colleagues (2008) report on the availability of the following forms of caregiver support in the six countries listed above: daycare centres for seniors, information and counselling for caregivers, self-help or support groups for caregivers, respite care, granny sitting, training in caring/protecting one's own health, formalized standard assessment of caregivers' needs, monetary transfers (a care allowance), and integrated planning of care. They found that few countries offered daycare services for seniors, that public-care allowances are received by only a marginal number of carers, and that the provision of services and supports for caregivers varies widely across the different regimes from a perceptible level (in terms of daycare, information, and self-help groups) only in Germany, Sweden, and the United Kingdom to a widespread perceived absence and/or inaccessibility of support in Poland, Greece, and Italy. The authors also note that even "in those countries that have introduced more widespread support programs and policies for carers – such as the United Kingdom, Sweden, and Germany – these interventions appear to reach only a limited proportion of the caregivers potentially needing them. This possibly reflects the largely 'reactive' rather than 'proactive' nature of these services" (Lamura et al. 2008, 768).

The authors close their paper by recommending the following: (1) The establishment and use of tailored specific services for carers should be encouraged; (2) Caregiver services should be made available by public financing of services or benefits for caregivers; (3) The development of "mixed care arrangements" (family carers, formal services, volunteers, privately paid carers) should be encouraged; (4) More research should be undertaken on the issue of caregiving; and (5) Legislation should be introduced to encourage increased flexibility between paid work and informal care of the elderly. With regard to this last recommendation, they note that "the overlapping of family and professional responsibilities in the employed population, especially for women of a mature age, represents a crucial challenge in the light of current EU policy goals of increasing employment rates of women and older workers" (Lamura et al. 2008, 769).

Caregiving issues are similar across industrialized economies

When reading the above summaries, one is struck, not by how much farther ahead countries in the OECD and Europe are than Canada with respect to policies to support caregivers but rather by how all countries are struggling with how best to deal with issues related to population aging and the need to support caregiving. In fact the similarities between Canada and its fellow OECD members with respect to the challenges caregiving poses to their citizens and their economies are far greater than the differences. Bauer and Sousa-Poza (2015, 8) perhaps put it best when they note the following: "Undoubtedly, if dignified aging is to be ensured, the increased demand for caregiving must be met with a satisfactory supply, yet formal care is expensive and public money short. Fostering informal care arrangements, therefore, seems tempting because it saves direct costs in professional care services and can postpone expensive hospitalization. These savings, however, may be offset by such indirect costs as reduced employment, possible loss in human capital, and higher health-care expenditures for caregivers."

It would appear, then, that we have the opportunity to learn from each other with respect to this issue. Many of the recommendations summarized above on how the OECD and Europe could best support caregivers within their populations are very similar to those proposed in this report and are applicable in Canada. Moreover, much of the very detailed data in this report on employed caregivers in the eldercare and sandwich groups should be relevant to policy makers in other industrialized nations as they debate what to do and how to do it. The findings from this report should also be relevant to policy makers across the OECD and Europe who seek to make the case for change in moving forward.

A Call to Action

The data presented in this book are a wake-up call to employers and government policy makers. The proportion of Canada's workforce with multigenerational caregiving demands is likely to increase in the next decade as our population continues to age and to delay parenthood. The consequences for the Canadian labour market of high levels of work-caregiving conflict are likely to be significant and consequential. As the very large baby boom demographic retires and the potential for labour shortages increases, either generally or in specific industries, pressures to keep older workers in the labour force will likely mount. To support the greater costs associated with the health, social, and income security of a proportionally larger population of retired senior citizens, Canada needs individuals of working age to participate actively in the paid labour market. To retain the services of older workers with specialized skills that are in short supply, it is likely that employers will need to make the workplace more "caregiver friendly." The aging of the workforce will also mean that a greater number of employers will experience at first hand the concerns of employees with multigenerational caregiving responsibilities and will need to adapt appropriate policies and practices to support these workers (Lero and Lewis 2008).

It is also important to note that the costs to Canada's health-care and social services systems would be onerous if employed caregivers were no longer available to provide care. Research has shown that the caregiving contributions of family members (i.e., informal caregivers) reduce or eliminate the need for some formal services. It is difficult to assign a precise dollar value to the cost of informal caregiving because methods to determine these costs are quite variable in the literature. It is very clear, however, that informal caregivers contribute an immense amount of value to society. One source estimates that informal caregivers for the elderly provide unpaid labour worth $5 billion annually (Fast et al. 2014), with informal caregiving totalling $25 billion. These informal sources of care offer significant savings to the Canadian health-care system and, consequently, to taxpayers (Chappell 2011). Family caregivers are a crucial part of sustainable public health care. They help ease health system challenges such as staffing shortages and wait times, while ensuring that care is available to the elderly and offering cost savings to the elderly in the process (Centers for Disease Control and Prevention 2008). Despite the importance of informal caregiving to the Canadian economy, there exists at this time an incomplete understanding of the "downstream consequences" of informal care on the caregivers themselves.

Taken together, the data reported in this book underline the need for employers and governments to develop a better understanding of the issues faced by employed caregivers (those in the sandwich group in particular) and how best to support employees in this group. Our research revealed that virtually none of the employed caregivers who participated in the interview process could identify any type of government support (municipal, provincial, or federal) offered to assist caregivers' efforts to support their elderly family members. This provides an opportunity for Canadian businesses to take ownership of an issue that is close to the heart of many Canadians – whether employed or re-tired. It is our hope that this report motivates Canadian businesses to add their voice to those of employees who struggle to care for their el-derly family members and help raise awareness of the issues faced by Canadian caregivers. Businesses can and should lead the charge for change in this area.

Closing Comments

The growing stress on the working population caused by conflict be-tween caregiving and paid employment is both an economic and a social problem. Productivity is impaired, costs of production are unnecessarily high, and personal health and family well-being are at risk. The extent of the problem has increased over the past decade and is likely to continue to increase as our population ages. The stress affects both men and wom-en in both professional and non-professional jobs. This is a societal issue. Individuals, families, employers, and governments can all take actions to moderate the stress, and they can all share in the benefits of taking action. Most of the actions are cost reducing in both the short and long term. What is required is a shift in attitudes: a recognition that workers are family members and family members are workers; a recognition that Canadians love their parents and wish to support them in the end stages of their lives; and an acknowledgment that Canadians deserve to end their lives with dignity. Canada relies on families to carry the responsi-bility for nurturing their children and caring for their elderly and other dependents. We also expect people of working age to work and earn their own living. Supporting them in meeting all those responsibilities is a win-win scenario. As stated eloquently by our respondents who are currently struggling in the trenches –

> I think the one thing that this experience has taught me is how important it is that when I become elderly, I've already made my own plans and decisions. My hus-band's parents did that, because they went through a similar exercise or experi-ence with my husband's grandmother, so they did their own research into retire-ment homes. They made sure that everything that they needed to settle in well was

in hand before they actually needed it to happen, whereas my mom waited too long, and so I know that my husband and I, we will go more towards his parents' direction. We will make sure we have everything lined up before we really need it. And it's taught me to never get too attached to things, because the emotional turmoil of giving up things is too difficult to deal with. So, I've come a long way for a lot of life lessons; I'm not sure they're all totally happy, but it will make the transition to being elderly easier – since I have no kids to inflict this upon, I want to make sure that we're ready for this.

It's the balance of everything, and learning how to be that middle person in the middle of a teeter-totter and being able to balance your whole life with your whole work. And like I said, there are things that could make things easier, as in accommodation with work schedules from employers to … allowing your mom to have more independence than what we think they can handle. Other than that, I think the only thing I can say is that all of this is all about time. When it comes right down to it, it has nothing to do with expense; it has to do with time and the emotional and the physical drain on the person who is caregiving …

Appendix:
Source of Measures Referred to
in the Book

Construct	Measure
	Role Overload
Total-role overload	Bohen, H., & Viveros-Long, A. (1981). *Balancing jobs and family life: Do flexible work schedules help?* Philadelphia: Temple University Press. 80.
Work-role overload	Caplan, R.D., Cobb, S., French, J.R.P., Jr, Harrison, R.V., & Pinneau, S.R., Jr. (1980). *Job demands and worker health: Main effects and occupational differences.* Ann Arbor, MI: University of Michigan, Institute for Social Research.
Family-role overload	Developed for this study to mirror the measures developed in Caplan et al. (1980) and Bohen & Viveros-Long (1981), cited above.
	Work-Family Conflict
Work interferes with family	Gutek, B., Searle, S., & Kelpa, L. (1991). Rational versus gender role explanations for work-family conflict. *Journal of Applied Psychology*, 76, 560–8.
Family interferes with work	
	Organizational Outcomes
Absenteeism	Developed by authors and tested in previous research.
Employment Changes Index	Pyper, W. (2006). *Balancing career and care*. (Cat. 75-001-XIE). Ottawa: Statistics Canada.
	Individual Outcomes
Perceived stress	Cohen, S., Kamarck, T., and Mermelstein, R. (1983). A global measure of perceived stress. *Journal of Health and Social Behaviour*, 24, 385–96.
Depressed mood / Perceived health	Moos, R.H., Cronkite, R.C., Billings, A.G., & Finney, J.W. (1988). *Health and daily living form manual*. Stanford, CA: Social Ecology Laboratory, Department of Psychiatry, Stanford University.

Construct	Measure
	Caregiving
Caregiving intensity	Montgomery, R., Gonyea, J., and Hooyman, N. (1985). Caregiving and the experience of subjective and objective burden. *Family Relations*, 34, 19–26.
	Supplemented with items from:Sims-Gould, J., & Martin-Matthews, A. (2008). Episodic crisis in the provision of care to elderly relatives. *Journal of Applied Gerontology*, 27 (2), 123–40.
Subjective burden	Montgomery, R., Gonyea, J., and Hooyman, N. (1985). Caregiving and the experience of subjective and objective burden. *Family Relations*, 34, 19–26.
Objective burden	
Caregiver strain	Robinson, B. (1983). Validation of a caregiver strain index. *Journal of Gerontology*, 38, 344–8.

References

Abel, E.K. (1991). *Who cares for the elderly? Public policy and the experiences of adult daughters*. Philadelphia, PA: Temple University Press.

Airey, L., McKie, L., & Backett-Milburn, K. (2007). Women's experiences of combined eldercare and paid work in the Scottish food retail sector. *Health Sociology Review, 16*(3-4), 292–303. http://dx.doi.org/10.5172/hesr.2007.16.3-4.292.

Albert, S.M., & Schulz, R. (2010). *The MetLife study of working caregivers and employer health care costs*. New York: Metropolitan Life Insurance Company.

Amirkhanyan, A.A., & Wolf, D.A. (2006, Sept.). Parent care and the stress process: Findings from panel data. *Journals of Gerontology. Series B, Psychological Sciences and Social Sciences, 61*(5), S248–S255. http://dx.doi.org/10.1093/geronb/61.5.S248 Medline:16960238.

Armstrong, P. (1994). Closer to home: More work for women. In P. Armstrong, J. Choiniere, G. Feldberg, & J. White (Eds), *Take care: Warning signals for Canada's health system* (95–110). Toronto: Garamond Press.

Armstrong, P., & Kitts, O. (2004). One hundred years of caregiving. In K. Grant, C. Amaratunga, P. Armstrong, M. Boscoe, A. Pederson, & K. Willson (Eds), *Caring for/Caring about caring for/Caring about: Women, home care, and unpaid caregiving* (45–74). Aurora: Garamond Press.

Autman, K., Galinski, E., Sakai, K., Bond, M., & Brown, J. (2010). *The eldercare study: Everyday realities and wishes for change*. New York: Families and Work Institute.

Barr, J.K., Johnson, K.W., & Warshaw, L.J. (1992). Supporting the elderly: Workplace programs for employed caregivers. *Milbank Quarterly, 70*(3), 509–33. http://dx.doi.org/10.2307/3350133 Medline:1406498.

Bauer, J., & Sousa-Poza, A. (2015): *Impacts of informal caregiving on caregiver employment, health, and family*. Institute for the Study of Labor (IZA) Discussion Paper No. 8851. Bonn. http://dx.doi.org/10.1007/s12062-015-9116-0.

Beach, S.R., Schulz, R., Williamson, G.M., Miller, L.S., Weiner, M.F., & Lance, C.E. (2005, Feb.). Risk factors for potentially harmful informal caregiver behavior. *Journal of the American Geriatrics Society, 53*(2), 255–61. http://dx.doi .org/10.1111/j.1532-5415.2005.53111.x Medline:15673349.

Boddy, J., Cameron, C., & Moss, P. (Eds). (2006). *Care work: Present and future.* London: Routledge.

Boise, L., & Neal, M.B. (1996). Family responsibilities and absenteeism: Employees caring for parents versus employees caring for children. *Journal of Managerial Issues, 8*(2), 218–38.

Bond, J., Galinsky, E., Kim, S., & Brownfield, E. (2005). *National study of employers.* New York: Families and Work Institute.

Briggs, R. (1998). *Caregiving daughters: Accepting the role of caregiver for elderly parents.* New York & London: Garland Publishing.

Brody, E.M. (1990). *Women in the middle: Their parent-care years.* New York: Springer.

Brody, E.M., & Schoonover, C.B. (1986, Aug.). Patterns of parent-care when adult daughters work and when they do not. *Gerontologist, 26*(4), 372–81. http://dx.doi.org/10.1093/geront/26.4.372 Medline:3732831.

Brody, J. (2012, 9 Apr.). Caregiving as a "rollercoaster ride from hell." *New York Times:* 1–9. Retrieved 17 Apr. 2012.

Bumagin, V.E., & Hirn, K.F. (2001). *Caregiving: A guide for those who give care and those who receive it.* New York: Springer.

Calvano, L. (2013). Tug of war: Caring for our elders while remaining productive at work. *Academy of Management Perspectives, 27*(3), 204–18. http:// dx.doi.org/10.5465/amp.2012.0095.

Canadian Caregiver Coalition. (2001). *Respite: A challenge for caregivers, service providers, and policy makers.* Retrieved from: http://www.seniorlivingmag. com/articles/2015/09/prescription-for-good-health.

Canadian Healthcare Association. (2009). Home care in Canada: From margins to the mainstream. Ottawa: Author. Retrieved from: http://www .healthcarecan.ca/wp-content/uploads/2012/11/Home_Care_in_Canada_ From_the_Margins_to_the_Mainstream_web.pdf.

Centers for Disease Control and Prevention. (2008). Caregiver facts. Retrieved from: http://www.cdc.gov/nchs/data/hus/hus08.pdf.

Chappell, N.L. (2011). *Population aging and the evolving care needs of older Canadians.* Montreal: Institute for Research on Public Policy. Retrieved from: http://www.carp.ca/wp-content/uploads/2011/10/IRPP_Study_no21.pdf .

Charmaz, K. (2014). Constructing grounded theory. (2nd ed.). Thousand Oaks, CA: Sage.

Chisholm, J.F. (1999). The sandwich generation. *Journal of Social Distress and the Homeless, 8*(3), 177–91. http://dx.doi.org/10.1023/A:1021368826791.

Chumbler, N., Pienta, A., & Dwyer, J. (2004). The depressive symptomatology of parent care among the near elderly. *Research on Aging*, 26(3), 330–51. http://dx.doi.org/10.1177/0164027503262425.

Cohen, S., Kamarck, T., & Mermelstein, R. (1983, Dec.). A global measure of perceived stress. *Journal of Health and Social Behavior*, 24(4), 385–96. http://dx.doi.org/10.2307/2136404 Medline:6668417.

Conner, K.A. (2000). *Continuing to care: Older Americans and their families*. New York: Falmer Press.

Cranswick, K. (2002). *General social survey, cycle 16: Caring for an aging society*. Statistics Canada, Housing, Family and Social Statistics Division, Catalogue No. 89-582-XIE. Ottawa: Statistics Canada.

Cranswick, K., & Dosman, D. (2008). Eldercare: What we know today. *Canadian Social Trends*, 86(1), 49–57.

Cranswick, K., & Thomas, D. (2005). *Elder care and the complexities of social networks. Canadian social trends*. Catalogue no. 11-008. Ottawa: Statistics Canada.

Cravey, T., & Mitra, A. (2011). Demographics of the sandwich generation by race and ethnicity in the United States. *The Journal of Socio-Economics*, 40(3), 306–11. http://dx.doi.org/10.1016/j.socec.2010.12.003.

Davey, A., & Szinovacz, M.E. (2008). Division of care among adult children. In M.E. Szinovacz & A. Davey (Eds), *Caregiving contexts: Cultural, familial, and societal implications* (133–59). New York: Springer.

Decima Research Inc. (2004). *Informal/family caregivers in Canada caring for someone with a mental illness*. Ottawa: Health Canada.

Dee, A.J., & Peter, T. (1992). Caring for the elderly dependants: Effects on the carer's quality of life. *Age and Ageing*, 21(6), 421–8.

De Graff, A.H. (2002). *Caregivers and personal assistants*. Fort Collins, CO: Saratoga Access Publications.

Duxbury, L., & Dole, G. (2014). Squeezed in the middle: Balancing paid employment, childcare and eldercare, In R. Burke, K. Page, & C. Cooper. (Eds), *Flourishing in life, work, and careers: Individual well-being and career experiences*. New Horizons in Management. Cheltenham: Edward Elgar Publishing. In Press.

Duxbury, L., & Gover, L. (2011). Exploring the link between organizational culture and work-family conflict. In C. Wilderom, M. Peterson, & N. Ashkanasy (Eds), *Handbook for organizational culture and climate* (2nd ed., 271–90). Newbury Park, CA: Sage. http://dx.doi.org/10.4135/9781483307961.n15.

Duxbury, L., & Higgins, C. (2003). *Work-life conflict in Canada in the new millennium: A status report (Report two)*. Ottawa: Health Canada. Retrieved from: http://publications.gc.ca/collections/Collection/H72-21-186-2003E.pdf.

Duxbury, L., & Higgins, C. (2009). *Key findings and conclusions from the 2001 national work-life conflict study*. Ottawa: Health Canada. Retrieved from:

http://www.hc-sc.gc.ca/ewh-semt/pubs/occup-travail/balancing_six-equilibre_six/index-eng.php/.

Duxbury, L., & Higgins, C. (2013a). *Balancing work, childcare and eldercare: A view from the trenches*. Retrieved from: http://sprott.carleton.ca/directory/duxbury-linda/.

Duxbury, L., & Higgins, C. (2013b). *Causes, consequences, and moderating factors of strain of caregiving among employed caregivers*. Retrieved from: http://sprott.carleton.ca/wp-content/files/2012NationalStudyWorkCaregiving_FinalReportTwo.pdf.

Duxbury, L., & Higgins, C. (2013c). *The Desjardins Insurance report: Balancing work, childcare and eldercare: A view from the trenches*. Montreal: Desjardins Insurance. Available from the authors on request.

Duxbury, L., & Higgins, C. (2013d). *Employed caregiving in Canada: A view from the trenches*. Retrieved from: http://sprott.carleton.ca/wp-content/files/2012NationalStudyWokCaregiving_FinalReportThree.pdf.

Duxbury, L., Higgins, C., & Schroder, B. (2009). *Balancing paid work and caregiving responsibilities: A closer look at family caregivers in Canada*. Ottawa: Canadian Policy Research Network. Retrieved from: www.cprn.org/doc.cfm?doc=1997&l=en.

Duxbury, L., Lyons, S., & Higgins, C. (2008). Too much to do and not enough time: An examination of role overload. In K. Korabik, D.S. Lero, & D.L. Whitehead (Eds), *Handbook of work-family integration: Research, theory and best practices* (125–40). Waltham, MA: Academic Press. http://dx.doi.org/10.1016/B978-012372574-5.50010-7.

Eales, J., Keating, N., & Fast, J. (2001). *Analysis of the impact of federal, provincial and regional policies on the economic well-being of informal caregivers of frail seniors, Final report*. Submitted to the Federal/Provincial/Territorial Committee of Officials (Seniors). Ottawa.

Eby, L.T., Casper, W.J., Lockwood, A., Bordeaux, C., & Brinley, A. (2005). Work and family research in IO/OB: Content analysis and review of the literature (1980–2002). *Journal of Vocational Behavior, 66*(1), 124–97. http://dx.doi.org/10.1016/j.jvb.2003.11.003.

Elliott, T.R., & Pezent, G.D. (2008). Family caregivers of older persons in rehabilitation. *NeuroRehabilitation, 23*(5), 439–46. Medline:18957730.

Evercare Survey (2009). *The Evercare survey of the economic downturn and its impact on family caregiving. Report of findings*. Bethesda, MD: National Alliance for Caregiving. Retrieved from: http://www.caregiving.org/pdf/research/EVC_Caregivers_Economy_Report%20FINAL_4-28-09.pdf.

Family Caregivers' Network Society (2010) *Supporting family caregivers: An action plan for British Columbia*. Victoria: British Columbia Ministry of Health Services. Full report available at: http://www.familycaregiversbc.ca/

wp-content/uploads/2010/10/Updated-Supporting-Family-Caregivers_
Action-Plan-for-British-Columbia-May-31_2010.pdf.

Fast, J. (2015). *Caregiving for older adults with disabilities: Present costs and future challenges*. Montreal: Institute for Research on Public Policy.

Fast, J., & Keating, N. (2000). *Family caregiving and consequences for carers: Toward a policy research agenda*. Canadian Policy Research Network Discussion Paper No. F/10-5. Retrieved from: http://www.cprn.org/documents/familycaregivingandconsequencesforcarers.pdf.

Fast, J., Lero, D., DeMarco, R., Ferreira, H., & Eales, J. (2014). *Fact sheet: Combining care work and paid work: Is it sustainable? Research on aging, policies and practice*. Edmonton: University of Alberta.

Fradkin, L.G., & Heath, A. (1992). *Caregiving of older adults*. Santa Barbara, CA: ABC-CLIO, Inc.

Frederick, J., & Fast, J. (1999). *Eldercare in Canada: Who does how much? Canadian Social Trends*, Catalogue No. 11–008. Ottawa: Statistics Canada.

Fredriksen, K., & Scharlach, A. (1999). Employee family care responsibilities. *Family Relations, 48*(2), 189–96. http://dx.doi.org/10.2307/585083.

Gahagan, J., Loppie, C., MacLellan, M., Rehman, L., & Side, K. (2004). *Caregiver resilience and the quest for balance: A report on findings from focus groups*. Retrieved from: http://www.dal.ca/content/dam/dalhousie/pdf/ace-women-health/Healthy%20Balance/ACEWH_hbpr_caregiver_resilience_quest_for_balance.pdf.

George, L.K., & Gwyther, L.P. (1986, Jun.). Caregiver well-being: A multidimensional examination of family caregivers of demented adults. *Gerontologist, 26*(3), 253–9. http://dx.doi.org/10.1093/geront/26.3.253 Medline:3721232.

Gilboa, S., Shirom, A., Fried, Y., & Cooper, C. (2008). A meta-analysis of work demand stressors and job performance: Examining main and moderating effects. *Personnel Psychiatry, 61,* 227–71.

Glynn, K., Maclean, H., Forte, T., & Cohen, M. (2009, Feb.). The association between role overload and women's mental health. *Journal of Women's Health, 18*(2), 217–23. http://dx.doi.org/10.1089/jwh.2007.0783 Medline:19183093.

Greenburg, L., and Decady, Y. (2014). Health at a glance – Ninety years of change in life expectancy (1921 to 2011). Statistics Canada, Catalogue Number: 82–624-X.

Grundy, E., & Henretta, J.C. (2006). Between elderly parents and adult children: A new look at the intergenerational care provided by the "sandwich generation." *Ageing and Society, 26*(5), 707–22. http://dx.doi.org/10.1017/S0144686X06004934.

Grunfeld, E., Glossop, R., McDowell, I., & Danbrook, C. (1997, 15 Oct.). Caring for elderly people at home: The consequences to caregivers. *Canadian Medical Association Journal, 157*(8), 1101–5. Medline:9347781.

Guberman, N. (1999). Caregivers and caregiving: New trends and their implications for policy. *Final Report Prepared for Health Canada*. Ottawa: Health Canada.

Haley, W.E., Roth, D.L., Howard, G., & Safford, M.M. (2010, Feb.). Caregiving strain and estimated risk for stroke and coronary heart disease among spouse caregivers: Differential effects by race and sex. *Stroke, 41*(2), 331–6. http://dx.doi.org/10.1161/STROKEAHA.109.568279 Medline:20075357.

Hammer, L.B., & Neal, M.B. (2008). Sandwiched-generation caregivers: Prevalence, characteristics, and outcomes. *Psychologist-Manager Journal, 11*(1), 93–112. http://dx.doi.org/10.1080/10887150801967324.

Harlton, S., Keating, N., & Fast, J. (1998). Defining eldercare for policy and practice: Perspectives matter. *Family Relations, 47*(3), 281–8. http://dx.doi.org/10.2307/584978.

Harris, P.B. (1998, Jun.). Listening to caregiving sons: Misunderstood realities. *Gerontologist, 38*(3), 342–52. http://dx.doi.org/10.1093/geront/38.3.342 Medline:9640854.

Hart, G., Meagher-Stewart, D., Stewart, M.J., MacPherson, K., Doble, S., & Makrides, L. (2000). Stroke and heart failure in seniors: Dyadic peer support for family caregivers. In M.J. Stewart (Ed.), *Chronic conditions and caregiving in Canada* (156–71). Toronto: University of Toronto Press.

Health Canada. (2002). *National profile of family caregivers in Canada – 2002: Final report*. Prepared for Health Canada by Decima Research, Ottawa. Retrieved from: http://www.hc-sc.gc.ca/hcs-sss/alt_formats/hpb-dgps/pdf/pubs/2002-caregiv-interven/2002-caregiv-interven-eng.pdf.

Henderson, K. (2002). Informal caregivers. In M. Stephenson & E.W. Sawyer (Eds), *Continuing the care: The issues and challenges for long-term care.* (2nd ed., 267–90). Ottawa: Canadian Healthcare Association Press.

Hicks, C., Rowe, G., & Gribble, S. (2007). The view from the middle: Taking care of the young and the old. In A. Gupta & A. Harding (Eds), *Modelling our future: Population ageing, health and aged care.* International Symposia in Economic Theory and Econometrics (261–80). Amsterdam: Elsevier.

Hollander, M.J., Liu, G., & Chappell, N.L. (2009). Who cares and how much? The imputed economic contribution to the Canadian healthcare system of middle-aged and older unpaid caregivers providing care to the elderly. *Healthcare Quarterly, 12*(2), 429.

Igarashi, H., Hooker, K., Coehlo, D.P., & Manoogian, M.M. (2013, Apr.). "My nest is full": Intergenerational relationships at midlife. *Journal of Aging Studies, 27*(2), 102–12. http://dx.doi.org/10.1016/j.jaging.2012.12.004 Medline:23561275.

Jacobs, J., & Gerson, K. (2001). Overworked individuals or overworked families? Explaining trends in work, leisure, and family time. *Work and Occupations, 28*(1), 40–63. http://dx.doi.org/10.1177/0730888401028001004.

Jacobs, J.C., Lilly, M.B., Ng, C., & Coyte, P.C. (2013, Mar.). The fiscal impact of informal caregiving to home care recipients in Canada: How the intensity of care influences costs and benefits to government. *Social Science & Medicine, 81*, 102–9. http://dx.doi.org/10.1016/j.socscimed.2012.12.015 Medline:23347496.

Johnson, R.W., & Lo Sasso, A.T. (2000). *Parental care at midlife: Balancing work and family responsibilities near retirement.* Washington, DC: The Urban Institute, The Retirement Project: Perspectives on Productive Aging Brief #9. Retrieved from: http://www.urban.org/sites/default/files/alfresco/publication-pdfs/309373-Parental-Care-at-Midlife.PDF.

Johnson, R.W., & Schaner, S.G. (2005). *Many older Americans engage in caregiving activities.* Washington, DC: The Urban Institute, The Retirement Project: Perspectives on Productive Aging Brief #3. Retrieved from: http://www.urban.org/sites/default/files/alfresco/publication-pdfs/311203-Many-Older-Americans-Engage-in-Caregiving-Activities.PDF.

Kahn, R.L., Wolfe, D.M., Quinn, R.P., Snoek, J.D., & Rosenthal, R.A. (1964). *Organizational stress: Studies in role conflict and ambiguity.* New York: John Wiley & Sons.

Karasek, R.A., Jr. (1979). Job demands, job decision latitude, and mental strain: Implications for job redesign. *Administrative Science Quarterly, 24*(2) (June), 285–308.

Karasek, R., & Theorell, T. (1990). *Healthy work: Stress, productivity, and the reconstructing of working life.* New York: Basic Books.

Katz, D., & Kahn, R.L. (1966). *The social psychology of organizations.* New York: John Wiley.

Katz, R., Lowenstein, A., Prilutzky, D., & Halperin, D. (2011, Apr.). Employers' knowledge and attitudes regarding organizational policy toward workers caring for aging family members. *Journal of Aging & Social Policy, 23*(2), 159–81. http://dx.doi.org/10.1080/08959420.2011.554120 Medline:21491305.

Keating, N., Fast, J., Lero, D., Lucas, S., & Eales, J. (2014). A taxonomy of the economic costs of family care to adults. *Journal of the Economics of Ageing, 3*, 11–20. http://dx.doi.org/10.1016/j.jeoa.2014.03.002.

Keefe, J. (1997). The likelihood of combining employment and helping elderly kin in rural and urban areas among regions. *Canadian Journal of Regional Science, 20*, 367–87.

Keefe, J. (2002). Home and community care. In E. Sawyer & M. Stephenson (Eds), *Continuing the care: The issues and challenges for long term care* (109–41). Ottawa: Canadian Healthcare Association Press.

Keefe, J., & Medjuck, S. (1997). The contribution of long term economic costs to predicting strain among employed women caregivers. *Journal of Women & Aging, 9*(3), 3–25. http://dx.doi.org/10.1300/J074v09n03_02.

Keene, J.R., & Prokos, A.H. (2007). The sandwiched generation: Multiple caregiving responsibilities and the mismatch between actual and preferred work hours. *Sociological Spectrum, 27*(4), 365–87. http://dx.doi.org/10.1080/02732170701313308.

Klein, G. (2007). Performing a project premortem. *Harvard Business Review, 85*(9), 18–19.

Kramer, B.J., & Kipnis, S. (1995, Jun.). Eldercare and work-role conflict: Toward an understanding of gender differences in caregiver burden. *Gerontologist, 35*(3), 340–8. http://dx.doi.org/10.1093/geront/35.3.340 Medline:7622087.

Krett, E. (2008, 11 Aug.). Boomers sandwiched between aging parents, children. *Canadian HR Reporter*.

Lamura, G., Mnich, E., Nolan, M., Wojszel, B., Krevers, B., Mestheneos, L., Döhner, H., & EUROFAMCARE Group. (2008, Dec.). Family carers' experiences using support services in Europe: Empirical evidence from the EUROFAMCARE study. *Gerontologist, 48*(6), 752–71. http://dx.doi.org/10.1093/geront/48.6.752 Medline:19139249.

Lazarus, R.S., & Folkman, S. (1984). *Stress, appraisal, and coping.* New York: Springer.

Lechner, V.M., & Gupta, C. (1996). Employed caregivers: A four-year follow-up. *Journal of Applied Gerontology, 15*(1), 102–15. http://dx.doi.org/10.1177/073346489601500107.

Lee, S., Colditz, G.A., Berkman, L.F., & Kawachi, I. (2003, Feb.). Caregiving and risk of coronary heart disease in U.S. women: A prospective study. *American Journal of Preventive Medicine, 24*(2), 113–19. http://dx.doi.org/10.1016/S0749-3797(02)00582-2 Medline:12568816.

Lero, D., & Lewis, S. (2008). Assumptions, research gaps and emerging issues: Implications for research, policy and practice. In K. Korabik, D. Lero, & D. Whitehead (Eds), *Handbook of work-family integration* (371–97). New York: Elsevier, Academic Press. http://dx.doi.org/10.1016/B978-012372574-5.50023-5.

Lesthaeghe, R. (2010). The unfolding story of the second demographic transition. *Population and Development Review, 36*(2), 211–51. http://dx.doi.org/10.1111/j.1728-4457.2010.00328.x Medline:20734551.

Lum, J. (2011). Informal caregiving. In *Focus.* Toronto: Canadian Research Network for Care in the Community. Retrieved from: http://www.ryerson.ca/content/dam/crncc/knowledge/infocus/informalcaregiving/InFocus-InformalCaregiving.pdf.

Margolies, L. (2004). *My mother's hip: Lessons from the world of eldercare.* Philadelphia, PA: Temple University Press.

Marshall, K. (2009). The family work week. *Perspectives.* Statistics Canada, Catalogue No. 75-001-X (5–25). Ottawa: Statistics Canada.

Mathew Greenwald and Associates (2009). *Caregiving in the U.S.* National Alliance for Caregiving with AARP (American Association of Retired Persons). Retrieved from: http://www.caregiving.org/pdf/research/Caregiving_in_the_US_2009_full_report.pdf.

Mature Market Institute. (1999). *The MetLife juggling act study: Balancing caregiving with work and the costs involved.* New York: Metropolitan Life Insurance Company.

Mature Market Institute (2011). *The MetLife study of caregiving costs to working caregivers: Double jeopardy for baby boomers caring for their parents.* New York: Metropolitan Life Insurance Company. Retrieved from: http://www .caregiving.org/wp-content/uploads/2011/06/mmi-caregiving-costs-working-caregivers.pdf.

McGowan, R. (2009). Managerial discourse of work and eldercare: (Re)producing, resisting, and negotiating boundaries between private and public. *Culture and Organization, 15*(3–4), 307–29. http://dx.doi.org/10.1080/14759550903119319.

MetLife. (1997). *MetLife study of employer costs for working caregivers.* New York: Metropolitan Life Insurance Company.

MetLife. (2003). *The MetLife study of sons at work: Balancing employment and eldercare.* New York: Metropolitan Life Insurance Company.

MetLife. (2006). *The MetLife caregiving cost study: Productivity losses to United States businesses.* Westport, CT: The MetLife Mature Market Institute.

MetLife. (2010). *The MetLife study of working caregivers and employer health care costs.* Westport, CT: The MetLife Mature Market Institute.

Montgomery, R.J.V. (1992). Gender differences in patterns of child-parent caregiving relationships. In J.W. Dwyer & R.T. Coward (Eds), *Gender, families, and elder care* (65–83). Newbury Park, CA: Sage Publications.

Montgomery, R.J.V., Borgatta, E.F., & Borgatta, M.L. (2000). Societal and family change in the burden of care. In W.T. Liu & H. Kendig (Eds), *Who should care for the elderly? An East-West value divide* (27–54). Singapore: Singapore University Press. http://dx.doi.org/10.1142/9789812793591_0002.

Montgomery, R., Gonyea, J., & Hooyman, N. (1985). Caregiving and the experience of subjective and objective burden. *Family Relations, 34*(1), 19–26. http://dx.doi.org/10.2307/583753.

Moos, R.H., Cronkite, R.C., Billings, A.G., & Finney, J.W. (1988). *Health and daily living form manual.* Stanford, CA: Social Ecology Laboratory, Department of Psychiatry, Stanford University.

Morris, M. (2001). *Gender sensitive home and community care and caregiving research: A synthesis paper.* Canada: Women's Health Bureau.

Neal, M.B., Chapman, N.J., Ingersoll-Dayton, B., & Emlen, A.C. (1993). *Balancing work and caregiving for children, adults and elders.* Family Caregiver

Applications Series, 3. Newbury Park, CA: Sage Publications. http://dx.doi.org/10.4135/9781483326160.

Neal, M.B., Chapman, N.J., Ingersoll-Dayton, B., Emlen, A.C., & Boise, L. (1990). Absenteeism and stress among employed caregivers of the elderly, disabled adults, and children. In D.E. Biegel & A. Blum (Eds), *Aging and caregiving: Theory, research, and policy,* 160–83. Newbury Park, CA: Sage Publications.

Neufeld, A., & Harrison, M.J. (2000). Family caregiving: Issues in gaining access to support. In M.J. Stewart (Ed.), *Chronic conditions and caregiving in Canada* (247–73). Toronto: University of Toronto Press.

Nichols, L.S., & Junk, V.W. (1997). The sandwich generation: Dependency, proximity, and task assistance needs of parents. *Journal of Family and Economic Issues, 18*(3), 299–326. http://dx.doi.org/10.1023/A:1024978930126.

Nolan, M., Grant, G., & Keady, J. (1996). *Understanding family care: A multidimensional model of caring and coping.* Buckingham: Open University Press.

OECD. (2011). *Help wanted? Providing and paying for long-term care.* English Summary. Paris: Author. (ISBN 978-92-6). Full report available at: https://www.oecd.org/els/health-systems/47836116.pdf.

Pavalko, E.K., & Gong, F. (2005). Work and family issues for midlife women and their families. In S. Bianchi, L. Casper, & R. King (Eds), *Work, family, health and well-being* (379–93). Mahwah, NJ: Erlbaum.

Pearlin, L.I., & Schooler, C. (1978, Mar.). The structure of coping. *Journal of Health and Social Behavior, 19*(1), 2–21. http://dx.doi.org/10.2307/2136319 Medline:649936.

Petrovich, A. (2008). Lessons learned in the sandwich. *Journal of Women and Social Work, 23*(3), 223–30. http://dx.doi.org/10.1177/0886109908319121.

PEW (2013). *Family caregivers are wired for health.* California Health Care Project, Pew Research Center's Internet & American Life Project. Retrieved from: http://www.pewinternet.org/2013/06/20/family-caregivers-are-wired-for-health/.

Pyper, W. (2006). *Balancing career and care.* Catalogue No. 75-001-XIE. Ottawa: Statistics Canada.

Rajnovich, B., Keefe, J., & Fast, J. (2005). *Supporting caregivers of dependent adults in the 21st century.* Background paper for Canadian Policy Research Networks policy workshop on family caregiving. Retrieved from: http://www.dal.ca/content/dam/dalhousie/pdf/ace-women-health/Healthy%20Balance/ACEWH_hbrp_supporting_caregivers_of_dependent_adults_21st_century.pdf.

Remennick, L.I. (1999). Women of the "sandwich" generation and multiple roles: The case of Russian immigrants of the 1990s in Israel. *Sex Roles, 40*(5/6), 347–78. http://dx.doi.org/10.1023/A:1018815425195.

Rice, D.P., & Fineman, N. (2004). Economic implications of increased longevity in the United States. *Annual Review of Public Health, 25*, 457–73. http://dx.doi.org/10.1146/annurev.publhealth.25.101802.123054 Medline:15015930.

Robinson, B.C. (1983, May). Validation of a caregiver strain index. *Journal of Gerontology, 38*(3), 344–8. http://dx.doi.org/10.1093/geronj/38.3.344 Medline:6841931.

Rosenthal, C.J., Hayward, L., Martin-Matthews, A., & Denton, M.A. (2004). Help to older parents and parents-in-law: Does paid employment constrain women's helping behaviour? *Canadian Journal on Aging / La revue canadienne du vieillissement, 23*(5 Suppl 1), S115–S130. http://dx.doi.org/10.1353/cja.2005.0042 Medline:15660305.

Rosenthal, C., & Martin-Matthews, A. (1999). *Families as care-providers versus care-managers? Gender and type of care in a sample of employed Canadians.* Research Institute for Quantitative Studies in Economic and Population Report No. 343.

Rousseau, D. (1995). *Psychological contract in organizations.* Newbury Park, CA: Sage Publications.

Rubin, R., & White-Means, S. (2009). Informal caregiving: Dilemmas of sandwiched caregivers. *Journal of Family and Economic Issues, 30*(3), 252–67. http://dx.doi.org/10.1007/s10834-009-9155-x.

Scharlach, A.E. (1994, Jun.). Caregiving and employment: Competing or complementary roles? *Gerontologist, 34*(3), 378–85. http://dx.doi.org/10.1093/geront/34.3.378 Medline:8076880.

Schulz, R., & Beach, S.R. (1999, 15 Dec.). Caregiving as a risk factor for mortality: The Caregiver Health Effects Study. *Journal of the American Medical Association, 282*(23), 2215–19. http://dx.doi.org/10.1001/jama.282.23.2215 Medline:10605972.

Schulz, R., & Martire, L.M. (2004, May-Jun.). Family caregiving of persons with dementia: Prevalence, health effects, and support strategies. *American Journal of Geriatric Psychiatry, 12*(3), 240–9. http://dx.doi.org/10.1097/00019442-200405000-00002 Medline:15126224.

Schulz, R., Newsom, J., Mittelmark, M., Burton, L., Hirsch, C., & Jackson, S. (1997, Spring). Health effects of caregiving: The caregiver health effects study: An ancillary study of the cardiovascular health study. *Annals of Behavioral Medicine, 19*(2), 110–16. http://dx.doi.org/10.1007/BF02883327 Medline:9603685.

Schulz, R., & Sherwood, P.R. (2008, Sept.). Physical and mental health effects of family caregiving. *American Journal of Nursing, 108*(9 Suppl), 23–7, quiz 27. http://dx.doi.org/10.1097/01.NAJ.0000336406.45248.4c Medline: 18797217.

Sims-Gould, J., & Martin-Matthews, A. (2007). Family caregiving or caregiving alone: Who helps the helper? *Canadian Journal on Aging / La revue canadienne du vieillissement, 26*(S1 Suppl 1), 27–45. http://dx.doi.org/10.3138/cja.26. suppl_1.027 Medline:18089527.

Sinah, M. (2013). *Portrait of caregivers.* In *Spotlight on Canadians: Results from the general social survey.* Ottawa: Statistics Canada, Catalogue no. 89-652-X — No. 001. (ISBN 978-1-100-22502-9).

Soldo, B.J., & Freedman, V.A. (1994). Care of the elderly: Division of labor among the family, market, and state. In L.G. Martin & S.H. Preston (Eds), *Demography of aging* (195–216). Washington, DC: Committee on Population, National Research Council.

Spillman, B.C., & Pezzin, L.E. (2000). Potential and active family caregivers: Changing networks and the "sandwich generation." *Milbank Quarterly, 78*(3), 347–74. http://dx.doi.org/10.1111/1468-0009.00177 Medline: 11028188.

Statistics Canada. (2010). *Population projections for Canada, provinces and territories 2009 to 2036.* Catalogue no. 91-520-X. Ottawa: Statistics Canada Demography Division.

Statistics Canada. (2011a). Chapter 28: Seniors. In *Canada year book 2011* (406–21). Catalogue No.11-402-XPE. Ottawa: Author.

Statistics Canada. (2011b). *Health trends.* Catalogue No. 82-213-XWE. Ottawa: Author.

Statistics Canada. (2012). *General social survey – Family (GSS).* Retrieved from: http://www.statcan.gc.ca/pub/89f0115x/89f0115x2013001-eng.htm.

Statistics Canada. (2014). *Canadian demographics at a glance,* Statistics Canada, Demography Division, Publication Number 91–003-X. Retrieved from: http://www.statcan.gc.ca/pub/91-003-x/91-003-x2014001-eng.htm.

Stobert, S., & Cranswick, K. (2004). *Looking after seniors: Who does what for whom? Canadian Social Trends.* Catalogue No. 11-008-XIE. Ottawa: Statistics Canada.

Stoller, E. (1983). Parental caregiving by adult children. *Journal of Marriage and the Family, 45*(4), 851–8. http://dx.doi.org/10.2307/351797.

Turcotte, M. (2013). Family caregiving: What are the consequences? *Insights on Canadian Society.* Ottawa: Statistics Canada, Catalogue no. 75-006-X, ISSN 2291-0840.

Uhlenberg, P., & Cheuk, M. (2008). Demographic change and the future of informal caregiving. In M.E. Szinovacz & A. Davey (Eds), *Caregiving contexts: Cultural, familial, and societal implications* (9–33). New York: Springer.

Vitaliano, P.P., Young, H.M., & Russo, J. (1991, Feb.). Burden: A review of measures used among caregivers of individuals with dementia. *Gerontologist, 31*(1), 67–75. http://dx.doi.org/10.1093/geront/31.1.67 Medline:2007476.

Wagner, D.L. (2003). *Workplace programs for family caregivers: Good business and good practice.* Family Caregiver Alliance, National Center on Caregiving. Retrieved from: https://www.caregiver.org/workplace-programs-family-caregivers-good-business-and-good-practice-2003.

Wagner, D.L., & Lottes, J. (2006). *The MetLife caregiving cost study: Productivity losses to U.S. business.* Westport, CT: MetLife Mature Market Institute; and Bethesda, MD: National Alliance for Caregiving.

Wagner, D., Lottes, J., & Neal, M. (2006). *The MetLife caregiving cost study: Productivity losses to U.S. business.* MetLife Mature Market Institute. Available at: https://www.metlife.com/assets/cao/mmi/publications/studies/mmi-caregiver-cost-study-productivity.pdf.

Williams, C. (2004). *The sandwich generation.* Statistics Canada, Catalogue No. 75-001-XPE. Ottawa: Statistics Canada.

World Bank. (2012). *The world bank annual report 2012.* Washington, DC: The World Bank.

Young, L. (2006, 8 Aug.). Coping with caregiving. *Chatelaine.* Retrieved from http://www.chatelaine.com/living/coping-with-caregiving/.

Index